The Marana Community in the Hohokam World

ANTHROPOLOGICAL PAPERS OF
THE UNIVERSITY OF ARIZONA
NUMBER 56

The Marana Community in the Hohokam World

Suzanne K. Fish, Paul R. Fish, and John H. Madsen, Editors

CONTRIBUTORS

John J. Field
Paul R. Fish
Suzanne K. Fish
John H. Madsen
Charles H. Miksicek
James M. Skibo
Alan P. Sullivan III
Christine R. Szuter
Mary Van Buren

THE UNIVERSITY OF ARIZONA PRESS
TUCSON
1992

About the Editors

SUZANNE K. FISH is a Research Archaeologist at the Arizona State Museum, University of Arizona. She has specialized in Hohokam archaeology for more than ten years; other areas of professional emphasis include ethnobotany, settlement patterns, and Mesoamerican prehistory. Recent publications include articles and books on the advantages of full-coverage archaeological survey, subsistence issues, demography, and Hohokam cultural ecology and social organization.

PAUL R. FISH is Curator of Archaeology at the Arizona State Museum and Research Professor in the Department of Anthropology, University of Arizona. His research focuses on the prehistory of the deserts in southern Arizona and northern Mexico. Recent publications address archaeological classification, settlement patterns, political and social organization, factors influencing regional abandonment, and cultural resource management.

JOHN H. MADSEN is a Research Archaeologist at the Arizona State Museum, University of Arizona. Over the past twelve years he has worked closely with the Arizona State Land Department as a cultural resource management advisor. His research interests include prehistoric and historic land use in the Sonoran Desert. In recent publications he has written about prehistoric agave use, raw material procurement strategies associated with stone tool manufacturing, full-coverage archaeological survey, and Hohokam political and social organization.

Cover: Early Classic period Hohokam settlements in the Marana survey area north of Tucson, Arizona (see Figure 3.2).

Contributors

John J. Field
    Department of Geosciences, University of Arizona, Tucson,

Charles H. Miksicek
    BioSystems Analysis, Inc., Santa Cruz, California

James M. Skibo
    Department of Anthropology, University of Arizona, Tucson

Alan P. Sullivan
    Department of Anthropology, University of Cincinnati, Ohio

Christine R. Szuter
    University of Arizona Press, Tucson

Mary Van Buren
    Colorado State University, Fort Collins

Second Printing
THE UNIVERSITY OF ARIZONA PRESS

Copyright © 1992

The Arizona Board of Regents
All Rights Reserved

This book was set in 10/12 Dutch Roman
⊗ This book is printed on acid-free, archival-quality paper.
Manufactured in the United States of America.

96 95 94   6 5 4 3 2

Library of Congress Cataloging-in-Publication Data

The Marana Community in the Hohokam world / Suzanne K. Fish, Paul
    R. Fish, and John H. Madsen, editors : contributors, John J. Field
    ...[et al.].
       p. cm. — (Anthropological papers of the University of Arizona;
no. 56)
    Includes bibliographical references and index.
    ISBN 0–8165–1314–7 (acid-free paper)
    1. Hohokam culture—Social conditions. 2. Hohokam culture—
Irrigation. 3. Hohokam culture—Agriculture. 4. Social archaeology—
Santa Cruz River Basin (Ariz. and Mexico). 5. Santa Cruz River Basin
(Ariz. and Mexico)—Antiquities. 6. Arizona—Antiquities. I. Fish,
Suzanne, K. II. Fish, Paul R. III. Madsen, John H. (John Henry),
1947– . IV. Field, John J. 1961– . V. Series.
E99.H68M35   1992
979. 1'7901--dc20   92-8510
                                        CIP

Contents

FIGURES

TABLES

Preface

The Marana Community is a social and territorial unit of Classic period Hohokam settlement in the Tucson Basin of southern Arizona during the twelfth and thirteenth centuries (A.D. 1150–1350). Prehistorically, this multisite entity drew its essence from the social relationships, settlements, and land use of a dynamic population of desert cultivators. Our ability to recognize and understand the Marana Community today derives in large part from marks on a map. The following pages trace our pathways to reconstructing production and society in this former time and place and present our findings to date. As a more general goal, we hope this study will serve as an argument for the potential of a survey methodology not yet fully realized in Southwestern archaeology.

The evolution, structure, and productive basis of the Marana Community became a focus of inquiry in the context of a larger project known as the Northern Tucson Basin Survey. The inadequacy of existing frameworks for interpreting Hohokam archaeology in the Tucson Basin and other Hohokam regions outside a "core area" surrounding Phoenix, Arizona became apparent following a small scale excavation in the future study area. In 1981 at the inception of the survey, even minimally comprehensive settlement patterns were lacking. Information pertaining to the kinds, frequencies, and distributions of sites for any time horizon or significant areal segment had not been obtained. Acquisition of such data in the northern Tucson Basin became the goal of an extended Arizona State Museum survey project directed by the volume editors.

To accomplish our objectives, we chose a survey strategy termed 100 percent, total, or full-coverage. Full-coverage survey involves the systematic examination of large contiguous blocks of terrain at a uniform level of intensity (Fish and Kowalewski 1990: 2). The value of this approach for regional and relational problems had been amply demonstrated in Mesoamerica (for example, Sanders and others 1979; Blanton and others 1981) and the Near East (Adams 1965, 1981; Wright 1979), but it had seldom been attempted in the Southwest. The major advantages of full-coverage survey for our research objectives were: (1) the recovery of spatial relationships among remains of all sizes, representing ephemeral activ-

ities as well as habitation; (2) the ability to evaluate settlement pattern against a full range of environmental variation; and (3) the ability to define territorial units of interrelated sites that included relatively low densities and dispersed distributions. Coverage of the study area at a spacing of 30 meters between surveyors was the eventual compromise between our desire to recover the greatest amount of detail and still achieve a pattern of regional scale (P. Fish and others 1991). In hindsight, we had no good idea of study area size or extent of regional data that would be required to define meaningful units of territory and society.

Aside from the obvious logistical advantage of proximity to a home base at the University of Arizona, a variety of considerations governed our decision to select the Tucson Basin for intensive study. This area had been recognized as a distinctive region within the Hohokam cultural tradition for some time. In the period of early Spanish contact, it appears that the Tucson Basin was the major aboriginal population center of southern Arizona. A fortunately low level of modern land use in the northern Basin meant that the desired regional scope could be achieved in conjunction with well-preserved surface remains.

Because rapid growth is under way north of the Tucson urban limit, this survey was a last opportunity to recover many aspects of archaeological settlement. In recognition of this fact, the Arizona State Historic Preservation Office provided initial support to the Arizona State Museum for the Northern Tucson Basin Survey. A basin segment of 260 square kilometers (100 square miles) was targeted in 1981. Spatial configurations of a large Classic period community near the modern town of Marana were beginning to emerge from this survey by 1984. The Bureau of Reclamation, the Arizona State Land Department, and the Museum cooperated at that time to continue the survey program northward in order to provide a regional context for excavations required by construction of the Central Arizona Project canal in the Tucson vicinity.

Results from the initial survey east of Marana were instrumental in refining our concept of the nature of Classic period communities near Tucson and in adjacent desert basins. A central site containing an earthen platform mound was surrounded by settlements of varying size and function in diverse environmental zones. This concept structured ensuing survey design, for which the goal became acquisition of full-coverage data characterizing three such communities (see Fig. 1.8). Full-coverage survey blocks were centered on the mound sites in each community and totaled 470 square kilometers (180 square miles). The three blocks were then connected by survey transects in a study area covering 1800 square kilometers (700 square miles). Access, funding, and results from ancillary excavations were most advantageous for the Marana Community and it received a proportionally large share of project effort.

Investigations in the Marana Community are unique in several ways. Full-coverage survey of more than 350 square kilometers (125 square miles) encompasses the entire community as well as substantial areas surrounding it. Although excavated information was limited to testing at one large site (Lange and Deaver 1989) when the survey began, the study area has since witnessed investigations both within and adjacent to the community. In addition to research reported in this volume, there have been a number of large and small excavations by various investigators (Bernard-Shaw 1988, 1989, 1990a; Czaplicki and Ravesloot 1988; Downum 1986; Henderson 1987a; G. Rice 1987a; Wallace 1983) and studies of agricultural strategy (S. Fish, P. Fish, and Madsen 1985, 1989; S. Fish, P. Fish, Miksicek, and Madsen 1985; S. Fish, P. Fish, and Downum 1984; Waters and Field 1986; S. Fish and Donaldson 1991).

These elements of project history provided the foundation for an interpretive emphasis on Marana Community organization and its economic basis. Prior interests of the principal investigators and their collaborators, combined with National Science Foundation support, led to particular analytical attention to agricultural production. Early survey efforts revealed impressive arrays of types of agricultural remains that had not previously received systematic attention. Furthermore, many of these agricultural features could be linked to the cultivation of agave. This intriguing evidence of large-scale production led us to continue focusing on agricultural strategies used by the Hohokam residents of the Marana Community.

We have drawn heavily upon aspects of settlement pattern, including systematic artifact collections, in our interpretation of community organization. The unequal availability of excavated data entails major reliance even now on surface distributions for recognizing attributes of organizational structure. The following chapters outline some of the most comprehensive data in the Hohokam tradition for architectural and settlement hierarchies and

for the variable distribution of population and subsistence production across a zonally differentiated landscape. Our results make it clear that convincing interpretations of these phenomena require broad-scale patterns of the type obtained for the Marana Community.

The major contributions of our research to date in the northern Tucson Basin can be summarized under three themes: (1) the evolutionary background and structure of Classic period Hohokam settlement in a region outside the Phoenix Basin (Chapters 1, 2, 3, 9); (2) the nature of differentiated productive patterns within a Classic community in response to environmental and settlement diversity (Chapters 4, 5, 6); and (3) recognition of the magnitude of agave cultivation and its economic role (Chapters 7, 8).

Although we attempted an ideal sequence of research stages from general to specific, this monograph reflects more than ten years of evolving project history. Varying levels of scope and detail are outcomes of the episodes by which our broader understanding progressed. We often had to delay ongoing efforts in order to resolve critical issues in interwoven themes. Availability of collaborators and funding tempered the degree to which individual topics could be explored. Thus, the following chapters embody the fits and starts of real life research, as will be recognized by those who have experienced the vicissitudes of long-term commitment to a regional study.

Acknowledgments

Marana Community research has benefitted from the support of numerous institutions and individuals. It is a pleasant task to recall our benefactors, coworkers, and advisors over the course of ten years. Early funding came from the Arizona State Historic Preservation Office (SP 8104). In their capacities as successive directors, James Ayres, Donna Shober, and Shereen Lerner aided us in obtaining grants for survey (SP 8315 and 9314) and later for the preparation of nominations to the National Register of Historic Places (SP 10735). An award from the National Science Foundation (BNS-8408141) permitted focused study of agricultural production. Gene Rogge was instrumental in initiating survey funding from the Bureau of Reclamation in order to provide a regional context for archaeological investigation occasioned by construction of the Central Arizona Project aqueduct. His successors as Bureau archaeologists, Tom Lincoln and Kathy Pedrick, have further facilitated project backing through the framework of a cooperative agreement with the Arizona State Land Department and the Arizona State Museum of The University of Arizona (Grant

4-CS-30-01380). Information, interest, and administrative oversight was generously supplied by Robert Larkin of the Arizona State Land Department.

Support and encouragement from the staff of the Arizona State Museum and its director, Raymond H. Thompson, have been central to the success of all investigative stages. Logistical arrangements, facilities, equipment, and professional expertise represent a significant level of research investment beyond that acquired from external sources. The Department of Anthropology provided teaching assistants and partial transportation costs for archaeological field methods classes that participated in survey and excavation over many semesters.

It is impossible to acknowledge or even to name all of the individuals who contributed to our present state of knowledge concerning the Marana Community. This volume is the product of the efforts of several hundred student employees, students in classes, members of the Arizona Archaeological and Historical Society, the Arizona Archaeological Society, and other volunteers and colleagues from multiple disciplines. However, the following persons deserve special recognition.

Among the many members of survey teams, we would like to single out the long-term survivors, who furnished ideas as well as energy: Chris Downum, Jim Bayman, Rich Lange, John Field, Barb Roth, Jim Skibo, and Jim Lombard. The organization of laboratory work was overseen by Carri VerPlank, Kim Beckwith, and Regina Chapin. Ceramic analyses were ably performed by Stephanie Whittlesey and Kim Beckwith. Jim Vint aided in analysis of lithic artifacts. Masa Tani and Regina Chapin assembled and organized endless survey data.

Our understanding of the northern Tucson Basin environment was enhanced by geomorphological studies undertaken by the late Keith Katzer, John Field, Jim Lombard, and Janette Schuster. Karen Reichhardt mapped and classified study area vegetation. Matts Myhrman and Gerald Matlock evaluated and quantified hydrological factors. Delores Lewis, a Tohono O'odham farmer, and Adalberto Cruz, a farmer from Cucurpe, Sonora, provided invaluable insights into traditional cultivators' perspectives on the Marana landscape. Gary Nabhan of the Phoenix Botanical Garden/Native Seed Search helped arrange the visits of these two agricultural experts and added his own experienced observations.

Information and resources for experimental agave plantings were gratefully received from Robert McDaniel of the Department of Plant Sciences at The University of Arizona. Jeff Parsons of the Museum of Anthropology at the University of Michigan shared data on Otomi Indian planting, processing, and use of agave in the state of Hidalgo, Mexico. Relevant ethnographic practices throughout northern Mexico and southern Arizona were related by Gary Nabhan from his extensive travels and studies. Charlie Miksicek was an indispensable partner in all aspects of our investigation of agave's role in Marana Community agricultural production. He also examined countless liters of ash from roasting pits to document this cultigen.

Numerous colleagues improved our methodology and interpretation through encouragement, advice, criticism, skepticism, intuition, and discussion. We express our particular appreciation to Emil Haury, Paul Martin, Vance Haynes, Charlie Miksicek, Jeff Parsons, Michael Schiffer, Norman Yoffee, Gary Nabhan, Dave Doyel, Dave Wilcox, Chris Downum, Stephanie Whittlesey, Henry Wallace, Jim Holmlund, Bill Doelle, Glen Rice, Kathy Henderson, Mary Bernard, Bill Doolittle, Vorsila Bohrer, Jeff Reid, Keith Kintigh, Ken Kvamme, Curtiss Brennan, and Jim Bayman. Linda Cordell and Paul Minnis read earlier versions of this manuscript and offered many valuable suggestions.

This volume owes its present form to the wisdom, persistence, and skill of Carol Gifford, who guided us through all stages of editing and production. Rose Slavin reproduced several versions of each chapter and helped us remain sufficiently organized to reach completion. We thank Axel E. Nielsen for his translation of the abstract into Spanish. Ron Beckwith's talents are apparent in all drafted figures. Photography by Helga Teiwes graces a number of pages, as indicated. Other credited photographs are by Charlie Miksicek, Wendy Hodgson, Marcus Fish, and Cooper Aerial Photo, Inc. Authors of respective chapters provided the remaining illustrations.

CHAPTER ONE

An Introduction to Time, Place, and Research

Suzanne K. Fish, Paul R. Fish, and John H. Madsen

The prehistoric residents of the Tucson Basin were participants in a Hohokam cultural tradition spanning 116,000 square kilometers (45,000 square miles) in the desert basins of south central Arizona (Fig. 1.1). The name Hohokam is usually reserved for pottery-making inhabitants of this territory, although Late Archaic occupants had adopted a farming lifestyle centuries prior to the earliest manufacture of ceramics about 2000 years ago. One of the major subdivisions of archaeological cultures in the southwestern United States, the Hohokam tradition is distinguished by designs in red paint on buff, brown, or gray pottery during all but the initial and final segments of the ceramic sequence.

The initial interval of ceramic manufacture is known from limited exposures, but has been documented in widespread locations during the first few centuries of the Christian Era. Compared to the precise, tree-ring-dated archaeological chronologies of the northern Southwest, Hohokam sequences are not internally refined or well synchronized among the regions of the tradition. An exhaustive review of chronological data has recently been completed by Jeffrey Dean (1991) and is the source for schema in Figure 1.2. The final years of the tradition remain a subject of debate, marked by a paucity of evidence between the early fifteenth century and reliable Spanish observation in the 1680s. Primarily Piman-speaking Indians of the historic period represent geographic successors in limited sectors of the former Hohokam domain and exhibit only a generalized level of cultural continuity.

CULTURAL DIAGNOSTICS

The Hohokam are distinguished from other prehistoric peoples of the southwestern United States by a strong cultural orientation toward the Mesoamerican fringe to the south (P. Fish 1989: 21). Both in stylistic elements and in settlement pattern the Hohokam resemble the historic, river-oriented, rancheria cultures of

adjacent Sonora and Sinaloa more than the Puebloans of uplands to the north and east. Hohokam ceramic traits with Mexican associations in a variety of periods include incising, grooving, repetitive small design elements, and vessel forms such as molcajetes (chili graters), comals (griddles), tripods, and censers. In the earlier part of the sequence, figurines, censers, and palettes form a suite of ritual items that are rare in the Southwest beyond the northern extent of Hohokam occupation. Similarly, mounds and ballcourts are classes of public architecture with distributional continuity to the south, in contrast to the kivas of Puebloan groups. More than other spheres of material culture, these ceremonial, ideological, and, by inference, organizational expressions have been the operative criteria in delimiting the boundaries of the Hohokam tradition.

The Hohokam lived in pit houses with wattle and daub or brush superstructures throughout the sequence. Adobe rooms were added about A.D. 1100 near the beginning of the Classic period and were often grouped within the walls of a compound. Earthen-banked ballcourts were the common form of public architecture before the Classic period, superseded thereafter by platform mounds supporting adobe structures. Public architecture was constructed at the large sites in differentiated settlement patterns. Hohokam agriculture was distinctive in its scale, intensity, and engineering feats that created hundreds of kilometers of canals along perennial rivers. A variety of alternate farming technologies were employed in other environmental settings.

A watershed in Hohokam cultural development is indicated by the transition to the Classic period about A.D. 1150, although more continuities with Preclassic times are now evident than previously. Canal systems reached their greatest extent, and acreage cultivated by alternate techniques was expanded in many areas. Maximum population densities at the largest settlements and highest overall densities for most regions were achieved after this transition. Greater investment in integrative

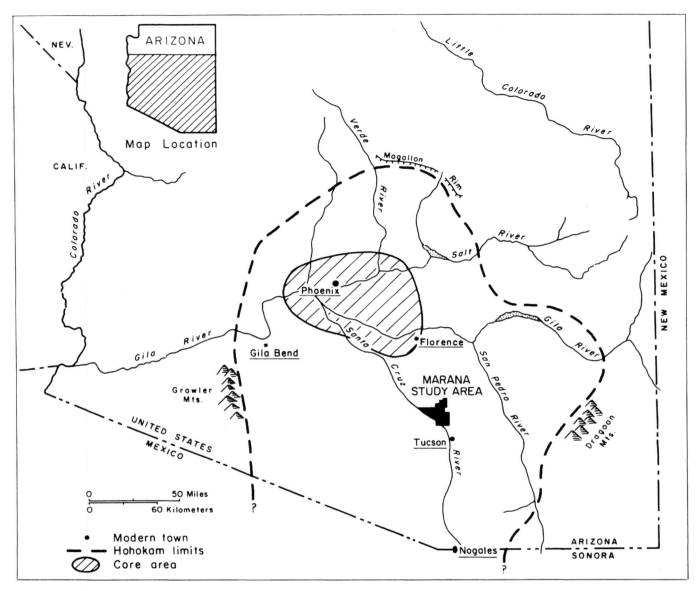

Figure 1.1. The Hohokam tradition of southern Arizona.

organization can be seen in the construction of the most massive examples of public architecture, with which socially differentiated personnel were now associated.

ENVIRONMENTAL SETTING

Hohokam in all reaches of the tradition shared the challenges of a relatively low, hot, desert environment. Their geographic extent to the north and east coincided closely with the vegetational attributes demarcating the Sonoran Desert. More tropical facies of this desert extend southward from Hohokam territory, and drier facies continue to the west and southwest. Even in the vicinity of the larger mountain ranges in the basin-and-range country of southern Arizona, Hohokam settlements were concentrated in basin interiors, seldom exceeding an elevation of 1100 m (3500 feet).

Bimodal rainfall in the Hohokam area is associated with a greater diversity in growth forms among plant communities and a more arborescent character of vegetation than under winter-dominant precipitation to the west and summer-dominant to the east (Turner and Brown 1982: 182). Associations of shrubby plants near basin floors (Fig. 1.3) predominantly contain mixes of creosote bush, bursage, saltbush, and similar species, but

A.D.	Major chronological subdivision	Period	Phoenix Basin Phase Sequence (Dean 1991: 91)	Tucson Basin Phase Sequence (Dean 1991: 91)	Temporal designations used in this book
1500					
1400			Civano	Tucson	LATE CLASSIC
1300	CLASSIC	CLASSIC			
1200			Soho	Tanque Verde	EARLY CLASSIC
1100					
1000		SEDENTARY	Sacaton	Rincon	LATE
900					
800		COLONIAL	Santa Cruz	Rillito	PRECLASSIC
700	PRECLASSIC		Gila Butte	Cañada del Oro	EARLY COLONIAL
600			Snaketown		
500			Sweetwater	No local	LATE PIONEER
400		PIONEER	Estrella	decorated	EARLY PIONEER
300			Vahki	pottery*	
200			Red Mountain		
100	LATE ARCHAIC	LATE ARCHAIC	LATE ARCHAIC	LATE ARCHAIC	LATE ARCHAIC

* The Tucson Basin Pioneer period recently has been subdivided into the Tortolita phase (A.D. 450–700), including red ware ceramics (Bernard-Shaw 1990a: 209–213), and an earlier phase with only plain ware pottery dating between A.D. 200 and 450 (Bernard-Shaw 1990a: 215; Huckell and others 1987: 293-296).

Figure 1.2. Correlation of Phoenix Basin and Tucson Basin Hohokam phase sequences.

larger plant forms are common in associations on basin slopes (Fig. 1.4). Distinctively large Sonoran Desert perennials include columnar saguaro cactus and the leguminous trees, mesquite, palo verde, and ironwood. Numbers and size of economically important trees and a comparative variety and abundance of edible cacti set off the plentiful plant resources of the Sonoran Desert basins from those of the adjacent Chihuahuan and Mohave deserts.

Parallel series of desert basins are bounded and separated by discontinuous mountain ranges of generally limited mass. Widths of well-defined basins range from 10 km to 32 km (6 to 20 miles), with the broadest rarely wider than 48 km (30 miles; S. Fish and Nabhan 1991: 31). Rock pediments along mountain flanks are overlain by relatively thin soils, but detrital sediments fill the basin interiors to great depth. Water in drainages from bordering uplands deposits suspended soil as it leaves the mountains, creating alluvial fans. These outwash fans coalesce on the lower slopes in zones of active deposition. Slopes descending from bordering ranges are the dominant landforms of inner basins and are called "bajadas," a term used throughout this monograph. The floodplains of axial drainages are positioned along the basin floors where the bajadas from opposite mountain borders meet.

Yearly precipitation in the area inhabited by the Hohokam rarely surpasses 400 mm (15 inches), but local averages vary by a factor of two. Totals between 175 mm and 300 mm (7 to 12 inches) are widespread, with a few locales receiving less than 150 mm (6 inches). Annual precipitation below 225 mm (9 inches) corresponds with greater variation about the mean and higher summer temperatures in the middle of the Hohokam domain near the modern city of Phoenix and in a swath to the southwest. Phoenix temperatures reach 40° C (100° F) about 90 days per year. To the north, east, and south, higher elevations and somewhat ameliorated conditions occur in conjunction with increasing proportions of rainfall during the summer months.

CORE AND PERIPHERAL REGIONS

Climatic extremes in the Phoenix Basin at the center of the Hohokam world (see Fig. 1.1) were countered by hydrological advantages for agriculturalists. The confluence of the Salt and Gila rivers lies just southwest of Phoenix. The two conjoined valley segments upstream from the confluence form the Phoenix Basin, which contains the broadest expanse of flat, irrigable floor in the entire Hohokam tradition. The Salt and Gila transport water from vast upland watersheds to the north and east outside the low desert. Peak flows in the spring carry mountain snowmelt. With insignificant seasonal frost, two cropping seasons were possible for Hohokam irrigators along canal networks of the largest scale in prehis-

Figure 1.3. Typical vegetation community near the basin floor
dominated by shrubs. (Photograph by Helga Teiwes.)

toric North America. More than 500 km (300 miles) of
main trunk lines have been mapped (Masse 1981; Nicholas and Feinman 1989).

The densest regional population and largest Hohokam
settlements occurred in the Phoenix Basin. Estimates for
maximum population range from a low of 30,000 persons
to more than 100,000 persons (Haury 1976: 356; Schroeder 1960; Doyel 1991; P. Fish and S. Fish 1991) in an
area of 2000 square kilometers (750 square miles).
Impressive remains attracted the great majority of early
field research by archaeologists, and urban construction
has continued to prompt intensive investigations in
recent years. In contrast with the archaeology of other
Southwestern areas, Hohokam studies have emphasized
comparison against the Phoenix sequence rather than the
definition of regional variants. This combination of
factors has resulted in a strong core-periphery model, in
which outlying regions have been considered imitative
and less developed.

The core-periphery dichotomy has also been cast as a
distinction between riverine and nonriverine or outlying

desert regions, based on the implications of differential
opportunities for large-scale irrigation (Haury 1950:
546–548). In spite of higher rainfall north, east, and
south of the Phoenix core, rivers lack sizable upland
watersheds and are intermittent rather than perennial.
Basin and floodplain morphologies restrict the width of
irrigable land. Peak flows in summer rather than spring
and greater frost hazards limit early crops. Settlement
was more dispersed in these areas, and it has been generally assumed that populations lacked the productive
base for an elaborated cultural development equal to
that in the Phoenix Basin. Spotty and sporadic research
in the vast geographic remainder of the Hohokam tradition outside the Phoenix Basin did little to modify these
perceptions before the last decade. Accelerated investigations elsewhere have now revealed unanticipated levels
of population and an equivalent array of material culture, including an increasing number of recorded sites
with public architecture.

In the Phoenix Basin, irrigation networks and large
sites were mapped in the early part of this century before

Figure 1.4. Typical vegetation community on basin slopes dominated
by leguminous trees and cacti. (Photograph by Marcus Fish.)

extensive modern land use, providing a means for recognizing clusters of interrelated sites along a shared canal line. A unit of settlement surrounding a central site with public architecture was termed a "community" on the basis of common interests in the acquisition and distribution of water (Doyel 1974, 1980). Integrative functions are ascribed to the central site, as embodied in communal construction and observances at ballcourts and mounds. Multiple community units along canals as long as 30 km (18 miles) could be inferred from the spacing of central sites at fairly regular intervals (Wilcox and Sternberg 1983: 195; Crown 1987: 154; Gregory and Nials 1985).

At the start of this study, sites with public architecture in outlying regions implied similar functions of multisite integration and some form of community organization outside the Phoenix Basin. These instances did not coincide with large-scale irrigation, however. Configurations of related settlement surrounding such sites, and their productive bases were unknown. In the Tucson

Basin, ballcourts and mounds were known to occur both near the Santa Cruz River and in other basin settings.

REGIONAL CHARACTER OF THE TUCSON BASIN

Defined by the drainage basin of the Santa Cruz, a major desert river, the Tucson Basin (Figs. 1.1, 1.5) is a typical focus of regional research in Southwestern archaeology. Mountains rimming the basin and dividing it from other drainage systems form physical barriers promoting a degree of both natural and cultural closure (Figs. 1.6, 1.7). Annual precipitation is between 225 mm and 300 mm (9 to 12 inches). Rainfall must be concentrated for successful cropping under conditions of rapid runoff and evaporation. Within an average horizontal distance of 24 km (15 miles) between mountains on the east and west, no internal barriers are present to inhibit travel, communication, and exchange.

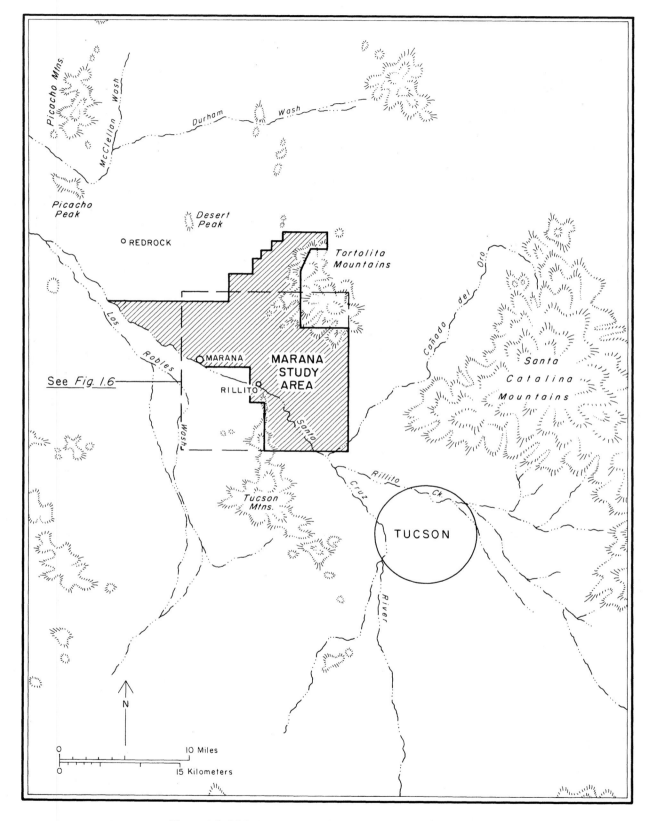

Figure 1.5. Major topographic features of the Tucson Basin.

Figure 1.6. Aerial view of the portion of the northern Tucson Basin between the Tucson and Tortolita mountains. (Photograph by Cooper Aerial Survey Company.)

Well-defined local sequences of decorated pottery, paralleling the ceramic sequence of the Phoenix core, have been established for few other Hohokam regions. The Tucson Basin is the major exception (Kelly 1978). The earliest Hohokam decorated pottery is rare and appears to be imported from the core among assemblages of Tucson plain and red-slipped wares. By the beginning of the eighth century A.D., however, a coherent regional style is evidenced by a series of local red-on-

brown designs exhibiting broadly similar trends with red-on-buff decoration of the Phoenix Basin. In the early 1980s, recorded distributions of ballcourt and mound sites were sufficient to suggest substantial levels of prehistoric population and community organization of settlement throughout the Tucson Basin.

Over its long history, the city of Tucson has erased Hohokam remains in a nucleus of most desirable land along the Santa Cruz River and successive outer zones,

Figure 1.7. View across the northern Tucson Basin from the Tucson Mountains on the west toward the Tortolita Mountains on the east. (Photograph by Helga Teiwes.)

with few records of even the largest former sites. As in the prehistoric era, however, population and agriculture are of lesser magnitude than in the Salt and Gila valleys. North of Tucson, historic settlement has been late (mainly after 1915) and clustered along a few roads. The dominant economic activity has been cattle raising. Modern agriculture is confined to localized and fragmented strips along the Santa Cruz River and one tributary. These conditions are in marked contrast to the Phoenix Basin where greater urban sprawl and highly mechanized irrigation in leveled fields have obliterated major portions of regional settlement pattern. The northern Tucson Basin promised preservation of a full range of surface remains in environmental settings representative of the basin as a whole.

THE MARANA STUDY AREA AND THE CLASSIC PERIOD COMMUNITY

Optimal conditions for recovering comprehensive settlement patterns and defining territorial organization are found in a broad trans-bajada area near the town of Marana, Arizona (Figs. 1.1, 1.8). A localized high water table on the Santa Cruz floodplain offers the greatest potential for riverine irrigation in the northern Tucson Basin. Elevational diversity is repeated between the river and the low volcanic Tucson Mountains on the west and the more massive Tortolita Mountains on the east.

Diachronic trends in agricultural production and territorial organization throughout the Hohokam sequence can be monitored in this Marana study area. Agricultural occupations beginning with Late Archaic cultivators are continuous until the late Classic period. Population, as measured by settlement, peaks during the early Classic period in tandem with the most expansive and intensive land use. The intersection of societal organization and agricultural production can be examined for technological combinations typifying Hohokam regions outside the core: irrigation on a smaller scale, diversions of short-term flow in ephemeral drainages or floodwater farming, and techniques for capturing overland runoff.

The trappings of community organization are reflected in a platform mound at a preeminent site within this

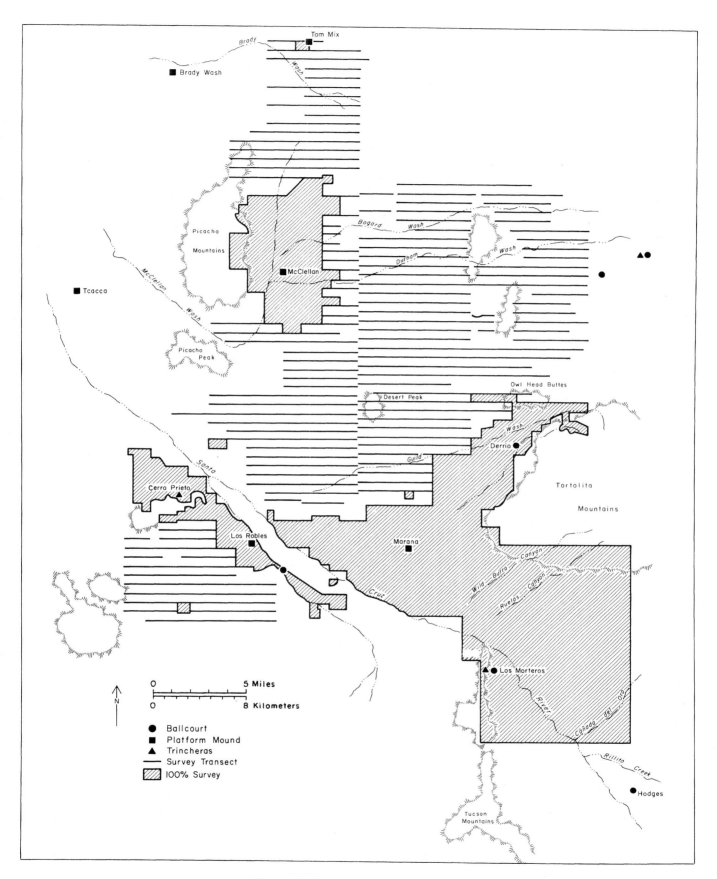

Figure 1.8. Survey coverage north of Tucson.

study area. Enclosing this center is a virtually intact framework of concentrated contemporary settlement, surrounded by markedly lower site densities and areas with scarce remains (see Fig. 3.2). Community units farther north, also surveyed in this study, offer comparative territorial configurations in somewhat different settings (Fig. 1.8). The mound center in the Robles Community is 19 km (12 miles) northwest and the center of the McClellan Community is 27 km (17 miles) north.

Because late Classic settlement is largely absent in the Marana study area, distributional evidence for agricultural production and settlement organization in the early

Classic period community is not obscured by subsequent prehistoric occupations. The abundant decorated pottery of the early Classic period Tanque Verde phase provides a reliable diagnostic for identifying even small community habitations and activity loci. Unlike the majority of large Hohokam sites with public architecture, the Marana Mound Site has been spared the ravages of serious pothunting. For understanding synchronic relationships in a noncore community, the early Classic configuration in the Marana study area comes as close to an ideal slice of time as can be achieved with Hohokam chronology and settlement.

CHAPTER TWO

Early Sedentism and Agriculture in the Northern Tucson Basin

Suzanne K. Fish, Paul R. Fish, and John H. Madsen

By the eighth century A.D., when emergent community organization can first be discerned in the northern Tucson Basin, regional inhabitants had already been cultivators for at least 1500 years. Only with the recent proliferation of radiocarbon dates for Late Archaic cultigens within the Hohokam domain has it become clear that farming preceded the appearance of pottery by as much as a millennium; therefore there are conceptual difficulties in considering the earliest ceramic occupations as times of "initial" agriculture. Both Late Archaic and Pioneer period settlements are without doubt underrepresented in survey data due to the relative scarcity of diagnostic artifacts and prolonged exposure to postoccupational processes. Nevertheless, the similar distributions of sites within this broad combined time span is striking (Fig. 2.1). This chapter emphasizes implications of Late Archaic settlement, locational continuities into early ceramic times, and the establishment of basic patterns of agricultural settlement.

A FRAMEWORK FOR TRANSITION IN THE TUCSON BASIN

Agriculture is already a significant factor in the earliest period for which settlement patterns can be obtained in the northern Tucson Basin. There is a virtual absence of evidence for the cultural and demographic background from which these first farmers arose. A long line of local predecessors is suggested by a Clovis point fragment (Agenbroad 1967) and a handful of Middle Archaic projectile points. Middle Archaic points, dating between approximately 5000 B.C. and 1500 B.C., occur in both upper basin and riverine zones of the Marana study area. Intensive later reuse of key locations such as springs and the scarcity of earlier Holocene alluvial surfaces on the bajadas, some of which experienced mid-Holocene scouring (Schuster and Katzer 1984), inhibit survey detection of pre-agricultural populations.

Although the Sonoran Desert today is exceptional for its array of edible plants for hunters and gatherers, packrat midden studies indicate that current distributions of species became established in the low southern deserts of Arizona only about 4000 years ago (Van Devender and Spaulding 1979; Anderson and Van Devender 1991). Sites dating substantially prior to 1000 B.C. have not been studied in the Tucson Basin and evidence for subsistence is lacking regionally. However, elsewhere in the southern portion of the Southwest probable structures (Martin and Rinaldo 1950: 430; O'Laughlin 1980), storage pits (Windmiller 1973; O'Laughlin 1980), and large sites with diverse artifact assemblages and high densities of well-made ground stone (Whalen 1971; Bayham and others 1986; Sayles and Antevs 1941; Agenbroad 1970; P. Fish 1967) suggest extended seasons of residence in some locations before the addition of cultigens.

The perception of Late Archaic occupations and often even the earliest ceramic ones as constituting a unitary "stage" in Southwestern cultural development, coupled with fragmentary regional data, tends to encourage the use of broad hunter-gatherer analogies in interpretation. For example, a generalized model of mobile band economy as reconstructed by Steward (1938) for the Great Basin has been widely applied across the regionally diverse environments of the Southwest. The possibility of a significant degree of sedentism in this early portion of the Southwestern archaeological record is seldom raised. For preceramic time, pronounced mobility in a seasonal round could be described as a widespread article of faith. However, analogy should be used even more judiciously for earlier than for later prehistoric times. Ethnographic observations of hunters and gatherers and less committed cultivators may not be representative of pre-agricultural settlement and subsistence in favored locales (Freeman 1968; S. Fish and P. Fish 1991; Mueller-Wille and Dickson 1991). Historic hunters and gatherers in the Southwest have been geographically

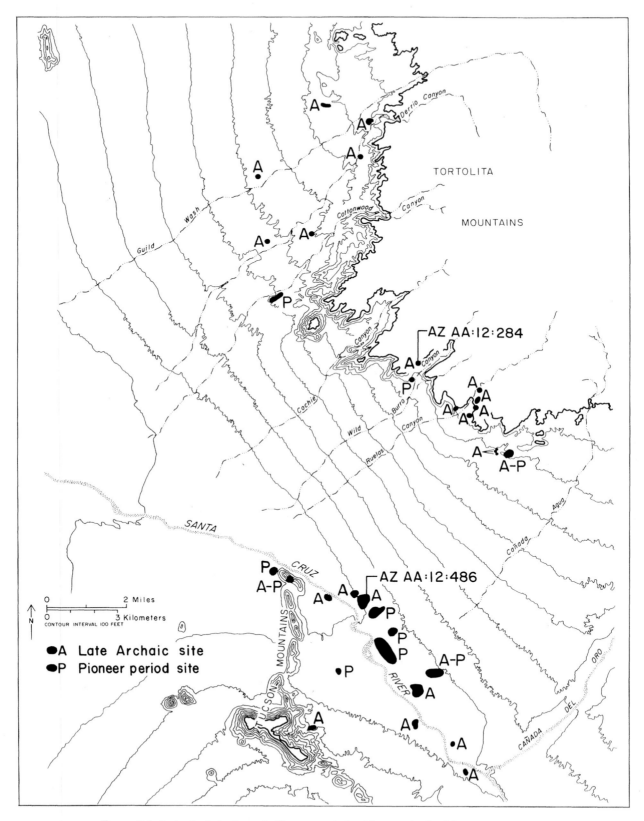

Figure 2.1. Late Archaic through Pioneer period settlement in the Marana survey area.

marginal to the territories of successful agriculturalists or have been strongly influenced by the presence of domesticated animals and other postcontact elements.

Direct ethnographic analogs for early cultivator sites are lacking in the accumulating evidence from survey and excavation in the Tucson Basin. Hunter-gatherer subsistence patterns have not been recorded historically or ethnographically in those areas of the Sonoran Desert where optimal environments for initial cultivation occur. The Seri and Sand Papago, Sonoran Desert people to the south of former Hohokam territory who practiced little or no agriculture, lived in regions receiving half to one-third of the relatively generous 250 mm to 300 mm (10 to 12 inches) of annual rainfall in the Tucson area. The Tohono O'odham (Papago) Indians near Tucson, who in historic times moved between winter villages and summer farming settlements, did not also occupy stretches along the Santa Cruz River with sustained surface flow; Hispanics, Anglos, and missionized Indian populations dominated those locales. Furthermore, the high water requirements of numerous cattle curtailed the duration of Tohono O'odham settlement in the vicinity of moderate water sources that might otherwise have sustained human needs (S. Fish and Nabhan 1991). By the time of ethnographic record, Apache residence patterns reflected horses and other livestock, guns, and a postcontact economy heavily influenced by raiding and trade with non-Indians.

Due to a lack of comprehensive settlement patterns for the Hohokam tradition, other than outlines derived from large irrigation networks, it has not previously been possible to place the relatively few identified sites of Late Archaic and early ceramic date within local or regional frameworks of contemporary settlement. In the northern Tucson Basin, sites recorded by systematic survey are modest in number but nevertheless exhibit a cohesive subset of locational correlates within the broader range encompassed by later occupations. In turn, the broader array of situations and more complete patterns during subsequent periods aid in understanding the overall agricultural potential of basin settings. In this way, regional settlement patterns provide a supplement to broad analogies for the interpretation of environmental selectivity and other aspects of early site distributions.

Similarity in some settlement pattern attributes with those of later times, and the occurrence of cultigens at most excavated sites, provide a basis for considering extended residence a likely correlate of food production for many Late Archaic and early ceramic residents of the Tucson Basin. This position is counter to the weight of recent archaeological opinion concerning early cultivators in the Southwest (for example, Simmons 1986;

Minnis 1985; Gilman 1987; Gumerman 1969; Rice 1980; Hard 1990; Nelson 1990) and undoubtedly is one of the more controversial conclusions arising from the present study. Issues regarding degrees of sedentism may not be conclusively resolved even with excavated data, which in the Marana study area are drawn from limited exposures at a few sites. Therefore, the proposed implications of Late Archaic and Pioneer period settlement patterns should be considered preliminary but are based on: (1) the unique availability of systematic distributional evidence from full-coverage survey; (2) attributes of regional environment in light of ethnographic analogy and later prehistoric land use; and (3) the model of agricultural transition and the potential for sedentism advanced in the following discussion (see also S. Fish, P. Fish, and Madsen 1990a; S. Fish and P. Fish 1991).

AGRICULTURAL TRANSITION AND THE TUCSON ENVIRONMENT

Variables Favoring Sedentism

In terms of multiseasonal abundance, diversity, and storability of plant foods, the Sonoran Desert has been described as one of the truly rich areas for the gatherer in North America (Nabhan 1985; Felger and Moser 1985; S. Fish and Nabhan 1991). Two seasonal peaks of rainfall in southern Arizona support a distinctive array of productive leguminous trees and succulents in addition to edible annuals. Linear valleys of the basin-and-range topography create elevational diversity within short trans-basin distances; most resources could have been acquired on a daily basis from settlements near permanent water at the river or mountain edge. In southern Arizona, constellations of conditions in favorable environments are consistent with both a substantial degree of preexisting sedentism and the early adoption of agriculture into compatible economic frameworks.

Of the critical combination of water, staples, and diverse resources in proximity that would permit extended residence in pre-agricultural times, perhaps the most limiting element in the Tucson Basin is a dependable water supply. Prolonged or permanent water in the Santa Cruz River occurs where igneous intrusions force underground flow to the surface. A second topographic location of permanent sources fed by upland watersheds is at the bases of the larger mountain masses bordering the basin.

The advantages of topographic and ecotonal diversity are well recognized (Flannery 1968; Gumerman and Johnson 1971). Diversity within short horizontal distances promotes the efficiency of logistical (Binford 1980,

1982) or more sedentary hunting and gathering strategies by increasing the range of resources within a convenient radius about a source of major dietary staples or long-term water. An optimal environmental constellation could be defined as: (1) a sustained water supply; (2) a dependable resource concentration, including an abundant staple; and (3) convenient access to environmental diversity. Indeed, such constellations should predict optimal locations for the earliest transitions to agricultural economies.

Both redundancy and diversity of resources contribute to the probability of a high degree of pre-agricultural sedentism in favorable locales of the Tucson Basin. Riparian species such as mesquite or saltbush occur widely but are densest near long-term water sources. Duplicate sets of diverse resources on opposing valley slopes or bajadas are accessible without residential mobility. Cacti such as saguaro, cholla, and prickly pear may be locally most dense on mid to upper bajadas, but distributions extend to the valley floor in many locations. The few additional species on relatively low mountain ranges such as the Tucsons and Tortolitas in the study area are generally within a day's round trip from a residential base near water. Only the occasional massive ranges of southern Arizona such as the Catalinas (Fig. 1.5) and Rincons east and south of the northern Tucson Basin study area offer unique (and, archaeobotanically, seldom documented) high-elevation resources. In fact, the mid to upper elevations of these mountains provide sparse evidence for prehistoric use during any period despite extensive survey (Arizona State Museum Site Survey File; Coronado National Forest Survey File).

In prime locations, no more than biseasonal movement and even year-round residence should be considered as possibilities for low-mobility hunters and gatherers and earliest farmers. Archaic occupations in these locations would have embodied a precondition of minimal conflict for the addition of cultivation to existing economic activities and schedules. Substantial duration of residence is a relevant variable both for situations of primary domestication and for those of secondary acceptance as in the Southwest. From this perspective, restricted residential mobility may be as much a prerequisite for a successful transition to agriculture as the result of such a transition.

Staple Resources

A few exceptional resources are usually pivotal in supporting the most sedentary lifestyles among groups who hunt and gather, such as salmon among tribes of the Northwest Coast or acorns among central California Indians. Dependable wild resources likely played a similar role as staples among those populations who were the earliest to adopt domesticates in any region. For example, in the Tehuacan Valley of Mexico, foxtail millet or *Setaria* was so consistently abundant in coprolites that it has been considered a potential early cultigen, although not cultivated in historic times (Smith 1967: 249; Callen 1967: 287). Sites with early corn in the Chaco Canyon area of New Mexico occur in dunes with dense stands of Indian rice grass. Caches of the seeds have also been recovered in contemporary rock shelters (Simmons 1982, 1986). These key resources recall the wild grasses that were heavily utilized just prior to the agricultural transition in the Old World, some of which gave rise to the first domesticates. Focused dependence and intensive tending of indigenous species are now demonstrated among Archaic populations of the eastern United States well prior to the advent of corn and other Mesoamerican domesticates (Smith 1989). If such practices constituted a widespread late Archaic pattern in North America, the potential for residential permanence in optimal locales of the Southwest would have been enhanced.

Mesquite beans exemplify a pivotal resource in southern Arizona. The pod yield from riparian mesquite groves is sufficiently prolific to serve as a staple for moderate populations. Except for the most severe droughts, freezes, or floods, and in spite of annual variability in individual trees, mesquite groves along larger drainages produce harvests year after year (Felger and Moser 1971, 1976; Aschmann 1959: 53; Bell and Castetter 1937: 18). In historic times, trees were pruned (Bean and Saubel 1972: 108) and yields are known to have been augmented by ditch irrigation (Bean and Lawton 1973: 27). The processed flour is highly nutritious and may be stored for up to two years. A single Cahuilla Indian worker might gather up to an estimated 80 kg of beans per day (Bean and Saubel 1972: 112). Average Seri production figures for flour are 40 kg per day with one man harvesting and two women pounding and winnowing (Felger and Moser 1971: 57). Raw or parched pods were stored for a year or longer in large basketry granaries by more sedentary historic groups (Castetter and Bell 1951; Bean and Saubel 1972; Bartlett 1854). Mesquite groves in some locales are thought to have permitted nonmigratory lifestyles among the California desert Cahuilla (Bean and Saubel 1972: 108).

Mesquites are distributed widely in the Tucson Basin but the largest and most abundant trees grow along the wide floodplains of drainages in the upper basin as well as in riverine groves. Both upland and riverine zones share optimal environmental combinations of potable water, accessible resource diversity, and this abundant staple. Thus, subsistence advantages involving both gathered and cultivated resources would have permitted extended residence at Late Archaic sites in riverine and upland zones of the study area.

LATE ARCHAIC AND EARLY CERAMIC SETTLEMENT PATTERNS

Visibility and Discovery Bias

Archaeological visibility presents a significant obstacle to the reconstruction of Tucson Basin settlement patterns of Late Archaic through Pioneer period age. Populations closely preceding the adoption of cultigens in the Late Archaic are virtually invisible due to the lack of chronologically sensitive diagnostic artifacts or features. It is not known whether projectile point styles associated with Late Archaic cultigens were also manufactured by hunters and gatherers during the several prior centuries. Furthermore, when isolated Archaic points are encountered at a site that also contains ceramics, it is difficult to distinguish between the presence of a Late Archaic component and the common Hohokam practice of retrieving older points.

Diagnostics are also a problem in the earliest ceramic assemblages of the Hohokam area, which contain no pottery types with painted or plastic decoration. In the recent past, initial plain wares were not readily distinguished from later ones in the Tucson area, although distinctive vessel forms are now known to occur (Huckell and others 1987; Bernard-Shaw 1990a). It is significant that the age of the earliest Tucson ceramic site now known was recognized only through the results of chronometric dating (Huckell and others 1987). Even for those subsequent Pioneer period occupations with decorated pottery, diagnostic sherds constitute no more than two percent of the ceramic assemblage and sherds assignable to particular phases are fewer still (see Chapter 6; Czaplicki and Ravesloot 1989b; Bernard-Shaw 1989; Kelly 1978).

Continuous occupation at hydrologically prime locations compounds recognition problems. Small artifact samples from alluvial profiles seldom contain decorated ceramics or diagnostic projectile points. Late Archaic and early ceramic sites are not all at great depths, but even in shallow contexts the rarity of diagnostics makes it difficult to distinguish early features interspersed among later ones. To achieve distributional data even partially comparable with settlement patterns of later ceramic times, both large numbers of sites and large artifact collections are essential.

Northern Tucson Basin Survey Patterns

The quantity of Late Archaic through Pioneer period sites in Figure 2.1 must be considered an abbreviated representation of occupation for the long time span in question. Surface indications of such age persist in a wide range of geomorphological settings, although site burial is greater for these earlier time periods in areas of active late Holocene deposition such as alluvial fans and drainage floodplains. The rarity of diagnostics, along with site burial, undoubtedly accentuate the perception of dual settlement clusters with few outliers, one concentration along the river near the end of the Tucson Mountains and another along the skirts of the Tortolita Mountains, separated by substantial unoccupied and unused territory. Loci of short-term activities that generated few artifacts are least likely to yield rare diagnostics, leading to an overemphasis on residential sites in these early settlement patterns.

Maximum size of individual sites and overall densities reflect the potential for concentrated populations in the vicinity of the Santa Cruz River. Domestic water, riparian resources such as mesquite groves, and water diversion opportunities impart long-standing attractions. As in ensuing ceramic phases, the largest sites occur near the river along the Tucson Mountains where igneous intrusions raise underground flow. Late Archaic facilities in the form of shallow wells or small reservoirs were constructed on the Santa Cruz floodplain to enhance and prolong water sources (Bernard-Shaw 1988).

An additional agricultural orientation for the band of settlement paralleling the river corresponds to cultivation of lower basin alluvial fans (described in Chapters 4 and 5). Alluvially active portions of the fans support dense stands of weedy annuals for gatherers and desirable conditions for floodwater farming through diversion of ephemeral drainages following storms. Recent excavations at three localities on these fans in the northern basin have revealed occupations containing Late Archaic cultigens (Chapter 6; Roth 1988, 1989; Mabry 1990). Aggradation and lateral movement of drainages across fans tend to obscure surface remains. Therefore, quantitative indications of fan settlement are underrepresented in overall distributions. All known Late Archaic and early ceramic fan settlements are located within 2 km (1 mile) of high water tables along the Santa Cruz. Although seasonal occupation of these sites is a possibility, structural remains are comparable with counterparts in floodplain sites of the Tucson Basin, and such distances for domestic water transport from the river are well within the ranges of ethnographic analogs.

The second concentration of Late Archaic through Pioneer period settlement is along the Tortolita flanks, again evoking a linkage with permanent rather than seasonal water. This is a preferred situation throughout the prehistoric sequence because accessible flow from mountain watersheds persists in drainages that provide

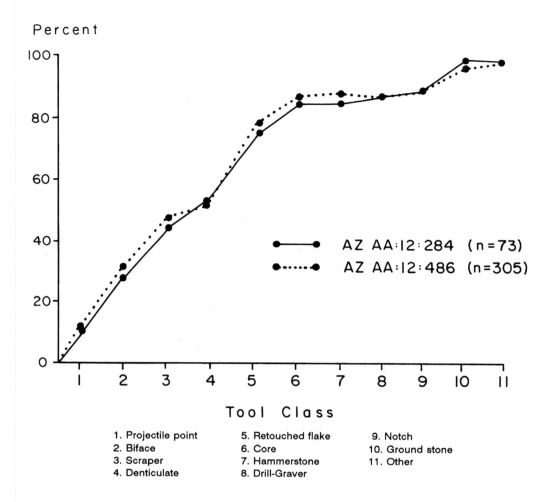

Figure 2.2. Cumulative frequency comparison of Late Archaic tool assemblages from a site on an alluvial fan near the Santa Cruz River (AZ AA:12:486) and a site on the upper bajada (AZ AA:12:284). Adapted from Roth 1989: 171–195. Using the Kolmogorov-Smirnov two-sample statistic, there is a probability of less than .001 that these samples were drawn from different populations.

domestic and agricultural water. Early sites tend to be located in the vicinity of easily diverted, small drainages as they emerge from the mountain front, and a few occur farther down the bajada along major water courses.

Although the largest upper bajada Archaic and early ceramic sites do not attain the size of the largest contemporary settlements along the river, maximum size exceeds 15 ha (35 acres). Artifact densities tend to be lower at higher elevation sites, but artifact assemblages, including frequencies of ground stone, are similar in some intensively occupied sites of both zones. This is illustrated by a comparison (Figs. 2.1, 2.2) of systematic artifact collections from an alluvial fan locality near the river (AZ AA:12:486) and from a site at the base of the Tortolitas (AZ AA:12:284). Early ceramic sites in both upper basin and river-oriented locations have produced

figurines and exotic items such as shell and include instances of trash mounds, the localized accumulations that typify Hohokam disposal of residential refuse.

Duration of Residence

A late historic Tohono O'odham or Papago analogy for riverine and upper basin settlement clusters would suggest annual movement between upland winter villages near permanent wells at the mountain edge and more temporary summer residences with seasonal reservoirs near low basin fields. However, this sort of biseasonal movement in the late nineteenth and early twentieth centuries described by Underhill (1939) and others was only one alternative among contemporary residence patterns (Fontana 1983a, 1983b). Additionally, the water needs of livestock seriously limited the duration of summer supplies at lower elevation settlements that were dependent on artificial water impoundments (S. Fish, P. Fish, and Madsen 1990b; S. Fish and Nabhan 1991).

Locales of early upper basin sites duplicate the same constellation of prolonged water availability and concentrated resources found at the river. Riparian vegetation is less areally extensive along upland drainages than along lusher stretches of the Santa Cruz floodplain, but mesquite and other species are abundant. Nonwoody plants that produce edible seeds, including saltbush, grasses, and various annuals, are similarly concentrated along both the river and drainages of the mountain edge. Mountain hunting and upland plant species such as wild grapes or yucca add supplementary resources only in the more massive Tortolita Mountains on the eastern basin edge. These minor resources could have been obtained through seasonal camps of brief duration. However, outside the mountain canyons, vegetation similar to that of the upper basin interior is predominant on all but the highest peaks bordering the northern basin. The subsistence advantage of seasonal movement of residence from either one of the settlement bands to the other would have been minor in view of the largely redundant wild resources and similar seasons of availability.

Environmental variables and archaeological remains suggest a potential for comparable degrees of persistence for both upper basin and riverine settlement clusters. Tohono O'odham ethnographic analogy would identify the higher sites with more extended occupations as winter settlements. As previously noted, upper basin sites reach substantial size but the largest are along the river. There are no excavated examples that can be used to compare details of settlement structure or subsistence. However, the diversity and proportions of artifact types for some upper basin settlements are similar to those of riverine counterparts.

Sites could have been advantageously located for both natural resource catchments and agricultural opportunity in a relatively uncrowded landscape. Lower population levels during the Late Archaic through Pioneer period apparently permitted habitation to be confined to optimal zones to a greater degree than in succeeding times. Undisturbed habitats for hunting and gathering also would have been more widespread and pressure on exploited resources lower.

BASIC PATTERNS OF SETTLEMENT AND PRODUCTION

The linkage of Late Archaic as well as early ceramic settlement patterns in the northern Tucson Basin with the requisites of farming is based on both direct evidence and on the emerging picture of Late Archaic subsistence throughout the Tucson Basin and surrounding areas of southern Arizona. Corn has been recovered from Late Archaic proveniences in excavations of limited scale on the Santa Cruz floodplain (Bernard-Shaw 1988), on two alluvial fans in the Marana study area (Chapter 6; Roth 1989), and on a third alluvial fan just to the south (Mabry 1990). By early ceramic times, botanical analyses in both these zones clearly demonstrate reliance on the range of later cultigens, with only minor exceptions that may reflect limited sample size (Chapter 6; Bernard-Shaw 1989).

An appreciable number of excavated Late Archaic sites with reliable complements of radiometric dates, subsistence remains, and artifact assemblages has now been recorded for the Tucson Basin and surrounding areas (Fig. 2.3, Table 2.1). However, these cases cannot be uncritically accepted as representative of overall spatial patterns. Compared to the systematic coverage in the northern basin, this sample registers a more pronounced influence of discovery bias. Recorded site locations largely coincide with intense modern development that prompts investigation and with floodplains of the Santa Cruz and major tributaries where channel cuts have created exposures. Excavations of any scope are few in the upper basin zones of permanent water and along mountain flanks that were used continuously for farming. Similar locational bias is evident among investigated ceramic sites through the Pioneer period.

Late Archaic sites for which subsistence analyses have been performed are dated as early as the beginning centuries of the first millennium B.C. and have yielded cultigens with remarkable consistency (Fig. 2.3, Table 2.1). When evidence is sufficient to first evaluate Late Archaic subsistence, domesticates are widespread. Almost every instance of analysis at a range of Tucson area site types and locations has revealed the presence of corn. Recovery at even small and ephemeral sites indicates the role of domesticates as important dietary elements. Furthermore, measures for cultigens at the earliest Late Archaic sites (Huckell 1987, 1988, 1990) are within the range of early ceramic settlements, and both compare favorably with later Hohokam riverine occupations (Miksicek 1988). Subsistence reconstruction suggested by these findings seems inconsistent with a predominance of seasonally mobile lifestyles in the Tucson Basin. Moreover, recent studies of diverse materials such as coprolites, charred plant remains, and human bone (Matson and Chisholm 1991; Minnis 1989; Wills and Huckell, in press) suggest that a number of Late Archaic and earliest ceramic populations across the Southwest shared a dietary reliance on corn.

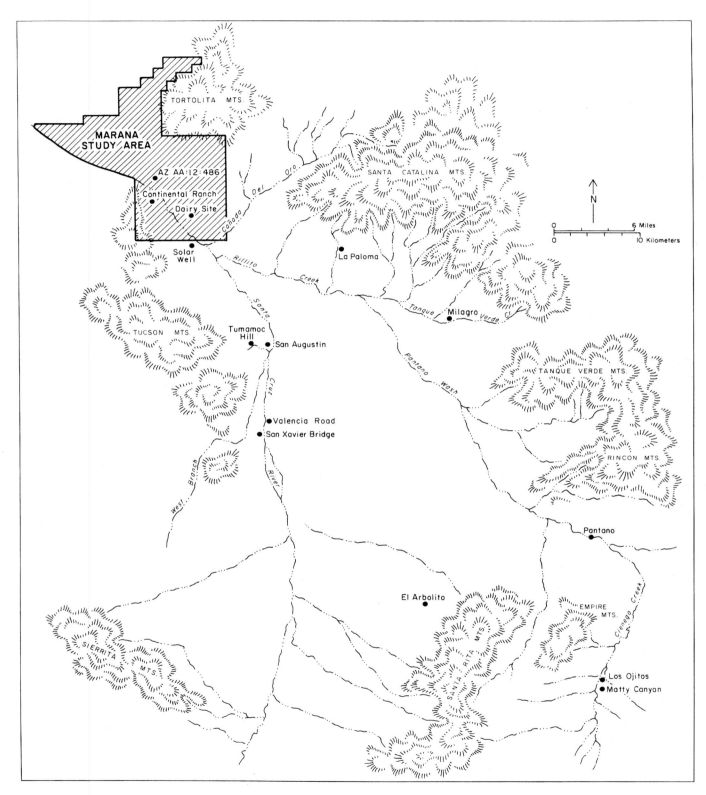

Figure 2.3. Locations of Late Archaic sites in Table 2.1.

Table 2.1. Late Archaic Sites in the Tucson Area with Evidence of Corn

Site	Topographic location	Component recognition	Radiocarbon dates	Corn confirmed in pit houses	References
Valencia Road AZ BB:13:15 AZ BB:13:74	Santa Cruz terrace	Excavated materials	2770 ± 90 B.P. 2740 ± 160 B.P.	x	Doelle 1985a
San Augustin AZ BB:13:6	Santa Cruz terrace	Excavated materials	None available	x	Elson and Doelle 1987
San Xavier Bridge AZ BB:13:14	Santa Cruz terrace	Channel cut, Excavated materials	2570 ± 210 B.P. 1840 ± 125 B.P.	x	Ravesloot 1987
Continental Ranch, Los Morteros AZ AA:12:57	Santa Cruz terrace	Excavated materials	2640 B.P. ± 100		Bernard-Shaw 1988
Pantano Site AZ EE:2:50	Major tributary terrace	Channel cut	1782 ± 105 B.P. 1678 ± 73 B.P.		Hemmings and others 1968
Milagro AZ BB:10:46	Major tributary terrace	Surface diagnostic	2800 ± 110 B.P. 2780 ± 90 B.P.*	x	Huckell 1988
Matty Canyon AZ EE:2:30	Major tributary terrace	Channel cut	2400 ± 90 B.P. 2380 ± 90 B.P.	x	Huckell 1988
Los Ojitos AZ EE:2:137	Major tributary terrace	Channel cut	2270 ± 200 B.P. 2170 ± 150 B.P.*	x	Huckell 1988
La Paloma AZ BB:9:127	Upper bajada pediment	Surface diagnostic	1690 ± 200 B.P.		Dart 1986
Tumamoc Hill AZ AA:16:6	Hill top	Excavated materials	2110 ± B.P. 2470 ± 270 B.P.* 1630 ± 270 B.P.* 1130 ± 270 B.P.*		P. Fish and others 1986
AZ AA:12:486	Alluvial fan	Surface diagnostic	2290 ± 24 B.P. 2270 ± 50 B.P.		Roth 1989
Dairy Site AZ AA:12:285	Alluvial fan	Excavated materials	1660 ± 45 B.P.		Chapter 6, this volume
Solar Well Site AZ AA:12:105	Alluvial fan	Excavated materials	3040 ± 110 B.P.	x	Mabry 1990

* Direct dates of corn remains.

The foregoing interpretation of Late Archaic and early ceramic remains in the northern Tucson Basin has been shaped primarily by the nature of settlement patterns rather than by comprehensive excavation at one or a few key sites. Perceptions based on study area survey have been subsequently strengthened by the accumulating densities of recorded sites throughout the Tucson area; by the presence of substantial structures, storage facilities, and burials in excavated residential contexts; and by the abundance and consistency of associated cultigens. Earlier versions of settlement history that postulated a peopling of the Tucson Basin by Preclassic immigrants from the Phoenix core and posited relatively late expansion away from riverine zones (Grebinger 1971; Haury 1976; Doyel 1977) have not been supported. Although the origin and incorporation of later organizational, ceremonial, and stylistic modes is not resolved by these findings, it is evident that a basic and persistent pattern of agricultural subsistence and settlement in the Tucson Basin was established well prior to the appearance of these distinctively Hohokam cultural forms. The locational and agricultural bases of the Marana Community are clearly foreshadowed in the settlement distributions of Late Archaic and early ceramic farmers.

CHAPTER THREE

Evolution and Structure of the Classic Period Marana Community

Suzanne K. Fish, Paul R. Fish, and John H. Madsen

The Marana Community of the early Classic period represents the height of population and organizational complexity in a major segment of the northern Tucson Basin. The final community configuration, emerging from nearly two thousand years of settlement history for desert cultivators, is a relatively short-lived phenomenon of about two centuries from A.D. 1150 to 1350. The centerpiece of a decade of survey, excavation, and analysis is the detailed definition of this community: its settlement components, productive bases, and developmental history.

Centers identified by public architecture and settlements integrated by a community structure are not tangibly and relationally linked by shared canals in the Tucson Basin as in the Phoenix core of the Hohokam territory. Present understanding of the Marana Community is an outcome of the availability of unusually complete settlement patterns on a regional scale. Comprehensive aspects of territorial and societal organization can be most effectively approached only through data of this scope. Hierarchies among sites expressed by size or unique features are of this nature, as are nonhierarchical distributions such as those pertaining to diversified production activities. Recognition of culturally meaningful boundaries in regional settlement also rests on patterns of extensive scale.

Full-coverage survey of more than 350 square kilometers (125 square miles) encompassing the Marana Community (Fig. 1.8) resulted in the identification of more than 700 sites spanning all time periods and thousands of isolated artifacts and scatters. Descriptive summaries of these sites are on file in the Arizona State Museum (Tani and Chapin 1991). Functionally and topographically differentiated segments of the Classic period community include a central site with a platform mound and walled residential compounds, three additional large sites with compounds, habitation sites without compounds, trincheras or hillside terraced sites with both residential and agricultural features, large communal agricultural fields, small agricultural fields, and a variety of specialized activity sites.

Basic patterns of land use, production, and settlement location were established early in the Tucson Basin. Combinations of environmental and agricultural parameters influencing settlement through the Classic period are apparent in the Late Archaic and earliest ceramic occupations (Chapter 2). Yet overlying these more stable configurations of residence and production is an evolution of elaborated cultural expressions and societal organization that progresses in tandem with developments in the Phoenix Basin and other Hohokam subareas. By the Classic period, these trends culminated in mound-centered communities.

DEVELOPMENTAL ASPECTS OF COMMUNITY ORGANIZATION

Definition of Community

Locational continuities in study area settlement are of a dual character. Sites of all ceramic periods parallel the Santa Cruz River. This concentration includes both sites at the edges of the floodplain itself and those situated on the adjoining lower edge of the bajada. Along the flanks of the Tortolita Mountains, sites and diagnostic artifacts also clearly indicate a second concentration from the earlier ceramic occupations onward. Each concentration appears to have begun with Late Archaic cultivators. Long-standing preferences for particular locales within riverine and mountain flank bands of settlement are demonstrated by numerous multicomponent sites and clusterings of discrete ones.

Although clearly patterned, such environmental correlates of settlement are not adequate bases for defining cultural boundaries in the past; these must be inferred from evidence of tangible distinctions and symbols by which segments of prehistoric populations might have differentiated themselves. Two kinds of settlement attributes have been foremost in defining the Marana Community and other regional units of territorial organization. One is the presence of architectural symbols believed to express prehistoric concepts of hierarchy and integration at preeminent centers within clusters of interrelated settlement. This approach rests upon a model of a fundamentally differentiated central place within concentrically structured geographical and cultural space, repetitions of which occur across a landscape (Christaller 1966; Wright and Johnson 1975; G. Johnson 1977). Prior applications of this approach in Hohokam settlement analyses include the definition of communities along canal networks with one or more centers (Wasley and Johnson 1965; Schroeder 1966; Doyel 1980; Crown 1987; Gregory and Nials 1985), of Preclassic ballcourt communities (Wilcox and Sternberg 1983), and of primary villages (Doelle and others 1987).

The second discriminant of community in this study is the spatial separation of a settlement cluster from other contemporary site aggregates that appear to be equivalent sociopolitical units. Boundaries of communities and the intervening areas, often termed buffer zones, can be reliably confirmed only through systematic survey recording of settlement patterns at sufficiently large scales. Such coverage is similarly essential in demonstrating the primacy or uniqueness of central places within areally extensive settlement arrays and the locational arrangement of these kinds of sites with regard to territorial boundaries.

Preclassic Community Definition

Prior to A.D. 1100, two dispersed site clusters can be recognized in settlement patterns of the Marana study area (Fig. 3.1). One centers on the Santa Cruz floodplain and lower bajada near the end of the Tucson Mountains. Northern outliers include settlements at favorable farming situations on the lower bajada edge for several kilometers north of the mountains. A second upland concentration skirts the Tortolita Mountains. Preclassic sites are grouped on the upper bajada between three large washes. Focal sites for upland and riverine clusters are marked by ballcourts at large sites on the west side of the Santa Cruz and below the Tortolitas. Ballcourts are usually considered communal structures and facilities for competitive sports. It has been suggested (Wilcox 1991) that activities associated with ballcourts served further integrative functions in communities involving mate exchange, craft production, labor procurement, and risk management.

Distributions in Figure 3.1 may most closely approximate settlement in the Late Preclassic interval encompassing the late Colonial (Rillito phase) and early Sedentary (Rincon phase) periods (Fig. 1.2) because diagnostics of these phases predominate at the typically multicomponent habitation sites. However, each of the two clusters has demonstrably earlier roots. Site clusters,

including ballcourts, characterize Preclassic settlement distributions in the Tucson Basin as a whole. For example, another riverine ballcourt site is located 17 km (10 miles) to the south (Kelly 1978) and a ballcourt in the next settlement cluster south along the Tortolita Mountains is 19 km (12 miles) distant from its Marana counterpart (Craig and Wallace 1987).

Both Preclassic communities exhibit indications of equally substantial and permanent occupations. Year-round flow in springs and canyons provides domestic water in the upper bajada community. Shallow wells or reservoirs could provide dry season water at the river in stretches of high water table. A range of site sizes and topographic settings in each cluster registers differentiation in functions and productive capacities. Agricultural features constructed of cobbles are present in both upper and lower bajada contexts. The variety of overall artifact classes is duplicated, including ground stone and shell, and vessel forms of all types are present in each. Ballcourts and trash mounds are found at the largest sites.

Classic Community Definition

A reorganization of settlement structure in the northern Tucson Basin occurs in the early Classic period. By the end of Preclassic time, a dynamic element has appeared between the persistent bands of occupation in riverine and mountain edge zones. This new locational orientation is evident in substantial remains covering middle elevations of the bajada (Fig. 3.2). Dense sites of a predominantly specialized nature span the previously unused area separating Preclassic communities. At the same time, terraced occupations on the slopes of the Tucson Mountains supplement long-term farming locations below. Beyond the end of the Tucson Mountains, settlement increases and is extended along the lower edge of the eastern bajada. Where this new settlement ends to the north, a mound center is established near the present town of Marana. Upland and riverine ballcourt centers are replaced by this single mound center that serves as the integrative focus for continuous Classic period settlement between the east and west basin borders.

Classic Community Chronology

The new settlement configuration appears to be a temporally restricted phenomenon of less than 200 years, beginning in the late Rincon phase just prior to the Classic period (Fig. 1.2), becoming fully developed in early Classic times, and terminating prior to the late Classic period as marked by the advent of Salado poly-

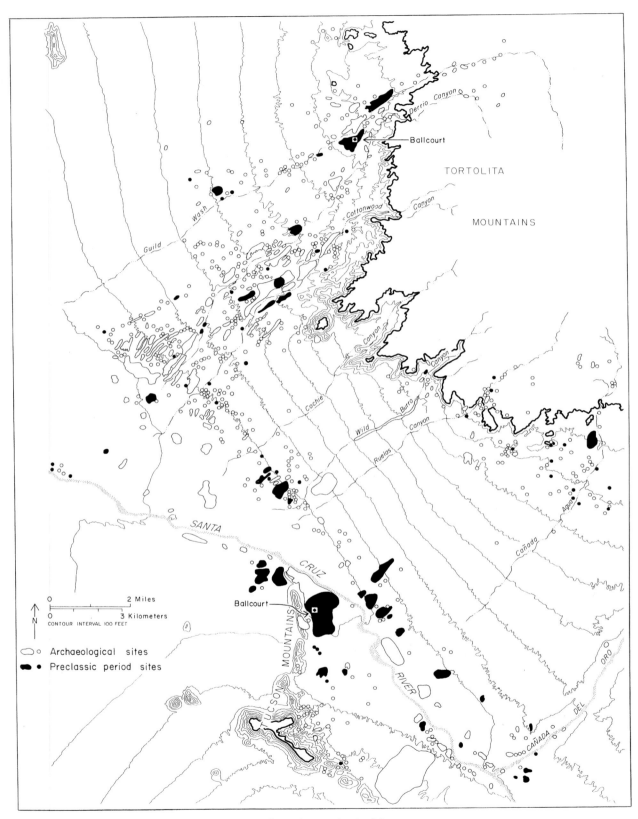

Figure 3.1. Preclassic settlement in the Marana survey area.

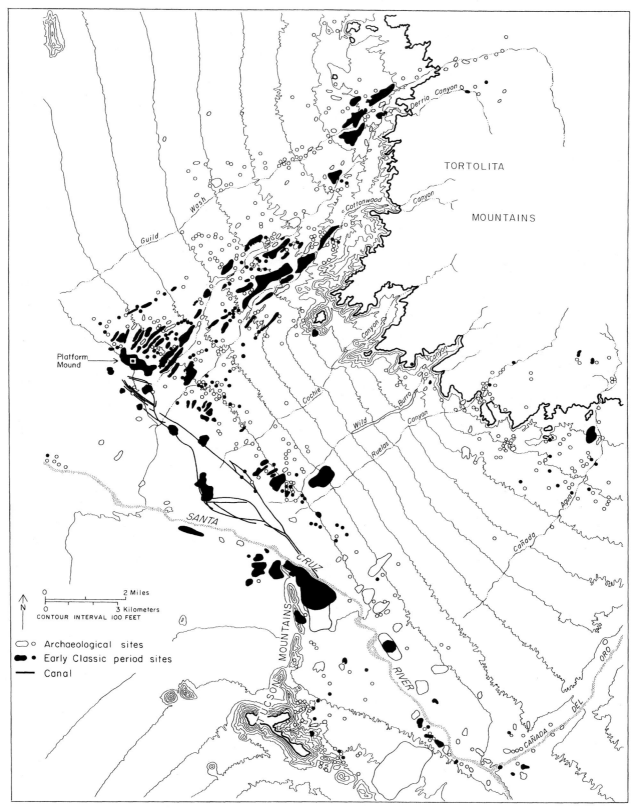

Figure 3.2. Early Classic period settlement in the Marana survey area.

Figure 3.3. Tanque Verde Red-on-brown ceramics of the early Classic period.

chrome pottery. Rincon phase components in several lower basin sites south of the mound (Czaplicki 1984; Henderson 1987b), occasional Rincon sherds at middle bajada sites, and possibly several late Rincon ceramics at the mound imply that reorganizational trends culminating in the Classic Marana Community may have begun slightly before the Classic period.

The Tanque Verde phase is synonymous with the early Classic period in the Tucson Basin, and Tanque Verde Red-on-brown ceramics (Fig. 3.3) are overwhelmingly predominant among diagnostics from the mound site and middle bajada portion of the community. Intrusive pottery at the Marana mound is chronologically consistent with local ceramic evidence and includes small quantities of Casa Grande Red-on-buff, McDonald Corrugated, Pinedale Black-on-white, San Carlos Smudged, Gila Black-on-red, and Little Colorado White Ware. Among more than 300 diagnostic sherds in collections of isolated artifacts below the Tortolita flanks, all are of Tanque Verde design.

Salado polychrome pottery of a quantity suggesting late Classic components occurs at only five sites in the southernmost portion of the northern Tucson Basin survey area (Fig. 3.4). These sites are outside the Marana Community by its broadest areal definition. Within the Community, such ceramics are represented at two specialized activity sites and by three isolated sherds near the northern end of the Tucson Mountains.

Preclassic to Classic Trajectories

Developmental Models

Previous reconstructions for the early Hohokam sequence in the Tucson Basin have posited entries of agricultural immigrants from the Phoenix core, who initiated succeeding developments according to the tenets of that cultural tradition. Comprehensive settlement data fail to support this assumption (Chapter 1) and instead document a primarily local development, although Pioneer period decorated ceramics may have been acquired

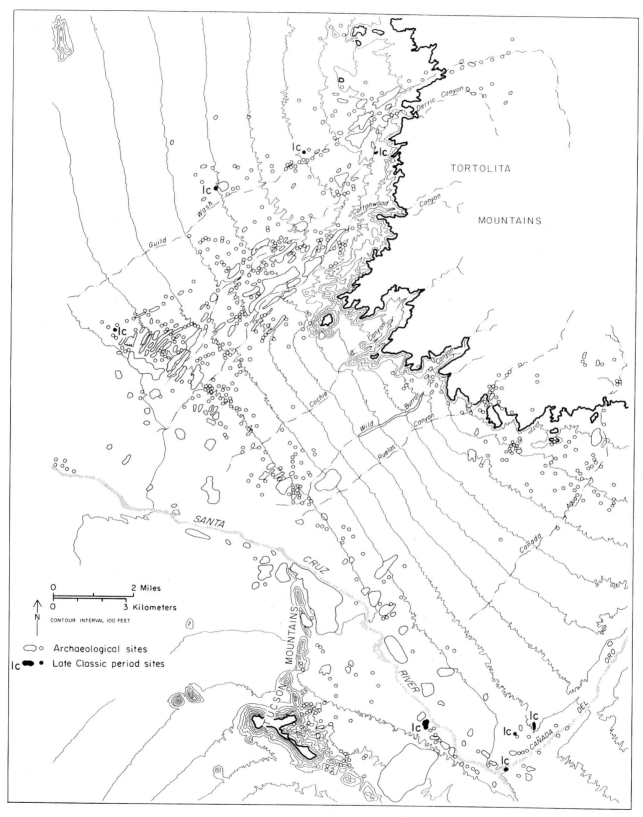

Figure 3.4. Late Classic period settlement in the Marana survey area.

from the Phoenix Basin (Lombard and Fish 1991). At most, these imports account for only a few percent in assemblages of unpainted local wares, and by A.D. 700, a distinctive Tucson decorative style had been established. Additionally, models of riverine-based organization with only minor settlement and use of the bajadas (Grebinger 1971; Doyel 1977) are contradicted by substantial Preclassic occupance in such zones, including ballcourt villages.

Regional settlement chronology of the Tucson Basin further indicates that the Classic period witnessed both continuing population growth and continuing development toward more complex organization. In the study area, Preclassic entities coalesced into a single Classic community of greater scale. Such a trajectory is counter to previous models of the Classic transition as a period of boundary retraction for the Hohokam tradition as a whole (Weaver 1972) and of reversal toward simpler organizational levels (Doyel 1980; Nelson 1981).

Settlement Measures

A comparative measure bearing on organizational complexity that can be derived from regional settlement patterns is the size of integrated area. An increase in area is usually assumed to imply some corresponding increase in integrated population. To the degree that area reflects population, this is a relevant consideration, since complexity is the outcome of relational rather than spatial attributes. However, some independent significance can be claimed for the spatial referent. Larger territories entail greater investment in maintaining integrative functions. Exchange of information and material and communal scheduling require greater effort. Regulatory or coordinating activities must be extended, and spatial costs of acquiring or dispensing benefits are similarly magnified.

The size of integrated territory for the riverine and upland Preclassic communities is similar. Extent along the Santa Cruz approaches 70 square kilometers (27 square miles) and on the Tortolita flanks approximates 57 square kilometers (22 square miles). Boundaries of the Classic period Marana Community enclose more than double these previous sizes, encompassing 146 square kilometers (56 square miles).

Population is notably difficult to estimate through surficial attributes of Hohokam sites because structures are dispersed and pit houses can seldom be tabulated from surface remains. Low ratios of decorated sherds in many site assemblages further hamper efforts to estimate the extent of individual components at multiphase localities. In this study, site area for separate components could be calculated for only a few of the larger sites.

Table 3.1. Comparison of Site Categories for the Preclassic and Classic Periods

	Preclassic	Classic
Habitation sites (number)	21	51
Habitation sites (square meters)	2,300,000	6,100,000
Nonhabitation sites (number)	13	48
Nonhabitation sites (square meters)	11,700	45,007
Nonhabitation:Habitation (number)	1:1.6	1:1.1
Nonhabitation:Habitation (square meters)	1:197	1:136
$\bar{x}$ area, Nonhabitation site (square meters)	900	938
Mid-bajada rockpile fields (square meters)	62,600	4,858,300
Rockpile fields:Habitation (square meters)	1:37	1:1.3

Nevertheless, comparison of site sizes and densities in Figures 3.1 and 3.2 establishes the magnitude of difference between all identified Preclassic sites and those with early Classic diagnostics. The total area of residential function in Preclassic sites is approximately 2,000,000 square meters compared to 6,000,000 square meters of Classic date.

In spite of higher population levels and organizational change in the Classic period, certain characteristics of settlement show continuity with basic Preclassic patterns (Table 3.1). Large, specialized sites (>10,000 square meters) on the middle bajada are Classic innovations. If these sites are excluded from consideration in the nonhabitation category, broad similarities can be seen in the quantitative relationships between nonhabitation and habitation sites of the Preclassic and Classic periods. These similarities likely represent continuity in aspects of land use practices, as reflected in ratios of extractive and agricultural activities to population. For each interval, there are more habitation sites than nonhabitation, partly because ephemeral sites frequently cannot be dated. Both for site numbers and area, the proportion of Preclassic habitation sites is somewhat higher, likely due to the scarcity of early Preclassic diagnostics. However, the average size of nonhabitation sites at about 900 square meters is surprisingly constant from period to period. Similar averages for area of nonhabitation sites in the two periods suggest that there are also continuities in activity group size, arrangements, frequency of reuse, or other factors influencing the size of such sites.

Some distributional measures and environmental correlates of settlement pattern remain constant, but others register responses to changing population and organization. The specialized site type of the middle bajada excluded from the nonhabitation category in the above comparison is associated with novel developments in the Classic settlement pattern. Quantitative measures for such sites are strongly divergent in the late period.

Complexes of cobble agricultural features known as rockpile fields (see Chapter 7) proliferate on unused portions of the middle bajada and large fields are constructed for the first time. The ratio between area in these fields and in habitation sites jumps sharply between the Preclassic and Classic periods.

DESCRIPTION OF THE MARANA COMMUNITY

Classic Linkage of Settlement Axes

Although the Marana Mound is a unique Classic period edifice in the study area, additional lines of evidence support a strong integration of the two conjoined axes of Tanque Verde phase settlement. These axes consist of the continuous, well-bounded settlement spanning the eastern bajada and the band of sites paralleling the lower bajada edge and floodplain near the end of the Tucson Mountains (Fig. 3.2). Simultaneous cessation of occupation after the early Classic period in both these axes with different environmental and technological parameters of production suggests interlinked fortunes among all segments of a unified community.

The Santa Cruz floodplain below the Marana Mound at the juncture of the two settlement axes is highly disturbed by modern agriculture. Site identification has been achieved only through multiple attempts at artifact collection under combinations of plowing and irrigation that improved surface visibility. Tanque Verde phase habitation and irrigation in the floodplain north of the Tucson Mountains remain imprecisely known.

A Classic period canal system represents tangible evidence of shared interests between residents in the two axes of Marana Community settlement. The potential existence of such canals was suggested by mapped irrigation lines of the nineteenth century. Historic canals headed in high water tables on the river at the mountain terminus and extended north over 10 km (6 miles) to the vicinity of the mound site (Roskruge 1896a, 1896b). Indications on aerial photographs and preserved stretches of prehistoric berm revealed the parallel course of Classic period alignments (see Fig. 3.2). These canals linked community inhabitants at the central site in the trans-bajada axis, populations along the river at the intake, and ones at intervening lower bajada locations. The acquiescence if not the active cooperation of riverine inhabitants near canal heads would have been needed by users to the north. At canal end, residents of the mound site were most dependent in this regard. The position of the Marana center parallels the phenomenon of pre-eminent sites near the ends of several Phoenix networks rather than in locations of direct control at intakes

(Upham and Rice 1980: 82; Nicholas and Neitzel 1984: 176; Masse 1981; Gregory and Nials 1985).

Preclassic site clusters are associated with sources of permanent water, in contrast to settlements on the intervening bajada occupied by the early Classic period. Drainages in these locations could have supported seasonal cropping but provide no year-round water. Northernmost Classic settlement on the lower bajada is 10 km (6 miles) from persistent surface water in the river. Canals extending north for this distance appear to have facilitated settlement in areas between the Preclassic concentrations. Progressive expansion from the early riverine community along the lower bajada follows the canal route to the north. Preclassic sites opposite the Tucson Mountains date as early as the Colonial period. In the succeeding Sedentary period, earlier site components precede later ones farther north. From midpoint to end of the canal, settlements are almost exclusively of early Classic date. This temporal succession strongly suggests a correlation between the timing of northward extension of the canals and initial occupations at adjacent sites.

Some means for ensuring domestic water at settlements near the mound would have been necessary, and reservoirs filled by the canals or directed runoff are highly likely. Numerous historic accounts prior to the late 1800s identify a seasonal source known as Mud Tanks or Desert Wells in the vicinity of Marana (Roskruge 1896a, 1896b). These descriptions may refer to a prehistoric reservoir still retaining water. The reported location would place this feature under currently plowed fields but at an elevation consistent with canal end points. Modern cattle tanks near the mound are constructed to fill from runoff, illustrating another potential water source. Although residents of the mound site must have resolved their needs for domestic supplies, limited seasonal flow in nearby drainages offered secondary potential for floodwater farming compared to lower bajada areas of earlier settlement.

The Marana Mound Site

The Marana platform mound appears today as a rounded adobe mass. Wall alignments are visible on some parts of the upper mound surface (Fig. 3.5). A compound wall around the mound, encompassing 2700 square meters, can still be traced for much of its length on the west, north, and east sides under optimal vegetation conditions. Rooms within the compound courtyard can also be identified.

A mapping and testing program has been initiated to investigate the layout of the mound site, an area of approximately 1,500,000 square meters. Refined mapping

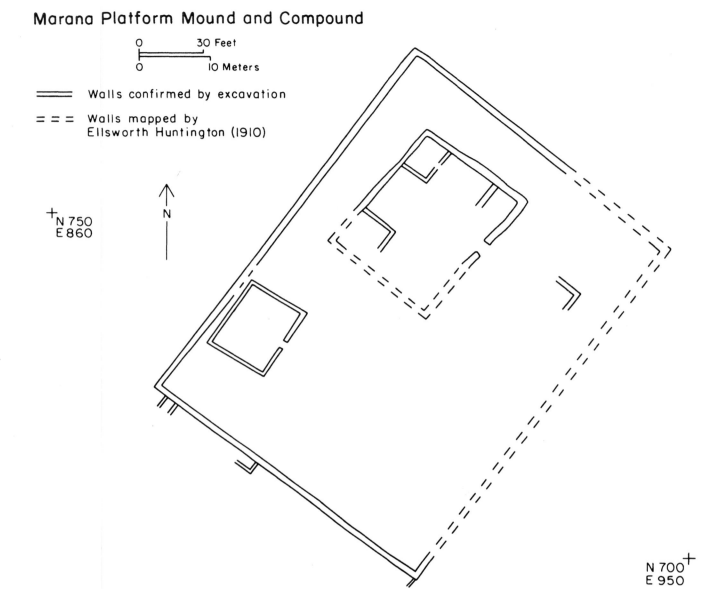

Figure 3.5. The Marana platform mound and surrounding compound.

of dispersed but continuous architectural distributions has substantially increased the area believed to be included within site boundaries over earlier estimates (S. Fish, P. Fish, and Madsen 1989). Compound loci, consisting of one to several compounds and adjacent trash mounds, can be identified by surface remains of melted adobe (Fig. 3.6).

In some instances within compounds, low mounded ridges reveal concentrations of rooms, which are built along compound walls and independently in interior positions. Cobbles used in footings and as bondings between adobe courses remain as surface alignments after surrounding adobe has melted, outlining portions of rooms and outer compound walls. Surface structures and, occasionally, pit houses are enclosed within the compounds. A partially excavated compound near the mound is unusually large for Hohokam compounds, enclosing approximately 5500 square meters and containing a minimum of 11 rooms (Fig. 3.7). Trenching to date in several site sectors lacking surface indications of architecture has confirmed an absence of structures outside the compounds.

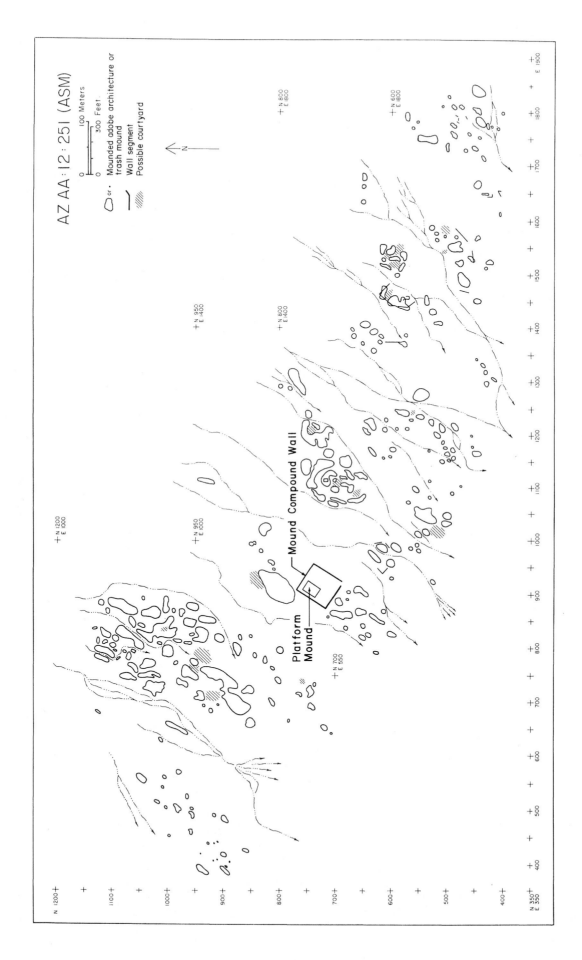

Figure 3.6. Distribution of adobe architectural remains and trash mounds associated with residential compounds at the Marana Mound Site.

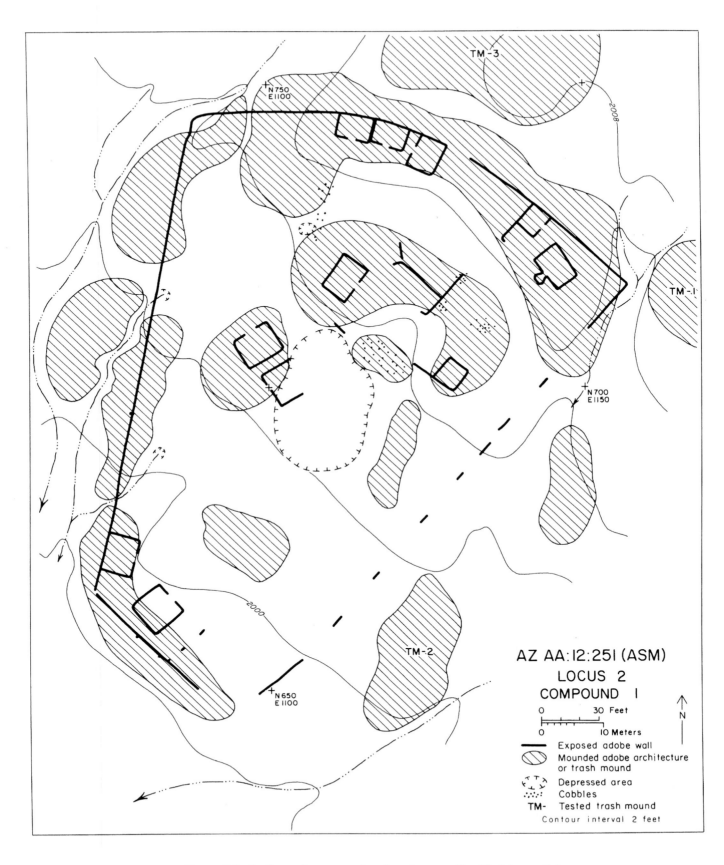

TM-3

N 750
E 1100

2008

TM-1

N 700
E 1150

2000

TM-2

N 650
E 1100

AZ AA:12:251 (ASM)

LOCUS 2

COMPOUND 1

N

| 0 | | 30 Feet |
| 0 | | 10 Meters |

Exposed adobe wall

Mounded adobe architecture
or trash mound

Depressed area

Cobbles

TM- Tested trash mound

Contour interval 2 feet

Figure 3.7. Outlines of compound wall and rooms identified by partial
excavation of a large residential compound at the Marana Mound Site.

Zonal Patterns

Six zones of settlement are defined within the Classic period Marana Community based on environment, habitation, and evidence for productive activities (Figs. 3.8, 3.9). The first four pertain to the eastern basin slope. Zone 1 sites, including the platform mound, occur in a more or less continuous band along the lower bajada. Coalescing alluvial fans in this zone create an active depositional environment. Abundant sherd, ground stone, and lithic scatters across these fan surfaces correlate with sites of mostly moderate size in a rancheria pattern of dispersed clusters of structures.

The density of Zone 1 settlement is the result of opportunity for floodwater farming in an area receiving runoff from the full expanse of the bajada. Geomorphological studies (Field 1985, Chapter 5 in this volume; Waters and Field 1986) have shown that fan edges and small fans associated with secondary drainages were favored. Easily diverted and controlled flows in small channels would have renewed fields with rich loads of suspended sediment and detritus in the course of supplying water.

The most desirable floodwater farming situations are concentrated in the southern third of Zone 1 (S. Fish 1987a: 236–238). This is the segment with the earliest settlement, predating developments in the Classic period. Later expansion to the north in Zone 1 is almost certainly correlated with dependable domestic water through canal construction, supplying the mound vicinity from the river. Although Zone 1 inhabitants may have realized some agricultural benefits from this canal, topographic placement suggests greatest irrigation potential for fields of floodplain inhabitants in Zone 5 below.

Zone 2 is uphill from the mound and lower bajada sites. Dominant remains in this zone consist of complexes of agricultural features without habitations. Heaps of cobbles, termed "rockpiles," are the prominent feature type, accompanied by low cobble terrace alignments, checkdams, and roasting pits (described in detail in Chapter 7). Over 485 hectares or more than two square miles of large rockpile fields (10 to 50 ha) have been located. A total of 42,000 rockpiles and 120,000 m of linear alignment is estimated for this zone.

Zone 2 fields occur on ridges between secondary drainages on gentle mid-bajada slopes. Broad, flat implements of tabular stone represent 19.2 percent of retouched tools in surface collections. Ethnographically, such "mescal knives" have been used in gathering agave. In all large fields, huge roasting "areas," with maximum dimensions up to 50 m, are processing facilities that have consistently yielded charred agave. Annual crops such as corn were probably attempted only in climatically favorable years in the small drainage bottoms. With less predictable and abundant water than in other zones, drought-adapted agaves provided dependable harvests on this agriculturally marginal land.

A third settlement zone in the middle elevations of the bajada extends to the upper basin slope nearer the foothills of the Tortolitas. A few small sherd, lithic, and ground stone scatters are widely dispersed in a rancheria pattern and located in more favorable situations for water diversion and utilization. Like Zone 2, Zone 3 is characterized by a scarcity of substantial habitation remains and by the occurrence of unique and specialized sites.

Surface scatters of ceramics with few or no other artifact classes comprise the only large Zone 3 sites. Sometimes huge (approaching almost 1.0 km or more than a half mile in length), these sites tend to be linearly arranged along ridge tops. Relatively dense distributions of sherds number as high as the tens of thousands at individual sites. Intensive backhoe trenching at one of the largest revealed no subsurface artifacts or features. Location in abundant stands of saguaro cacti suggests repetitive and intensive seasonal resource gathering as a probable function of these obviously specialized sites. Rock rings, documented ethnographically as supports for conical baskets in saguaro fruit procurement (Goodyear 1975; Raab 1973), are the only surface features, offering support for this hypothesis. High sherd densities would have been generated over the years by vessels, mostly jars, supplying water for gatherers and fruit processing.

Zone 3 settlement patterns intergrade with a fourth zonal type nearest the mountains and between three major drainages. Unlike the lower zones that are underlain by deep colluvial basin fill, Zone 4 corresponds with mountain pediment where shallow bedrock prevents deep percolation of water originating on the Tortolita slopes. A relatively high and accessible water table is therefore maintained in the drainages. Large and small habitation sites in this zone undoubtedly reflect the availability of water. Both the three major drainages and secondary ones appear to have supported cultivation. Agricultural features such as terraces, rockpiles, and checkdams occur in substantial numbers in Zone 4 in conjunction with large and small sites, but never independently of adjoining habitation as in Zone 2.

The largest Zone 4 sites (a few approach or exceed one square kilometer) are found on ridges overlooking the floodplains of Derrio Wash and Cottonwood Wash. Structural remains include a number of architectural forms: compounds enclosing mounded adobe from substantial structures, cobble outlines of contiguous rooms, isolated cobble-outlined structures, and dry-laid masonry structures.

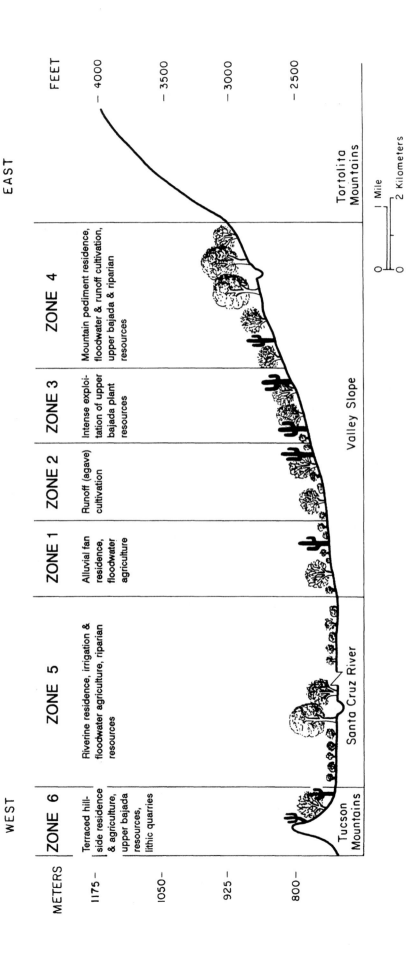

Figure 3.8. Idealized basin cross section, showing zonal divisions of the Marana Community.

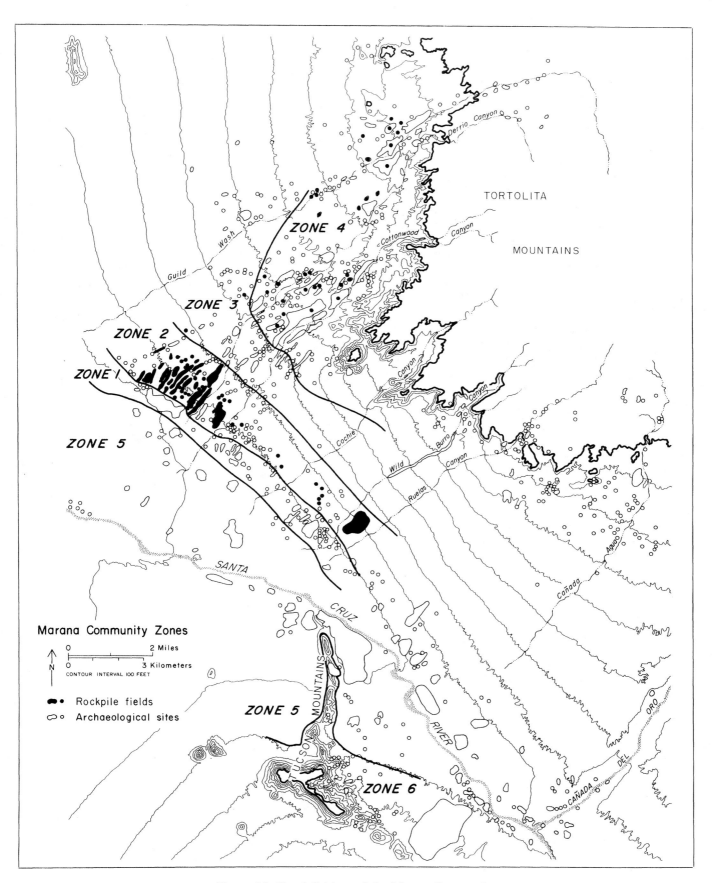

Figure 3.9. Zonal divisions of the Marana Community.

The floodplain and terraces of the Santa Cruz River constitute Zone 5. From the southern boundary of the study area to the end of the Tucson Mountains, the river channel and floodplain are concisely delimited. Igneous intrusions near the end of the mountains force underground flow to the surface, creating an elevated water table and more persistent surface water. Large and small sites of all periods occur on both sides of the river as it parallels the mountains. Irrigation from the river imparted the most concentrated productive capacity to this area. Two of the largest sites with the longest settlement histories in the community, Los Morteros and the Huntington Site, are located on either side of the mountain terminus. To the north, surface flow in the river is more infrequent and the floodplain broadens substantially. Maximum site size appears to be smaller and overall site densities reduced.

The highly foreshortened bajada between the Tucson Mountains and the Santa Cruz compresses the succession of zonal topography compared to that on the eastern bajada. A few sites at the western floodplain edge seem oriented toward floodwater situations. Riverine canals undoubtedly account for the denser populations and consistently preferred locales.

The Tucson Mountains define Zone 6. In the study area, they form a low chain of less than 130 m (400 feet) in elevation above the floodplain. Dark volcanic hills are covered with a variety of cacti and leguminous trees, providing immediate access to upper bajada resources for inhabitants of the river edge.

Trincheras sites, characterized by terraces and walls of dry-laid masonry, occur on Tucson Mountain hill slopes (Wallace 1983). The largest concentration of these features is immediately above the largest riverine site of Los Morteros, along the western edge of the Santa Cruz (Figs. 1.8, 3.2). Some of the 250 terraces in this trincheras site (Fig. 3.10) yielded evidence of agricultural function, and excavated pit houses (Fig. 3.11) in several other terraces have all the appearances of permanent habitations (S. Fish, P. Fish, and Downum 1984; Downum 1986). A cobble-outlined compound and a few masonry surface structures are also present. A single radiocarbon date and the design treatment on Tanque Verde phase ceramics suggest that some features of the trincheras site date to the latest interval of Marana Community occupation, although still predating the late Classic period advent of Salado polychromes.

ECONOMIC DIFFERENTIATION

Economic implications of the coalescence of the Preclassic ballcourt communities are illuminated by a body of data concerning environmental diversity, productive specialization, and increasing population, particularly in agriculturally marginal areas. Locations of the Preclassic communities entailed reciprocal environmental hazards: storms that flooded riverine zones might ensure bountiful upland harvests, whereas rains posing no floodplain threat might be insufficient for good harvests above (Lightfoot and Plog 1984; Abruzzi 1989). A strategy of diversification of efforts at various societal levels was followed historically by many Southwestern groups to counteract such localized environmental threats. In the Marana Classic period reorganization, diversification was shifted above the level of individual households, villages, and zones to include the broader productive spectrum of the enlarged community. Localized risks were diffused to the extent that fortunes were shared and resources circulated within the larger entity.

The specialization apparent in the scale of rockpile fields may well portend complementary processes that are more subtly expressed in the archaeological record. Specialization to maximize returns or to minimize individual risks, as in an emphasis on drought-resistant agave, simultaneously heightens the need for exchange. Classic settlement and dense populations expanding beyond earlier topographic concentrations probably were viable only in a differentiated and well-integrated economic context.

Data concerning productive activities in the Classic period Marana Community illustrate horizontal differentiation of an economic nature, but with likely implications for other social spheres. Entrepreneurial opportunities and managerial requirements may have been fostered under such conditions. Conversely, the coordination of differentiated or specialized components is a key function of elevated social roles and institutions.

Subsistence Specialization

The strength of the argument for a differentiated subsistence economy in the Marana Community derives from access to a regional perspective. Diversity in zonal resources and opportunities can be related to economic organization in that it can be shown to occur within a single, integrated territorial and sociopolitical unit. However, a degree of extractive redundancy would have existed across a community encompassing riparian, creosote bush-bursage, and palo verde-saguaro vegetation associations with highly overlapping species. Similarly, a basic suite of cultigens undoubtedly was grown by means of riverine irrigation, floodwater farming, and slope runoff. Nevertheless, zonal patterns document differing magnitudes, emphases, and organization of subsistence production across the different segments and correspond to differential risks and benefits for gatherers and cultivators (Chapter 4).

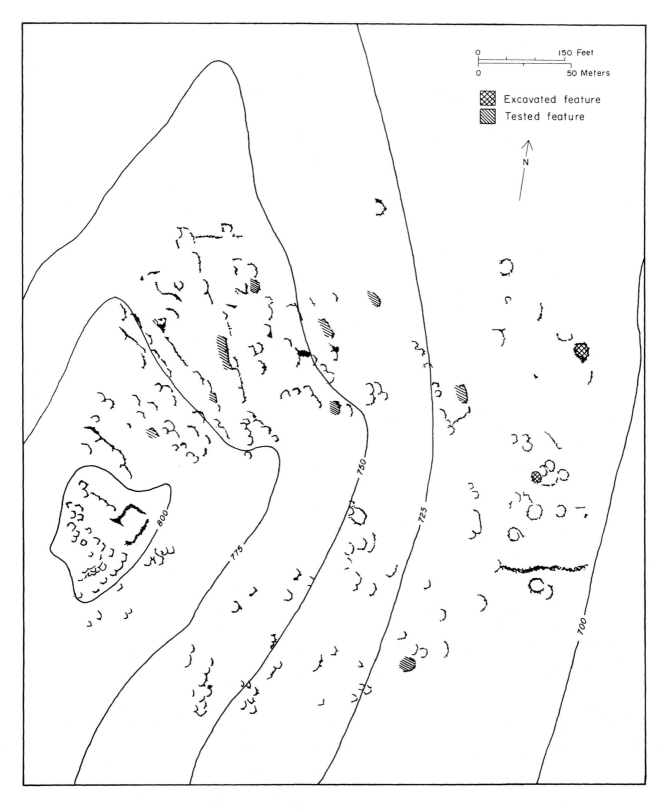

Figure 3.10. Terraces and other masonry features at the largest
Tucson Mountain trincheras site in the Marana Community.

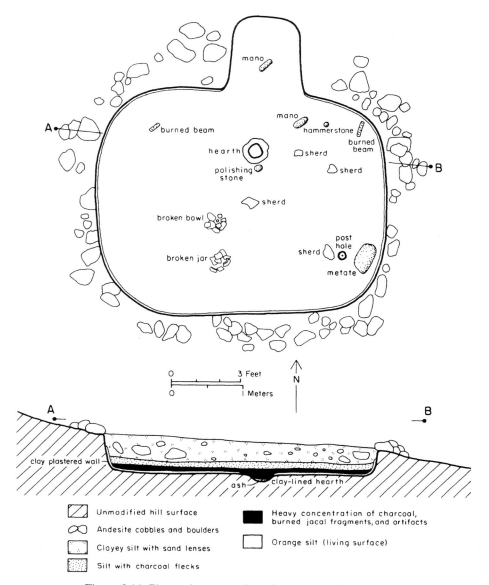

Figure 3.11. Plan and cross section of an excavated pit house
on a trincheras site terrace in the Marana Community.

Each of the defined zones subsume finer environmental variation. Excavations at six Zone 1 loci south of the mound (Henderson 1987a; G. Rice 1987a) supplement insights derived from settlement patterns. Artifacts, facilities, and botanical remains suggest that residents of settlements with differing floodwater potential for annual crops counterbalanced these lesser opportunities by emphasizing agave from Zone 2 fields, or by more intensively gathering resources such as cacti. Some patterns have no obvious environmental correlates and seem to represent economic choice (S. Fish 1987a). To the extent that evidence for production and consumption could be discriminated (S. Fish and Donaldson 1991), circulation

of differentially emphasized products appears to have broadened and homogenized consumption at individual Zone 1 settlements.

The most compelling data for subsistence specialization are a class of agricultural remains unequivocally linked to production. Large-scale agave cultivation in Zone 2 occurs in close tandem with temporal and spatial parameters of early Classic expansion. Within this milieu, the emphasis on rockpile fields seems best understood in the light of secondary floodwater land and higher population densities at the new mound center and nearby settlements initiated at the beginning of the Classic period. Only the densely settled inhabitants of northernmost Zone 1 near the mound specialized to a degree that covered middle bajada slopes with thousands of stone features (Fig. 3.9).

Nonsubsistence Specialization

Nonsubsistence specialization is currently documented only in broad strokes for the Marana Community. Small habitation sites in Zone 1 provide excavated data that as yet lack a comparative framework from other community segments. Craft specialization need not have coincided with locations of raw material production or procurement, although dense populations with poorer agricultural land, as at the Mound, might have found it desirable to engage in all phases of manufacture. Artifacts used in processing agave fiber and making fiber products are prominent at the six excavated Zone 1 sites. Estimated yields from Zone 2 fields (Chapter 7; S. Fish, P. Fish, Miksicek, and Madsen 1985: 112) likely surpassed the consumptive needs of the growers and provided conveniently portable items for exchange.

Evidence for ceramic and shell craft activities was relatively widespread in Zone 1 excavations (Kisselberg 1987; G. Rice 1987a). Residues of other manufacturing activities were more localized. Nearly two-thirds of all turquoise, including unworked pieces, was encountered in one site and mostly in a single structure. Only finished red stone jewelry is reported from the six excavated sites. Stylistically identical items have been recovered in one compound locus at the Mound site, where surface collections also contain plentiful manufacturing debris. Artisans at the community center apparently shaped ornaments for consumers at other sites.

Obsidian occurs sporadically in survey collections throughout the community. However, nearly 80 percent of all excavated Zone 1 obsidian was from a pit cache that included partially flaked nodules and flakes (G. Rice 1987b: 136). Contents of the adjacent large pit house at the site were also unusual (James 1987). Multiple bighorn sheep skulls and horn cores may represent hunting disguises or ceremonial garb. Pelves of 18 deer and big horn sheep are further anomalies among faunal assemblages that were otherwise dominated by lagomorphs.

As with subsistence, part of the basis for nonsubsistence specialization is localized opportunity. Lithic sources with signs of prehistoric quarrying have been identified for ground stone raw materials: tabular-fracturing stone for knives; fine-grained rhyolites, andesites, and metamorphosed limestone for chipped artifacts; and a cryptocrystalline series including jasper and agates. With the exception of one rhyolite type, these sources are in the largely volcanic Tucson Mountains on the west rather than in the predominantly granitic Tortolitas on the east. Even with this variety of community sources, preference is shown in some common utilitarian artifact classes for raw materials originating elsewhere in the Tucson Basin. Formal ground stone and tabular knives are commonly of stone quarried near Cerro Prieto in the Robles Community (Fig. 1.8), 30 km (18.5 miles) west of the Mound.

Circulated raw materials and finished products constitute an important fraction of everyday equipment for Marana residents. Manufacturing debris for tabular knives and ground stone is plentiful near the external quarry sources but absent within the community, suggesting importation of finished products through trade. By contrast, quarried chipping stone from west of the Santa Cruz River was made into tools throughout the community. These lithic types account for 30 percent or more of assemblages in an analyzed sample of Tortolita bajada sites. The abundance of circulated items implies economic differentiation on the part of suppliers near the sources and consumers elsewhere, who likely offered some form of exchangeable surplus.

EVIDENCE FOR VERTICAL ORGANIZATION

Settlement Patterns

Vertical differentiation in the Marana Community can be systematically approached from the perspective of settlement pattern (G. Johnson 1977; Kowalewski and others 1983; Steponaitis 1981). In this study, site hierarchy combines criteria of size and certain categories of unequally distributed architectural and artifactual remains. Since difficulties in separating components may affect estimates of site size and occupational intensities may not be uniform over time, these additional attributes are fortunate complements. The two bases for ranking discriminate among sites in a similar manner.

The distribution of site areas in square meters is presented in Figure 3.12. This compilation is based only on habitation area and only on sites of known Classic period affiliation; areas of agricultural function adjoining residential sites and specialized activity sites are not included. Components have been separated for large riverine settlements. Three size classes appear significant. Over three-fourths of the sites are under 100,000 square meters, with most less than 50,000 square meters. Small sites without diagnostics would increase this proportion. An intermediate class from 150,000 to 350,000 square meters contains 15 percent of the habitation sites. Only 7 percent or four sites exceed 350,000 square meters, and these are of a clearly distinctive magnitude between 550,000 and 1,500,000 square meters.

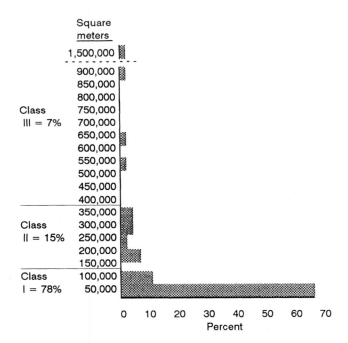

Figure 3.12. Histogram of habitation site sizes in the Marana Community. Classes defined on the basis of site size are correlated with differential distributions of architecture and decorated ceramics.

Architectural Distributions

Architectural indications are absent on the surface of sites in the smallest size class. Excavated sites of this class in Zone 1 contained adobe surface structures as well as pit houses. Floor area and contents of the two kinds of structures did not reveal consistent differences between assemblages or functions. Small habitation sites occur throughout the community.

Only two sites in the intermediate size class lack visible structural stone. In most of the remaining cases, structures incorporating cobbles as additions to coursed adobe appear to represent a minor fraction of residential units among more abundant pit houses or other types of surface structures. Sites of this intermediate size range occur in all zones of denser habitation, and utilization of cobbles in construction cannot be explained by the differential availability of stone. Cobble outlines that have eroded in place from substantial adobe walls of both isolated and contiguous rooms account for almost all the structural stone. Low walls of dry-laid masonry, again for single and multiple rooms, are found at a single upper bajada site.

The four sites larger than 500,000 square meters occur in zones of denser habitation along with the preceding size class. Two of these sites, Los Morteros and the Huntington Site, are near the end of the Tucson Moun-

tains where irrigation could support many people. A third site overlooks one of the largest upper bajada drainages. The Marana Mound Site is the fourth, constituting the largest early Classic period settlement. These four sites are unique in containing compounds in addition to the cobble-outlined structures previously described.

Compounds are not equally distributed among the four sites, although precise numbers at each are not known. On the upper bajada, preservation of surface remains is so comprehensive that the presence of a single compound seems certain. Maximum counts are not possible at the riverine sites, but from two to five compounds seem likely. At the Marana Mound Site (Fig. 3.6) there are multiple clusters of adobe architectural remains, some containing more than one compound. If compounds equate with elite residence, elites are clearly concentrated at the central site. If compounds reflect localization of craft activities, storage, stockpiling, or other specialized functions, these are similarly clustered.

Ceramic Assemblages

Ceramic assemblages provide a third measure of site hierarchy. Consumption of higher value items can be contrasted among sites by comparing proportions of decorated to plain pottery in surface collections. The presence of multiple components at most large habitation sites weakens this comparison as a measure of inequalities solely during the Classic period. However, occupation of the Mound site was limited to the early Classic period, and comparative assemblages from the two largest riverine settlements were collected in site areas with the best segregation of the Classic period component. Decorated sherds at the Mound site, the two largest riverine sites, and the upper bajada compound site exceed proportions at all other settlements. Intermediate and small sites consistently contain less than five percent.

Imported types of Classic period date are virtually nonexistent in surface collections from the two smaller size classes (I and II), a rarity reinforced by recovery from Zone 1 small-site excavations. The four compound sites of size Class III are distinguished by multiple nonlocal wares. Other infrequent high-cost items are less easily quantified from surface collections but seem most closely associated with these compound sites.

INSTITUTIONS AND SOCIAL PERSONAE

A case has been made for a three-tiered settlement hierarchy based on site size, architecture, and ceramics. More than three-fourths of all sites fall into a "small" category. Surface indications of structures occur at a small number of intermediate-sized sites. The largest sites set apart by compounds and differential ceramic consumption represent a still smaller settlement fraction. The mound at one of these compound sites is the ultimate symbol of community integration, sociopolitical hierarchy, or both.

Cumulative evidence for vertical differentiation in the Marana Community is internally consistent and convincing. The resulting hierarchical structure could have been socially generated in more than one way. The institutional framework of community integration and the social personae corresponding to evidence for inequalities in settlement, architecture, and consumption of higher value goods are the missing pieces of the puzzle of organizational character and complexity. In contrast to Puebloan cultures of the northern Southwest, the nature of Hohokam institutions is not illuminated by ethnographic continuity in highly relevant spheres or by even early historic observations. Piman analogs are absent for mounds, compounds, and settlement hierarchy among the Hohokam.

Construction of the Marana Mound in a geographically central location (Fig. 3.2) would seem to indicate communal concern with an edifice that symbolized the integration of the expanded Classic period boundaries. The Mound was situated not among long-term populations in favorable riverine or upper bajada locales, but in a recently settled and agriculturally marginal area. Separation of the Classic mound from Preclassic ballcourt centers signals a divergence from prior organizational bases and, inferentially, from traditional sources of local authority, such as established kinship lines and land tenure. The placement of compounds reenforces the appearance of societal realignment. The location of the Mound center was not previously occupied. Where riverine settlement was continuous from the Preclassic into the Classic period, compounds were built at a distance from the earlier ballcourt.

The significance of the Marana Mound in Classic period societal organization is unclear. As the most imposing and visible product of collective effort, a strong association with community identity is likely. Religious observances apparently were centered here. An additional referent of the mound, unlike ballcourts, is the exclusivity of activities, precincts, and personnel enclosed by a massive adobe wall. Enclosures similarly demarcate groups occupying other compounds, whose institutional roles are also presently obscure.

Several lines of evidence suggest a close relationship between resource circulation and hierarchical structure in the Marana Community. Routine use of nonlocal raw materials and a degree of specialized subsistence production would have created a widespread base for exchange. Geographic centrality of the mound site would have represented an advantage for performers or regulators of transport and communication in the surrounding community. As densely settled, specialized producers with arable land of secondary quality, compound dwellers at the Mound had high stakes in a comprehensive and dependable system of exchange. The correlation of nonlocal ceramics with compound sites suggests additional roles in long distance trade. Glen Rice (1987c) has proposed Marana Community exchange as redistribution in a chiefdom context. However, no evidence as yet contradicts additional possibilities of periodic marketlike transactions, ritually organized exchange among relatively equal social units as in the pueblos (Ford 1972), or multiple forms of exchange according to resource type.

ABANDONMENT OF THE MARANA COMMUNITY

Identifiable habitation ceases by about A.D. 1350 throughout the early Classic period Marana Community (Fig. 3.4), a segment of the northern Tucson Basin continuously inhabited since before the beginning of the Hohokam sequence. The abandonment appears generally synchronous as measured with the low resolution of Hohokam ceramic phases. Salado polychromes, the markers for the transition from the Tanque Verde to the following late Classic Tucson phase, are exceedingly rare and virtually absent from contexts of probable residence.

An environmental trigger for this abandonment is not apparent. Locally derived environmental sequences are unavailable for the Tucson Basin. In a reconstruction from tree-ring records above the Mogollon Rim by Graybill (1989), summer precipitation, the critical factor in Tucson agricultural production, was found to be surprisingly complacent between A.D. 750 and 1350. Irreparable, systemic disruptions of the Salt River canals are posited at about A.D. 1350 (Nials, Gregory, and Graybill 1989) due to a flood of unusual magnitude that caused changes in channel structure in the vicinity of Phoenix intakes. The morphology and seasonal flow regime of the Santa Cruz River is unlike that of the Salt River, but even if Tucson flood damage had coincided with hypothesized Phoenix events, occupation and production could have continued in the long-standing mountain flank settlements. A separate Preclassic community demonstrated the independent viability of upper bajada zones. The diversity of agricultural production in the Marana Community further implies that residential populations could have persisted in some locations under any conceivable environmental scenarios. Nevertheless, a consensus for abandonment was reached by all inhabitants. In this sense, abandonment can be viewed as a social as well as an economic choice among a large population whose vital interconnections are emphasized by such joint action.

The abandonment phenomenon of the later Tanque Verde phase is of a truly regional scale and involves more than the Marana Community. Residential occupations in the late Classic period are absent in an area of approximately 1300 square kilometers (500 square miles) between the confluence of the Cañada del Oro and the Santa Cruz River and the southern edge of the Picacho Mountains 44 km (27 miles) to the north (Fig. 1.8). Continuing occupations both to the north and to the south are marked by Salado polychromes. Barring catastrophic population loss, it is reasonable to assume that inhabitants of the abandoned portion of the northern Tucson Basin were incorporated into these late Classic period settlement concentrations. Later Classic settlements to the south occur in situations with high potential for agricultural intensification along stretches of intermittent water courses with sustained flow and along ephemeral drainages with vast watersheds to the north. Productive capacities must have been sufficient to absorb the increased labor force as well as to satisfy the additional consumptive demands. Large, late Classic sites in these areas exhibit surface remains suggesting the highest residential densities for any period and the greatest investment in public architecture of presumed integrative function. A corollary of increasing aggregation is the development of social structures capable of integrating significant numbers of immigrants.

THE MARANA COMMUNITY IN
REGIONAL PERSPECTIVE

Settlement organization in the Marana Community reflects trends within the greater Hohokam tradition and refines knowledge of the variability within those larger developments. Just as ceramic styles progress in broad tandem, so do stylistic aspects of social differentiation and hierarchy. The ballcourt-to-platform mound transition in the Tucson area generally parallels but also shows divergences from Salt-Gila sequences. Organizational and spatial realignment between Preclassic ballcourt communities and mound-centered entities (Wilcox and Sternberg 1983) occurs in the northern Tucson Basin as elsewhere. However, unlike the Phoenix core area (Gregory 1987, 1991), no formal arrangements are found between early Classic period mounds and ballcourts in the Tucson regional context. In fact, ballcourts and mounds do not co-occur at any site. Tucson Basin arrangements appear to reflect differential applications of the tenets of public architecture and perhaps also of the underlying ideology, rather than temporal variation in the dates of construction.

Hohokam communities in regions lacking the massive irrigation systems of the core cannot be explained by interactions surrounding shared canal use, nor are settlement expressions of community necessarily isomorphic. Classic period communities in the core cover smaller areas, as calculated by an average 5-km spacing between mound sites along canals (Chapter 8; Gregory and Nials 1985; Gregory 1987). They also appear to contain denser populations and are more closely packed. The Marana Community, by contrast, is expansive in terms of population and settlement and is environmentally more diverse. With less irrigable land in the northern Tucson Basin, a substantially larger territory would be required to support populations of a given size than in the Phoenix core.

The Marana Community adds regional substance and detail to broader Hohokam issues. An economic base has been documented for populations of sufficient size and prosperity to support organizational structures resembling those of the large-scale irrigators along perennial rivers. Levels of productive specialization and some consumption patterns have been demonstrated that are commensurate with a strong and integral network of exchange. Regional settlement data have provided quantified distributions for components of horizontal and vertical differentiation. These are the building blocks for understanding Hohokam regions and interregional interactions.

CHAPTER FOUR

Parameters of Agricultural Production in the Northern Tucson Basin

Suzanne K. Fish, Paul R. Fish, and John H. Madsen

As a microcosm of environmental variation in the portion of the Sonoran Desert inhabited by the Hohokam, the Tucson Basin is an ideal location for investigating a diversified but integrated system of Hohokam agricultural production. Regional demography, settlement, social organization, and exchange were shaped by specific resource needs, technological capabilities, and environmental potential for production in an agricultural economy. The productive landscape of the Marana Community and of the larger study area can be examined in detail by reference to environmental variables, settlement pattern, and agricultural features, and by comparison with the practices of traditional farmers in historic times.

A number of excavation and survey reports document localized occurrences of Hohokam agricultural features and complexes. At a higher synthetic level, extensive canal networks have been analyzed by integrating historic records, aerial photography, and settlement data (for example, Haury 1976; Masse 1981, 1987, 1991; Nicholas and Neitzel 1984; Nials and others 1989; Ackerly and others 1987). Combinations of canal irrigation and runoff devices also have been described for a few substantial study areas (Gumerman and Johnson 1971; Crown 1987; Doyel 1984). However, in none of these cases has a systematic regional sample of non-canal features been available. Archaeologists attempting to deal with agricultural patterns at this scale (Masse 1979, 1991; Doyel 1984) have had to interpolate from geographically restricted and noncomparable survey findings.

The most important qualification of the northern Tucson Basin for a regional perspective is the presence of undisturbed land in all environmental zones. Granitic mountain ranges on the east reach approximately 1325 m (4300 feet). To the west, rough basalt peaks form a lower chain mostly below 860 m (2700 feet). Elevational diversity is repeated on opposing sides of the basin. Major and minor Santa Cruz River tributaries carry runoff from both orographic rainfall in the mountains

and storm-fed watersheds of bajadas. The hydrologic system includes surface flow and a second component of less rapidly mobile groundwater. Distributions of agricultural remains across the varied zones of the Marana Community offer a uniquely comprehensive testament to past productive relationships between noncore Hohokam and their desert basin environments.

CONSULTATION WITH TRADITIONAL FARMERS

Ethnographic practices of traditional farmers in environments similar to the study area furnish insights into natural and cultural factors influencing agricultural production. Piman analogies have been applied to the interpretation of Tucson archaeological patterns, particularly with reference to floodwater farming or the diversion of short-term flows in ephemeral drainages (Wilson 1985; Field 1985, Chapter 5 in this volume; Waters and Field 1986). However, historic Piman floodwater farming (ak chin farming) is a method with few remaining practitioners on isolated remnants of previously productive acreage (Reichhardt and Nabhan 1982; Nabhan 1986a, 1986b). Although well documented, the ethnographic instances do not duplicate prehistoric situations that involved higher population densities and, necessarily, more intensive land use. Other prehistoric techniques such as the northern basin forms of riverine irrigation and cultivation in rockpile fields lack analogs altogether.

Traditional farmers from two cultural and agricultural backgrounds in the Sonoran Desert were consulted in order to include multiple approaches, to broaden the range of associated population and land use intensity, and to explore agricultural alternatives and decision making. Visits to the study area by a traditional Tohono O'odham (Papago) farmer from an area southwest of Tucson and a farmer from Cucurpe in northern Sonora, Mexico, were arranged with the aid of Gary Nabhan of the Phoenix Botanical Garden, who participated in all

[41]

Table 4.1. Annual Precipitation Measures for Stations in the Tucson Basin and Other Hohokam Subareas

Station	Elevation (ASL) (m)	(feet)	Years of record	Mean annual precipitation (mm)	(inches)	Range of annual precipitation (mm)	(inches)	Variability index	Percent of years > 10 inches
Gila Bend	275	900	77	145	5.8	52–340	2.1–13.6	34.3	7
Phoenix Airport	335	1100	34	175	7.1	60–335	2.4–13.4	29.1	16
Sacaton	365	1200	72	195	7.9	47–392	1.9–15.7	27.9	26
Florence	460	1500	69	250	9.9	103–470	4.1–18.8	24.6	27
Casa Grande National Monument	425	1400	59	220	8.8	97–480	3.9–19.2	27.1	26
Cortaro (Marana Study Area)	670	2200	27	280	11.2	158–463	6.3–18.5	23.9	65
Tucson, University of Arizona	700	2300	82	275	11.1	143–408	5.7–16.3	23.7	60

Sources: Range of annual precipitation from Green and Sellers 1964; other data from Sellers and others 1985.

phases of consultation. Both individuals engage in variants of floodwater farming, and the Cucurpe farmer irrigates with gravity-fed canals from a small Sonoran river. Evaluations and comments by these consultants are cited in relevant sections of this chapter.

PRECIPITATION AND REGIONAL POTENTIAL

Tucson Basin agriculture must be understood in the context of local risks and opportunities. The potential for riverine canals is lower than along the Salt and Gila rivers near Phoenix, based on volume and duration of flow in the Santa Cruz River, terrace morphology, and extent of topographically irrigable basin floor. Alternative prehistoric technologies for securing agricultural water were concomitantly more prominent. Precipitation measures for Hohokam subareas reveal variation in the

Table 4.2. July, August, and September Precipitation for Stations in the Tucson Basin and Other Hohokam Subareas

Station	Years of record	Mean summer precipitation (mm)	(inches)	Mean no. of summer days with > 0.25 inches precipitation
Gila Bend	77	52	2.1	2
Phoenix Airport	34	57	2.3	3
Sacaton	72	90	3.6	5
Florence	69	87	3.5	5
Casa Grande National Monument	59	77	3.1	3
Cortaro (Marana Study Area)	27	135	5.4	7
Tucson University of Arizona	82	145	5.8	6

Source: Sellers and others 1985

abundance and predictability of local rainfall corresponding to differential risks and returns for fields more directly dependent on this source for water than irrigated land (Tables 4.1, 4.2; Fig. 4.1). Substantial investment in such fields in the Tucson Basin may be explained as much by comparatively favorable precipitation regimes as by fewer possibilities for riverine canals.

Mean annual precipitation for the Marana study area at 280 mm (11.2 inches) is among the highest for basin interiors in all of Hohokam territory. For agriculturalists in arid environments, annual variability may be as critical as average amounts. Table 4.1 confirms that higher annual Tucson precipitation corresponds with lower variability, as measured by departures from the long-term mean. Likewise, precipitation minima in dry years are higher in the northern Tucson Basin than at other stations. Tucson riverine irrigators as well as farmers using channelized floodwater and overland flow depended on relatively abundant local precipitation. Because upland snow melt is too limited to generate high flows in the Santa Cruz and its tributaries during the spring and because summer precipitation predominates in south-central Arizona, rainfall in this season is the major factor in total agricultural production. As in the case of annual amounts, summer precipitation for the Tucson Basin is more favorable than for much of the territory inhabited by the Hohokam (Table 4.2).

AGRICULTURAL ATTRIBUTES OF BASIN SETTINGS

Mountain Slopes

At higher elevations, orographic rainfall delivers a more abundant and predictable water supply for crops dependent on direct precipitation than at lower elevations. The Tucson Mountains on the west edge of the Tucson Basin (Zone 6 of the Marana Community) exert

Figure 4.1. Locations of weather stations in Tables 4.1 and 4.2.

lesser influence on precipitation patterns than the more massive ranges on the east (Figs. 3.8, 3.9). However, the benefits of orographic rainfall are balanced against two drawbacks of mountain slope cultivation. Parcels of suitable soil depth and flatness are restricted. At altitudes above 925 m (3000 feet), frost hazards increase, although lower mountain flanks may be warmer than valley floors exposed to cold air drainage.

In the Tucson Basin, temperature inversion has significant elevational consequences for early or late season planting. The impact of cold air flowing down slope is illustrated by five years of weather records for a station on the shoulder of a hill in the Tucson Mountains and for a second station on the basin floor below, near the Santa Cruz River (Hastings and Turner 1965: 17). The stations are separated by a horizontal distance of only 0.8 km (0.5 mile) and by a vertical distance of only 100 m (330 feet). A difference of 10.1° C (20° F) was recorded on some nights. Over the five-year period there was a total of only 38 freezing nights on the hill in contrast to 263 nights on the floodplain. The frost-danger period

between first and last freezes for a winter averaged 36 days on the hill and 157 days below. Low temperatures were of shorter duration on the hill as well. These elevational contrasts would be critical for spring crops planted sufficiently early to benefit from winter rains.

Two mountain slope situations appear most advantageous for agricultural pursuits. One occurs on the flat land of ridge tops or plateaus at higher elevations where more abundant rainfall is available. Alternately, gentle slopes at intermediate elevations with less orographic rainfall have less frost, better soil accumulations, and offer opportunities for water catchment and concentration through such features as terraces and checkdams.

The Tortolita mountain slopes have been covered less fully in survey than other zones. The best coverage is in the northeast sector of the study area (Fig. 3.2). Here, a number of habitation sites are located away from canyons on flatter land at elevations as high as 1128 m (3700 feet). It seems probable that orographic rainfall and relatively small catchments supplied water for agriculture. Survey transects (Hewitt and Stephen 1981) located agricultural terraces near sites at still higher elevations on the eastern Tortolita slopes facing into the adjoining basin.

The Tucson Mountains are much less massive than the Tortolitas and were fully surveyed. The relative sparsity of sites in the Tucson Mountains (Zone 6) may be related to preferred habitation on the immediately adjacent Santa Cruz floodplain (Zone 5), but potential use of western mountain land also seems limited. Terraced slope sites in southern Arizona of the type found in the Tucson Mountains correlate almost exclusively with the kind of dark volcanic substrates occurring in this range; locations of such sites in the Marana Community additionally coincide with large populations on the adjoining floodplain.

Four clusters of stone terraces or trincheras features were constructed in the Tucson Mountains within the study area. The two largest coincide with dense occupations around the northern end of the mountain chain. Many of these terraces appear to have been agricultural in function, and corn pollen has been recovered from several (S. Fish, P. Fish, and Downum 1984). The agricultural benefits of terraces on mountain slopes include water concentrated from slope catchments above and between terraces, protection from freezing winter temperatures threatening lower elevations through inversion, and relief from high summer temperatures by preferential use of north and east exposures. Trincheras cultivation probably ranged from kitchen gardens around the houses built on some terraces to clusters of features of solely agricultural function (Downum and others 1985; Downum 1991) as described for a large site in the Robles Community to the northeast (Fig. 1.8).

Canyon Bottoms

Tortolita canyon bottoms represent a topographic class related to mountain slopes, but with distinctive agricultural potential. Canyons carry streams with large uphill watersheds. Effluent water continues to be discharged into these stream beds for extended periods and supports perennial flow in some cases. The quantity of effluent stream flow may be reduced in the summer, however (Chapter 5). Flat bottomland with adequate soil depth is often quite narrow. Since high-energy floods occur, smaller tributaries to main canyon drainages may have been easier to divert in some cases. Cold air, which flows down canyons, represents one environmental drawback for early crops. Wider canyon bottomland in the Tortolitas is associated with a number of settlements in uppermost Zone 4 of the Marana Community in contrast to the Tucson Mountains (Zone 6), where canyons are smaller and drain restricted slope areas.

Tortolita canyon sites tend to be located along the floodplain edges, no doubt above the contour of most floods. The only recorded habitation sites are small. Farming in the canyon bottoms may often have been carried out on a daily basis by inhabitants of settlements on the adjacent upper bajada. Deeper soils are typically associated with shallow, meandering channel segments from which water could be diverted. It is likely that diversion structures, agricultural features, and perhaps even habitation remains on canyon floodplains have been removed or buried by the larger floods occurring between prehistoric and modern times. The absence of sites in canyons of the Cochie and Cottonwood drainages (Fig. 3.2) reflects survey coverage rather than a departure from the general distributional pattern in the northern Tucson Basin.

Upper Bajadas

West of the river in the southern community (Zone 5), the width of the bajada is greatly compressed between the Tucson Mountains and the Santa Cruz, increasingly so toward the northern end of those mountains (Fig. 3.9). Relatively few sites have been recorded on the slope below these mountains and only small ones with evidence for habitation are located here. Farmers with floodwater fields along the mountain edge may have resided in nearby settlements along the river.

Two situations for agriculture predominate on the upper bajada below the Tortolitas (Zone 4), where substantial habitation sites of all periods are found. The first involves areas between major trans-slope washes that originate in the mountains. Secondary and less incised drainages of various sizes in these areas also carry water from more localized upland watersheds. Precipitation at the base of the mountain front, heightened by the initial uplift of moisture-laden air passing over the peaks, adds to flow in the smaller streams. Numerous instances of low-density but extensive arrays of simple stone alignments indicate the agricultural use of overland runoff in broad, gentle swales as well as water diverted from channels.

To the southeast of the Marana Community, a dispersed pattern of small habitations and other sites on the bajada occurs in the vicinity of Cañada Agua (Fig. 3.9). These sites are primarily oriented toward moderate-sized drainages. Farther from the mountains here, slopes flatten over deeper valley fill, and many smaller channels become shallow, braided, and easier to divert (Fig. 4.2). A continuous scatter of isolated artifacts corresponds to the vicinity of braided channels even where sites are lacking and appears to represent remains resulting from farming activities. Sites at the southeastern edge of this

Figure 4.2. Braided channel of a drainage on the upper bajada downslope from the Tortolita
Mountain pediment in the Marana survey area. (Photograph by Helga Teiwes.)

area are located outside the Marana Community and are affiliated with Preclassic or Classic period communities with centers farther east.

It is difficult to assess the relative agricultural reliance on primary and secondary drainages on the upper bajada within the Marana Community. In the Classic period and earlier, both large and small sites tend to cluster along the major Cottonwood, Derrio, and Guild washes. Smaller habitation sites are located between these on secondary channels, but distances would have permitted additional land in such situations to be cultivated by residents of settlements along the major watercourses.

Near the upper reaches of Guild Wash as it leaves the Tortolitas, the placement of dispersed small habitations on minor drainages resembles site locations about Cañada Agua. Agricultural features such as rockpiles and alignments are also concentrated here. Both within the Marana Community and to the south near Cañada Agua, remains oriented toward secondary drainages extend a limited distance beyond the mountain front onto the upper bajada. Contours of approximately 875 m (2700 feet) delimit the southern sites and the same elevation bounds similar sites within the Marana Community. Agricultural parameters probably figure in this pattern. Near the mountain front, sediment over pediment bedrock is typically no deeper than a few meters; water tables in drainages are correspondingly close to the surface. As drainages continue downhill across the bajada, surface flow tends to diminish or disappear in channels through infiltration into increasingly deep valley fill. The lower elevational limit of sites on small drainages likely marks the downslope extent of significant surface flow from all but the largest precipitation events.

Another factor in agricultural production involves the opportunity for early cropping at elevations above the level of cold air drainage. Winter frontal systems pass from the west and north toward the east across southern Arizona. Therefore, the greatest precipitation benefits from orographic uplift are experienced during this season along the western edge of the Tortolitas. In most years, winter rains cease well before May. The ensuing fore-summer drought lasts under high temperatures until July, preventing satisfactory maturation of mid to late spring plantings. To effectively use winter moisture, the earliest possible planting date would have been necessary. A relationship between upper bajada settlement near small drainages and the elevational limits of inversion is illustrated by the fact that urban smog can be observed to hover in the valley bottom just below these sites. Crops may have been planted sufficiently early on these warmer slopes for spring harvests as well as summer ones.

Water in the large trans-bajada washes supported the second major farming orientation in Zone 4 on the upper bajada. Bottomland with high agricultural potential is not evenly distributed along the major washes, but varies with factors such as width and morphology of the floodplain, water table depth, watershed size, and drainage gradient. The importance of such acreage for supporting relatively dense populations is indicated by the locations of large habitation sites along those stretches of the major drainages suitable for floodplain fields.

A proliferation of both large and small settlements on Guild, Derrio, and Cottonwood washes occurred during the Classic period. To some extent, this density may reflect cultural preference: the desire of expanding populations to locate new habitations within community boundaries and near sites of origin. However, the largest upper bajada sites of Preclassic times also occur here, indicating a long-term productive advantage.

Compared to Derrio and Cottonwood drainages, Guild, Cañada Agua, Ruelas, Wild Burro, and Cochie washes are characterized by small watersheds (Table 4.3), lesser volume and frequency of flow, and narrower floodplains. The greater length of Guild than these others along the mountain front, where bedrock depth is shallowest, and its course across a gentler slope likely account for larger sites along the upper reaches. Cañada Agua, with only one large site, and Guild, with numerous large and small ones, traverse less steep portions of the upper bajada on which water diversion and control of flow was easier. Evidence of the strength of flow in Wild Burro Wash was considered disadvantageous by the Tohono O'odham and Mexican traditional farmers. Wild Burro, Ruelas, and Cochie have steeper courses, and sites along them extend for only short distances beyond the mountains.

Compared to those washes, Derrio and Cottonwood cross flatter topography and are lined by clusters of large sites farther downhill on the upper bajada. Bedrock visible in bank cuts indicates a favorably high water table. These large sites coincide with segments of wide, arable floodplain and lush riparian vegetation within the wash bottoms (Fig. 4.3). Width of the floodplains is sufficient

Table 4.3 Mountain Watershed Sizes for Trans-bajada Drainages in the Marana Survey Area

Drainage	Watershed Area	
	(square km)	(square miles)
Cañada Agua	4.22	1.63
Guild	6.76	2.61
Ruelas	8.26	3.19
Cochie	14.06	5.43
Wild Burro	17.95	6.93
Cottonwood	18.78	7.25
Derrio	27.07	10.45

Prepared by Matts Myhrman

for water diversion from shallow channels onto fields at the side above flood limits. Trenching in Derrio and Cottonwood floodplains (Chapter 5) revealed intact features such as hearths in these floodplain edge situations at depths less than a meter. The greater upland watersheds of Derrio and Cottonwood (Table 4.3) may have supplied effluent flow from winter rains into the spring season as far downslope as these large sites or within short distances from them. Peak flow from summer rains in the two drainages would also reflect watershed size through frequency and volume of flow.

Derrio and Cottonwood floodplains were judged to be agriculturally desirable by the traditional farming consultants on the basis of vegetation indicators. The Mexican informant noted the size of mesquite trees. The Tohono O'odham farmer additionally commented on the intense green color of palo verde trees, the presence of catclaw (*Acacia greggii*), and a potential for hand-dug floodplain wells. In situations resembling Derrio and Cottonwood floodplains, highly productive fields are still cultivated today along major tributaries in the Rio Sonora valley of Mexico (Doolittle 1984: 124–135). Series of adjacent fields share diverted water from canals of moderate length. Such fields are also cultivated within tributaries of the San Miguel River in Sonora by means of short diversion ditches and floodwater techniques (Nabhan and Sheridan 1977).

Middle Bajadas

Middle reaches of the valley slope, representing large areas in Zones 2 and 3 (Figs. 3.8, 3.9) on the eastern side of the basin, were not a significant factor in agricultural production prior to the Classic period. Drinking water is inconveniently distant at the river or above at the mountain edge. Potential agricultural water appears as brief flows in the major trans-bajada drainages following only the largest storms. Water from lesser precipitation events typically generates local floods, which are

Figure 4.3. Segment of Derrio Wash with arable bottomland on the upper
bajada in the Marana survey area. (Photograph by Helga Teiwes.)

not sustained over long distances and infiltrate channels
over deep valley fill. These drainages are incised beyond
a depth for easy diversion even when water is available.

Many small drainages with bajada rather than mountain catchments are sufficiently shallow for successful
diversion. However, such water would have been available only in cases of thunderstorms directly over the
watershed, a relatively unpredictable event compared to
higher elevation precipitation triggered by uplift of air
over the mountains. The use of small drainages by means
of earthen checkdams in Zone 2, which likely was
attempted only in seasons of more promising rainfall,
correlates exclusively with the Classic period proliferation of an agricultural technology fed by surface runoff.
Simple mulches of piled cobbles, or rockpiles, enhanced
and conserved soil moisture for drought-adapted crops of
agave in vast fields (see Chapter 7). Overland runoff and
direct rainfall were the sole water sources on gentle
middle bajadas that were too marginal for annual crops
such as corn, beans, and squash.

Lower Bajadas

Alluvial fans composed of outwash sediment from the
uplands coalesce on the lower bajada in Zone 1 on the
east and Zone 6 on the west (Figs. 3.8, 3.9). In portions
nearer the floodplain, gentle slopes providing an active
depositional environment and controllable water flow
were favored by cultivators of every period. In these situations, floodwaters following storms provided both moisture and simultaneous enrichment for crops in the form
of suspended nutrients and organic detritus. Dispersed
settlements of farmers rather than the remains of agricultural activities register the reliance on lower bajada
cultivation. Analogy with historic Sonoran Desert cultivators suggests brush, earth, and stone diversion structures on watercourses (Fig. 4.4), intrafield constructions
of similar materials for water distribution (Fig. 4.5), and
ditches or canals of moderate length (Fig. 4.6), all of
which would rarely leave evidence in the archaeological
record.

Figure 4.4. Water diversion structure on a tributary of the Rio Sonora near Baviacora, Sonora.

Figure 4.5. Earthen embankment for intrafield distribution of water along a tributary of the Rio Sonora near Baviacora, Sonora.

Figure 4.6. Canal carrying diverted floodwaters to multiple fields
along a tributary of the Rio Sonora near Baviacora, Sonora.

Tohono O'odham ak chin or floodwater farming in late historic time has provided the foremost model for understanding strategies of land use on alluvial fans. The ideal location of fields coincides with down-fan positions in which floodwater overflows increasingly shallow channels and spreads laterally over the fan surface, delivering water of sufficiently low force to avoid disruption of plantings. The closer the correspondence between these conditions and field location, the less labor investment would be necessary to divert water and construct ditches or protective barriers. Locations of optimal conditions shift on fans over time as hydrological activity changes in response to continuing geomorphological processes.

Geomorphological variables affecting floodwater farming in the study area are discussed by Field (1985; Chapter 5 in this volume), Waters (1987, 1988), and Waters and Field (1986). Advantages of small fans over large ones include higher proportions of fine-grained soil, lower thresholds of overbank flow, and less erosive force of flow when it occurs. Greater distance from the

mountain front, also correlated with fan size, as in Zone 1 further enhances the accessibility of agricultural water. However, these advantages on small fans, as in the Tucson Mountains of Zone 6 must be balanced against the lower chance for thunderstorms over watersheds of more limited extent.

Late nineteenth century and more recent observations emphasize Tohono O'odham field placement with respect to points of natural water spreading (Bryan 1925, 1929), but ethnographic accounts recall more intensive past practices. Constructions are reported for runoff concentration in watershed areas upslope from fields and for water delivery from drainages to conjoined series of fields (Underhill 1939; Castetter and Bell 1942; Clotts 1915, 1917). Collective efforts were involved in constructing canals up to 1 km (0.5 mile) in length and even longer walls to divert runoff to plots or reservoirs. Nabhan (1986a, 1986b) notes that such efforts suggest a broader range of former field locations than at loci of natural water spreading, and he documents more varied situations of late historic Tohono O'odham cultivation. Downcutting and channel incision of major washes in southern Arizona in the late 1800s may have prevented their diversion, increasing subsequent use of smaller tributaries and watersheds with less predictable flood-water flow (Nabhan 1986a: 74). Higher densities of farmers in prehistoric times and greater dependence on their own agricultural yields may have occasioned other departures from idealized Tohono O'odham practices of the late historic period.

Possible evidence for more intensive methods of water management on alluvial fans has been found in excavated cross sections of buried drainages. Trenches dug on the lower bajadas in Zone 1 of the Marana Community (Katzer and Schuster 1984) intersected several secondary channels that differ in morphology from current natural drainages and that may have been constructed to direct overland flow. Compared with modern drainages, these channels are shallower and less concave, are unrelated to present drainage patterns, exhibit unusual lateral and vertical continuity, and contain indications of introduced flow greater than that to which the fluvial system was adjusted (Katzer and Schuster 1984). They appear to be contemporary with adjacent Hohokam occupations. Canals revealed by excavations on a fan west of the Tucson Basin (Withers 1973) represent another alternative to reliance on purely natural water-spreading processes. Canals would have permitted upstream diversion from large drainages with substantial watersheds that were less prone to natural overbank flow and floodwater spreading.

Late historic floodwater farming of isolated fields allowed ideal positioning for minimal labor investment and relocation whenever events such as massive floods altered favorable conditions. Use of fan areas by larger numbers of farmers prehistorically would have restricted relocations and prompted cultivation of less easily farmed locales. In a variety of situations with divertible water within the Marana Community, both the Mexican and Tohono O'odham consultants considered soils too sandy to achieve high yields. They suggested that finer-grained and more water-retentive planting mediums could be created by water diversion and resultant silt deposition for one to several years prior to cultivation. Such improvements might encourage further modifications toward field permanence, such as ditches or canals of moderate size from upstream diversions. Along the Rio Sonora, Doolittle (1984) describes the incremental growth of such improved and locationally stable field systems over the course of long-term use.

Particular site locations on the lower bajada were used over long intervals of time, indicating commensurate stability in general farming locations. A dense concentration of lower bajada sites of all periods occurs in Zone 1 to the north of Wild Burro Wash. Observations of sediment deposition and organic flood detritus that were made over several years document frequent flow in the larger secondary drainages of this area. This kind of evidence and vegetational indications convinced both traditional farming consultants that this zone was among the most desirable settings for farming in the Marana Community. A second likely factor in concentrated settlement of the lower bajada is the prolonged availability of domestic water. Portions of Zone 1 with substantial early settlement are those close to the high water table along the Santa Cruz near the end of the Tucson Mountains.

Irrigation by canal from the river may have augmented agricultural production on the eastern segments of the lower bajada. Terrace height diminishes and width of the floodplain increases rapidly downstream from the Tucson Mountains, topographically permitting canal paths to diverge from the river and traverse the lower edges of Tortolita alluvial fans. A series of prehistoric canals paralleling historic ones has been identified in aerial photographs and by surface remains, passing near or through a number of sites (Fig. 3.2). It appears that these canals supplied drinking water for permanent residence and also may have supported some irrigated acreage.

Santa Cruz Floodplain

Risks and opportunities for Hohokam agriculturalists in Zone 5 on the river floodplain cannot be judged precisely by present conditions (Figs. 3.8, 3.9). Historically, perennial surface flow in the Santa Cruz has been absent north of Tucson. Pre-Columbian runoff would have been less rapid due to wooded stream courses and the grass cover heavier before the appearance of livestock. Floods would have been poorly contained when the river channel was less incised. Current entrenchment and associated lowering of water tables began prior to this century (Cooke and Reeves 1976; Betancourt and Turner 1988).

It is not clear whether episodes of channel incision apply equally and simultaneously to the Santa Cruz throughout its length in the Tucson Basin. An instance of downcutting prior to the Classic period in the southern Tucson Basin apparently caused the abandonment of riverine settlements dependent on irrigation (Waters 1988: 217). The lack of later occupations at several Preclassic settlements along the river near the southern boundary of the Marana Community (Figs. 3.1, 3.2) may also have followed the disruption of canal intakes through vertical or horizontal shifts of the river channel.

Historically, localized areas of high water table and sustained flow of surface water were created in the Tucson Basin by igneous intrusions related to the mountain masses. Without such impervious barriers, water infiltrates the porous riverbed in other stretches and flows underground after short-term floods. In the northern basin, a volcanic intrusion, higher water table, and more prolonged flow occur near the end of the Tucson Mountains in Zone 5. Accessibility and duration of flow create the best situation for canal intakes, and a variety of historic lines headed here.

Compared to the Phoenix Basin, floodplain width and terrace morphology in the Tucson region significantly restrict the extent of irrigable land. Nevertheless, irrigated fields along the floodplain supported the densest populations in the study area. Intensive production of annual crops by irrigation likely played a significant role in community-wide population levels. Riverine settlement in both Preclassic and Classic periods was greatest in the area of high water table surrounding the mountain end.

Floodplain surfaces of the Santa Cruz have been alternately scoured and buried. Lateral channel movement that has obscured prehistoric activity is indicated by archaeological materials eroding from a west bank cut at the Tucson Mountain terminus. Remains of prehistoric canals are not visible on the surface of this zone and have only been identified in excavation. Evidence of buried canals has been encountered on the west side of the river just south of the study area (Kinkade and Fritz 1975) and within the Marana Community near the end of the mountains (Bernard-Shaw 1988). Due to overlying deposits, it is doubtful that the extent of Hohokam irrigation along the Santa Cruz can ever be comprehensively documented.

North and downstream from the Tucson Mountains, the river floodplain widens rapidly and terrace barriers to the lateral extension of canals diminish. At the same time, the channel becomes more poorly defined and surface flow disappears underground except during large flood events. Floodplain expanses are subject to extensive shallow flooding over fine-grained alluvial soils.

Canal headings are not feasible on this stretch of the river, but irrigated fields were supplied historically by lines with intakes near the end of the mountains. Gravity canals on the east side of the river extended as far north as the modern town of Marana (Roskruge 1896a, 1896b). It is likely that Hohokam canals irrigated more land in this area prior to historic river channel incision. The broad floodplain is under cultivation today, and surface indications of prehistoric canals are preserved only at higher elevation along the lower edge of the bajada. Similarly, the outlines of settlements in these modern fields

are poorly defined. As a second method of prehistoric floodplain cultivation in this area, a large set of rockpiles on an undisturbed stretch of a low west terrace just north of the mountains may have functioned to control the dispersion of shallow floods.

AGRICULTURAL PARAMETERS AND REGIONAL LAND USE

A perspective of regional scale provides richer insights into land-use patterns than would be possible through a compilation of isolated evidence. With the emergence of an overall settlement configuration in the northern Tucson Basin, the insufficiency of ethnographic analogy for understanding the breadth of Hohokam subsistence has become apparent. Some agricultural technologies and environmental situations were similar to those used by Piman Indians, but other components of Hohokam production are without analogs even in the earliest Spanish accounts. There are no descriptions of agricultural patterns similar to those in upper and middle bajada zones. Ethnographic parallels are also lacking for productive modes that were capable of underwriting the higher range of Hohokam population densities and the occupation of settings that were historically abandoned.

The availability of regional distributions sharpens the discrimination of environmental variables affecting land-use patterns. Elements of the technological repertoire represent incomplete information without reference to the regional variety of associated environmental contexts. For example, rockpile devices occur in more than one relationship to water and topography. In most instances, rockpiles were constructed on middle bajada ridge tops where runoff follows the general elevational trend from uplands to valley floor. Other rockpiles were located on the broad, gently angled sides of bajada drainages. Here, overland flow of water is at right angles to the downhill slope toward the valley bottom and coincides with the path of runoff as it joins streams laterally. Still another setting for rockpiles is on a low terrace of the Santa Cruz River. In this location, water originated from shallow overbank flooding or canals.

From one viewpoint, stability in Hohokam land use characterizes the northern Tucson Basin. A dual site distribution, with one band along the floodplain and adjacent lower bajada and one band paralleling the flanks of the eastern mountains, was established early in the sequence and remained constant. Harshness of the Hohokam environment has been viewed as imposing a modicum of settlement stability through the topographic requirements for canal systems and labor investments in them (Haury 1976: 354; Nicholas and Neitzel 1984;

Masse 1981, 1991). Restricted opportunities to concentrate water for floodwater farming or surface runoff management likely crystallized land use in additional topographic situations. Technological conservatism is reflected by construction of the same feature types for hundreds of years. In the Tucson Basin, the long-standing relationship between settlement patterns and hydrological opportunity suggests continuity in agricultural approaches.

These observations do not imply, however, that the system of Hohokam production was static or without identifiable trajectories. Dynamic elements were interjected by changing economic needs and aspirations of Basin inhabitants over time. The Classic period proliferation of rockpile fields above the Marana Mound Site illustrates a dramatic agricultural reorientation based on preexisting technology (see Chapter 7).

An understanding of environmental opportunity and available technology are not sufficient to predict prehistoric decisions as to the form and extent of implementation in agricultural production. Additional natural but nonagricultural variables may impinge, such as the co-occurrence of suitable domestic water. More importantly, agricultural production is the outcome of economic decisions on the part of individuals and groups, who consider cost, risk, expectations, and cultural values in formulating their responses. During successive periods, agricultural parameters of the northern Tucson Basin influenced economic behavior in changing contexts of regional settlement and demography.

CHAPTER FIVE

An Evaluation of Alluvial Fan Agriculture

John J. Field

Floodwater farming on alluvial fans takes advantage of water that rapidly moves through desert basins following storms. Settlement patterns in the Marana Community indicate widespread dependence on cultivation by this method, primarily in Zones 1 and 4 of the bajada below the Tortolita Mountains on the east, but also in the areally limited portion of Zone 6 between the Tucson Mountains and the Santa Cruz floodplain (Figs. 3.8, 3.9). Knowledge of floodwater methods comes in large part from Piman Indian practices of the late nineteenth and early twentieth centuries in topographic situations resembling those of Zone 1 (Bryan 1922, 1925, 1929; Castetter and Bell 1942; Underhill 1939). As described, this ak chin farming of the late historic period emphasized positioning of fields in ideal locations of natural overflow from drainages with a minimum of structural improvements for managing water. Additional studies of historic Piman agriculture (Nabhan 1983, 1986) and traditional farming methods in northwestern Mexico (Doolittle 1984, 1988) illustrate a wider latitude of more labor-intensive floodwater field systems that also have parallels in the Marana Community.

GEOMORPHOLOGY OF LATE HOLOCENE ALLUVIAL FANS

Approximately 390 square kilometers (150 square miles) of the lower bajadas in the surveyed area north of Tucson are composed of late Holocene alluvial fans (Figs. 1.8, 5.1). These fans are formed primarily from the erosion and redeposition of older Pleistocene and early Holocene alluvial fans found farther upslope. The late Holocene fans are actively prograding onto floodplains and terraces of the Santa Cruz River. Two depositional facies are ubiquitous on the late Holocene fans: channel gravelly sand facies and sheetwash silty sand facies. Facies are units of sediment deposited by a single depositional process (Reading 1978). By analyzing the distribution of depositional processes on an alluvial fan, paleoenvironmental reconstructions can be made to help assess the prehistoric agricultural potential of a particular fan.

The channel gravelly sand deposits are well-stratified, relatively well-sorted, loose, light colored sands containing up to 30 percent gravel (Fig. 5.2). Silt content is never greater than 5 percent. Agricultural drawbacks of coarse texture would be rapid infiltration of water to depths beyond crop roots and rapid evaporation of moisture content. The facies is typically 1 m to 2 m thick with sharp erosive bases and extends laterally for 50 m to 400 m before interfingering with silty sand deposits. The top of each channel unit also grades into sheetwash sediments.

The sheetwash silty sand facies, in contrast, is composed of very poorly sorted, massive, slightly hard, yellow orange (10 YR 6/3) silty sands containing between 5 and 50 percent silt (Fig. 5.3). Moisture retention would be greater than for the channel gravelly sand facies because of the higher proportion of silt. Gravel content rarely exceeds 10 percent. Massive textures result from heavy bioturbation of originally laminated silts and interstratified gravel lenses. Silty sand deposits completely enclose channel units, and are frequently over 3 m thick where channel deposits are absent. Archaeological features are abundant and well preserved in this facies.

The coarse texture, erosive nature, and stratification of the gravelly sand facies indicate deposition in confined high-energy environments characteristic of ephemeral washes or channels seen on active alluvial fan surfaces. The high percentage of silt, excellent preservation of archaeological features, and heavy bioturbation are evidence for low-energy processes operating in the silty sand facies. Laminated silts and sands are characteristic of sheetflood deposits below the fan intersection point (Packard 1974). The intersection point on an alluvial fan is where channel depth becomes zero, below which the

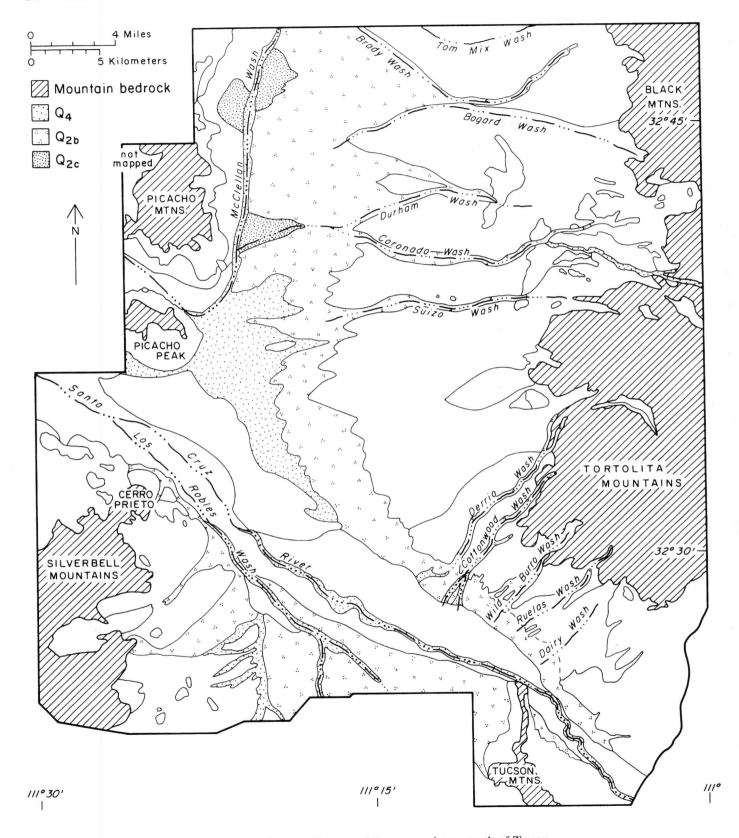

Figure 5.1. Geomorphic map of the surveyed area north of Tucson.

Figure 5.2. Typical exposure of well-stratified channel gravelly sand facies. Erosional contact with underlying silty sand facies is visible at bottom of trowel.

Figure 5.3. Typical exposure of sheetwash silty sand facies, showing massive textures enclosing a gravel lens to the right of the trowel.

stream flow becomes unconfined (Hooke 1967). This position equates with the location of natural water spreading described historically as preferred for Tohono O'odham ak chin (floodwater) farming (Bryan 1929: 449; Castetter and Bell 1942: 125).

By comparing depositional processes on active alluvial surfaces with those discussed above, a depositional model can be developed to reconstruct the paleohydrology of prehistoric surfaces. Portions of the fan accumulating sediment of a particular facies are revealed by surface indications of depositional processes. In stratigraphic profile, vertical variations in facies reflect changes in and document lateral migration of depositional processes through time at a single point.

Figure 5.4 is an aerial photograph of Cottonwood Fan displaying several active processes as well as inactive surfaces in Zone 1 of the Marana Community. Cottonwood Wash is well confined and channelized at the fan head. Farther down the fan a decrease in channel depth results in an increase in channel branches and a decrease in channel width. Below the intersection point where channel depth becomes zero, stream flow becomes unconfined and the aerial extent of deposition increases greatly. Sedimentary facies deposited in various reaches on the fan surface reflect the observed processes. Confined washes at the fan head are eroded into older fan sediments and are filled with gravelly sand channel deposits. The silty sand facies dominates below the intersection point. Similar longitudinal variations in depositional processes on alluvial fans are recorded elsewhere (Hooke 1967; Rahn 1967; Packard 1974; Bull 1977).

Subsurface longitudinal profiles constructed from evenly spaced backhoe trenches provide evidence for prehistoric distributions of depositional processes. Like surficial variations, channel deposits are most prevalent at the fan head and sheetflows dominate at the fan toe (Figs. 5.5, 5.6). Sections through Derrio Fan (Fig. 5.5) display a basal channel grading into silty sands. Upward trends in depositional processes observed in vertical profiles are similar to downfan longitudinal variations and indicate a headward (upstream) migration of facies. As channels at headward portions of the fan begin to fill due to low and intermediate stage flows, the intersection point is restricted to higher portions of the fan (Packard 1974). As a result, sheetflow sediments are deposited above channel fill. When channels at the fan head become completely choked with sediment, evulsion or cutoff of the main trunk stream occurs, a lower portion of the fan becomes active, and the depositional sequence outlined above is repeated. Each sequence creates a fan lobe that becomes a small portion of the entire alluvial fan; each alluvial fan is comprised of several vertically stacked and laterally adjacent fan lobes.

Although deposition on all fans is consistent with the processes and model presented above, variability in fan configuration exists because of differences in drainage basin area and distance from the mountain fronts. Thicknesses of fan lobes, channel dimensions, and aggradation rates increase with increased drainage basin area or proximity to mountain fronts. Because channel dimensions and the corresponding ability to contain high flows increase with fan size, channel deposits on large fans extend to the fan toe (Fig. 5.5). Sheetflows, which occur where floodwater overflows established channels, are more easily induced on small fans because the smaller channels are unable to contain flow converging on the fan surface. Also, the intersection point on small fans is

Table 5.1. Drainage Characteristics of Selected Washes in the Surveyed Area North of Tucson

Wash name	Drainage basin area (sq. km)	(sq. mi.)	Percent area on piedmont	Distance fan head to mountain front (km)	(mi.)	Drainage basin length (km)	(mi.)
Tom Mix	8.177	3.134	44.6	4.8	3.0	8.2	5.1
Brady	150.816	58.230	28.4	13.0	8.1	24.2	15.1
Bogard	62.310	24.058	87.3	18.7	11.7	23.3	14.5
Durham-Coronado	266.863	103.036	69.0	26.0	16.3	34.6	21.6
Suizo	83.600	32.278	84.9	27.2	17.0	32.8	20.5
Parker	77.154	29.789	72.6	20.0	12.5	27.5	17.2
Picacho							
I	3.245	1.253	none	1.9	1.2	4.2	2.6
II	5.828	2.250	none	0.5	0.3	5.0	3.2
III	2.642	1.020	none	1.0	0.7	3.4	2.1
Cerro Prieto							
I	21.523	8.310	84.8	2.4	1.5	11.8	7.4
II	4.944	1.909	56.5	3.5	2.2	4.0	2.5
III	9.088	3.509	100.0	4.8	3.0	8.2	5.1
IV	11.131	4.298	86.6	5.4	3.4	8.3	5.2
Robles							
I	14.613	5.642	90.0	13.4	8.4	15.5	9.7
II	5.607	2.165	100.0	13.1	8.2	10.2	6.4
III	21.751	8.398	71.9	14.0	8.7	15.8	9.9
IV	2.471	0.954	100.0	10.4	6.5	7.5	4.7
V	11.349	4.382	100.0	10.7	6.7	11.5	7.2
VI	2.844	1.098	50.8	3.2	2.0	4.3	2.7
Derrio	37.995	14.670	29.0	10.6	6.6	21.6	13.5
Cottonwood	34.551	13.340	29.0	10.3	6.4	17.3	10.8
Marana							
I	0.855	0.330	100.0	5.0	3.1	4.8	3.0
II	1.502	0.580	100.0	5.0	3.1	4.8	3.0
III	1.632	0.630	100.0	4.8	3.0	4.8	3.0
IV	2.745	1.060	100.0	7.2	4.5	6.1	3.9
Wild Burro	16.343	6.310	(mtn.)	6.9	4.3	14.4	9.0
Ruelas	8.262	3.190	(mtn.)	6.2	3.9	11.2	7.0
Dairy	13.675	5.280	97.0	9.1	5.7	16.0	10.0

Figure 5.4. Aerial photograph of Cottonwood Fan in the Marana survey area. There is an increase in channel branching and extent of deposits down the fan on both active and inactive surfaces. Fan head is at top. Area in photograph is 1.2 km across.

closer to the fan head, causing proportionally greater deposition of the silty sand facies (Fig. 5.6). Regardless of drainage basin area, alluvial fans are larger, much siltier, and contain very few channel deposits when mountain fronts are a great distance from the fan head such as with Durham Fan near McClellan Wash in the far northern part of the surveyed area (Fig. 5.1, Table 5.1). In contrast, alluvial fans relatively close to the mountain front, as in the Marana Community, are much sandier and more channelized.

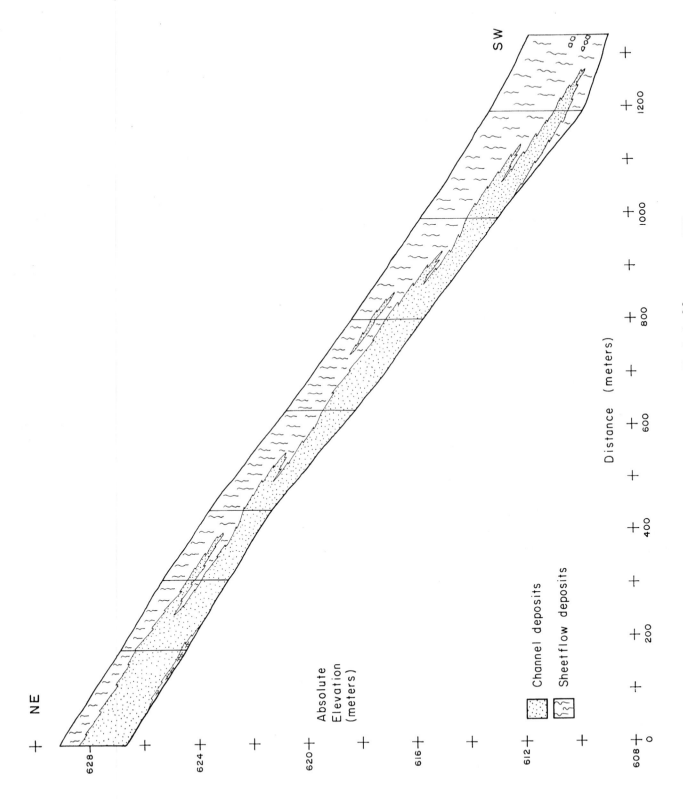

NE

SW

Absolute
Elevation
(meters)

Channel deposits

Sheetflow deposits

Distance (meters)

628

624

620

616

612

608

0

200

400

600

800

1000

1200

Figure 5.5. Longitudinal profile of Derrio Fan in the Marana survey area.

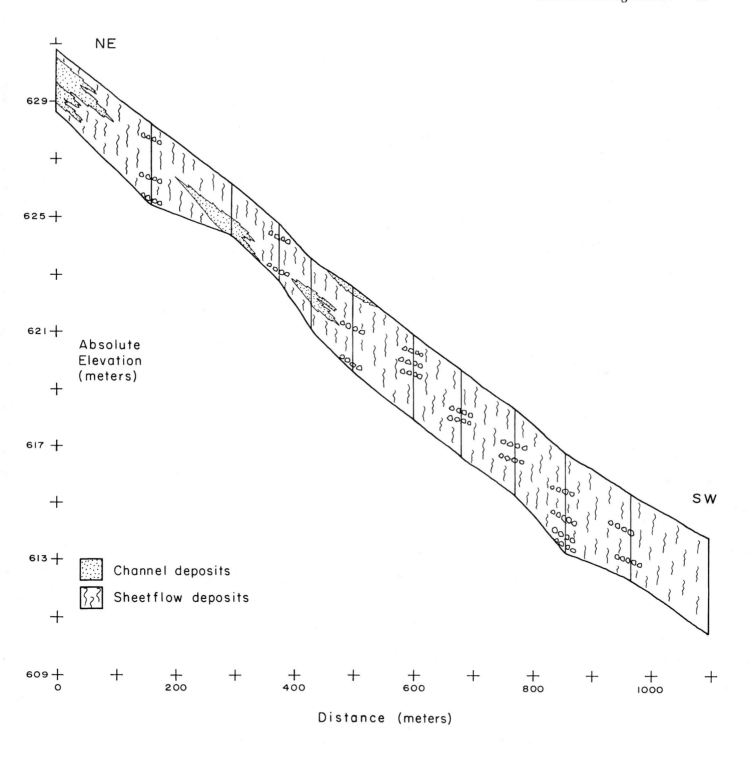

Figure 5.6. Longitudinal profile of a small fan in the Marana survey area, showing the dominance of sheetflow deposits.

AGRICULTURAL POTENTIAL
OF ALLUVIAL FANS

Several factors influence the potential for direct agricultural use of floodwaters on late Holocene alluvial fans: location and areal extent of sheetflooding on active fan lobes, frequency and intensity of rains, and minimum discharge needed to induce overbank flow. When depositional facies are considered as records of water flow over an alluvial surface, the farming potential of each fan can be analyzed. Areas frequently inundated by sheetfloods provide the ideal conditions for floodwater farming of the type preferred in late historic times, because water evenly wets the entire active surface and the need for water diversion or labor-intensive irrigation is alleviated. Water residence time is much greater on sheetflow surfaces than in areas where flow and the corresponding opportunity for soil infiltration is confined to channels; denser vegetative growth is found in these areas than in adjacent channelized and depositionally inactive reaches of the fan (Packard 1974). As discussed above, both drainage basin area and distance from the mountain front affect the amount of fan area experiencing sheetflooding. Hence, fans far from the mountain front or fans with small drainage basins are most suitable for water distribution on floodwater fields with a minimum of human intervention and labor.

The entire surface of a fan is not active at any given time; conditions are conducive to floodwater farming only in active reaches. Inactive portions of the fan remain dry because large, deep channels contain flow and thus adjoining surfaces are isolated from water supplied by the drainage basin. By calculating the amount of area on each fan that is presently active, an estimate can be made of the relative amount of land available to floodwater use through natural water spreading during prehistoric times. Because the percentage of area actively aggrading varies from fan to fan depending on size, a sampling of both large and small fans was used (Table 5.2). By extrapolating the data presented in Table 5.2, 15.3 percent of the 390 square kilometers (150 square miles) of late Holocene fans is presently active. This area was perhaps greater in prehistoric times because recent channel cutting has reduced viable agricultural land.

Given equal volumes of incoming water, minimum bankful discharge calculations for channels on different alluvial fans establish the relative likelihood of overland flow (surface flooding) occurring on one fan as compared to another. Sheetflow is induced when channels become filled beyond capacity. As a result, fans with small channels tend to produce overbank flow more readily and therefore may be particularly convenient for floodwater techniques.

Table 5.2. Amount of Active Fan Area on Selected Fans in the Surveyed Area North of Tucson

Fan Location	Fan Area (sq. km)	(sq. miles)	Active Fan Area (sq. km)	(sq. miles)	% Active Fan
Dairy Site Area					
Dairy Site	1.339	0.517	0.271	0.105	20.3
Unnamed	0.356	0.137	0.096	0.037	27.0
Marana Area					
Cottonwood	2.620	1.010	0.335	0.129	12.8
Unnamed I	0.396	0.152	0.080	0.031	20.4
Unnamed II	0.172	0.067	0.009	0.004	5.9
Unnamed III	0.256	0.099	0.029	0.011	11.1
Unnamed IV	0.109	0.042	0.015	0.006	14.3
Picacho Mountains	0.104	0.040	0.013	0.005	12.5
Cerro Prieto	0.808	0.312	0.116	0.045	14.4
Robles Area	2.217	0.856	0.314	0.121	14.1
Totals	8.377	3.232	1.278	0.494	15.3*

* Average

Table 5.3. Minimum Bankful Discharge Calculations for Channels on Three Fans in the Marana Survey Area

Wash name	Channel Area (sq. m)	Channel Slope	Channel Depth (meters)	Channel Roughness	Bankful Discharge (cu. m/sec.)
Derrio	25.10	.0154	2.87	.0275	203.00
Cottonwood	6.00	.0090	2.00	.0370	24.00
Marana II	2.24	.0125	0.17	.0350	2.35

Calculations use the Manning equation: $Q = A(1/n)r^{2/3}s^{1/2}$, where Q = discharge, A = channel cross-sectional area, r = channel depth, and s = channel slope.

Channel area, slope, depth, and roughness are needed to calculate bankful discharge. Minimum discharges for three channels in the Marana area were calculated (Fig. 5.7, Table 5.3). The relative ranking of agricultural potential through natural flooding determined from these measurements is consistent with other factors already discussed. The lowest minimum discharge occurs on the fan with the smallest drainage basin and highest percentage of sheetflow deposits. The highest minimum discharge occurs in the present channel of Derrio Wash, which is eroded into a late Holocene aggradational surface at the bottom of a permanently entrenched channel cut into Pleistocene alluvium. This situation stresses that the once arable aggrading surface on the floodplain of the wash bottom is presently isolated from all but the largest flood events.

Far from the mountain front, drainage basin area has a reverse influence. Floodwater potential may be high on fans far from the mountain front, where sheetflooding is

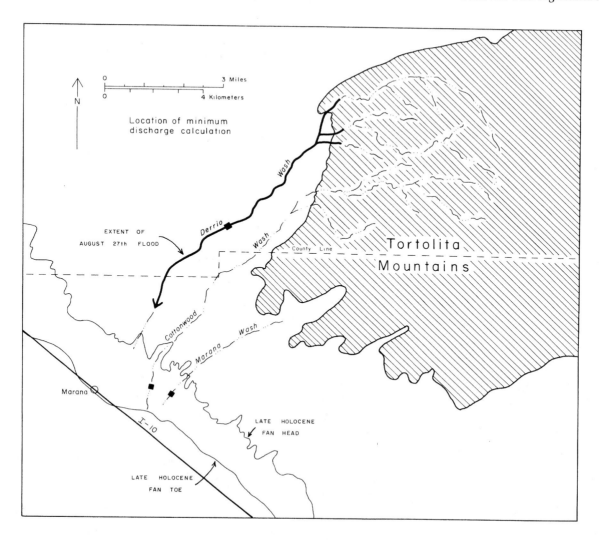

Figure 5.7. Locations of fan channel calculations in Table 5.3.

easily induced because of the low slopes and rapid loss of channel depth. Furthermore, large portions of the basin slope near the fan head are included in the drainage area supplying water for sheetflows; a majority of the drainage basin is located on the piedmont when the fan head is far from the mountain front (Table 5.1).

FLOW OBSERVATIONS ON COTTONWOOD WASH AND DERRIO WASH

The frequency at which discharge conditions are reached and surface flooding occurs on alluvial fans is impossible to calculate without considerable data on rainfall patterns, duration, and intensity. Observations and data were collected during the summer of 1985 to aid in understanding the frequency and intensity of floods on different portions of the bajada along the two

largest drainages of the Tortolita piedmont, Cottonwood and Derrio washes (Fig. 5.7). Although direct observations were difficult because of accessibility, data were gathered by monitoring geomorphic gauges and conducting personal interviews with local residents. Observations provide additional information on water resources.

Seven scour chains were placed in various locations along the length of Cottonwood and Derrio washes to see how a flood could differentially affect portions of the bajada. The four chains in the Cottonwood drainage were placed (1) at the mountain front, (2) on the upper bajada, (3) on the upper portion of the Holocene fan, and (4) downfan from the previous position, where extensive branching of the wash begins. Scour chains along the Derrio drainage were placed (1) at the mountain front, (2) at the channel fan head, and (3) at the Holocene fan head. The scour chains were made from a

5-foot length of link chain attached at one end to a piece of 7-foot rebar. The attached end is placed in a 5-foot hole standing straight up, so that when the hole is filled, the chain is completely buried by sediment. Two feet of rebar remains above ground for relocation. At times of flooding, sediment is washed away and the portion of chain exposed lies flat on the surface. During waning stages of the flow, sediment is redeposited over the chain. By measuring the depth to which the chain is covered and the length of chain lying flat, both the amount of deposition and erosion, respectively, can be determined. By subtracting the amount of fill from the amount of scour, a net sum of erosion or deposition can be obtained for each flood event.

The seven localities were revisited several times during the summer rainy season. Measurable scour and fill was recorded at all stations at least once except for the farthest downslope Cottonwood station, which is apparently too far downfan to be affected by moderate flows. Net scour and fill is nearly zero throughout the drainage systems, with total depth of scouring increasing toward the mountain front. Vegetation backed up behind the rebar gives a relative measure of depth of water flow and also appears to increase toward the mountain front. Through the 1985 summer season only two flow events affected the entire drainage basin; the 1985 summer rains were considered below average in length, intensity, and duration.

Interviews with local residents and personal observations provided some of the most useful information concerning flow in Cottonwood and Derrio washes. Discussions with residents revealed that the late August storm that washed out the Derrio mountain front station occurred only in the mountains; no rain fell on the bajada itself. Despite this, the county line road crossing Derrio Wash 10 km (6 miles) from the mountains was washed out the same night (Fig. 5.7). These observations indicate large storms in the mountains can induce significant flows on the bajada several miles from the mountain front, and that in some instances these flows may reach the Holocene fans near the Santa Cruz River. A resident also noted that pulses of sediment were occasionally washed out of the mountain canyon of Cottonwood Wash and were redeposited as a lobe of sediment in the wash floodplain at the mountain front. Migration of these pulses downstream with successive flood events would eventually supply sediment to active alluvial fans near the river.

On several visits through the summer, observations of stream flow out of Derrio Canyon at the mountain front (Zone 4 of the Marana Community in Fig. 3.9) reflected the flashiness and short duration of flow during the 1985 summer rainy season. During an initial visit to the

canyon in April, water was flowing out of the mountain front and continuing along the flank of the mountains for over 2 km (1.2 miles). In June, before the summer rains began, flow continued past the mountain front for only 75 m before soaking into the sand and disappearing underground. Continued observations through the rainy season revealed that despite the summer rains, water flow in the canyon was found farther and farther upstream with each visit. These observations suggest that the rains do not appreciably add to the water table and thus do not affect the effluent nature of Derrio Canyon, although they may produce peak flow in short-lived floods.

The sudden and rapid nature of the rains result in flash floods that rapidly run off overland without soaking into the ground or recharging the water table. In contrast, winter rains are of a lower intensity and longer duration, which promotes saturation of the ground and replenishing of the water table. Because of these differences in rainfall patterns, upland perennial flow in Derrio Wash is at its peak at the end of the winter rains. Both perennial flow and summer floods may be used to produce crops with different techniques and in different locations. (A related discussion of temperature inversion and spring crops on upper bajadas is in Chapter 4.)

Variations in rainfall patterns may also affect sediment supply in the drainage basins. During the low-intensity winter rains, sediment is supplied to the washes from adjacent hillsides but cannot be transported long distances downstream. Channel filling would be promoted and the creation of low terraces would be favored. In contrast, the high-intensity summer rains favor erosion, sediment transport, and redeposition where stream flow infiltrates sandy channels.

APPLICATIONS TO PREHISTORIC AGRICULTURE

Information from interviews and scour chain analysis are helpful in understanding prehistoric settlement patterns and subsistence strategies along Derrio and Cottonwood washes. First, perennial flow in Derrio Canyon provides a year-round water supply, although slightly longer distances into the mountain canyon must be traversed in the summer and fall than during the rest of the year. Second, the late August flood that originated in the mountains but induced flow far down on the bajada has interesting implications for farming along these drainages. Successful floodwater farming is dependent on flash floods reaching the surfaces being farmed. If floods in the mountains can reach surfaces several miles away, the farming potential is much higher than if only local rains provide water. Channel fans aggrading on bottomland in larger washes during Hohokam occupation would have been flooded by storms similar to the one in late August; that flow did not overflow onto the current surfaces of the prehistoric channel fans because of the present entrenchment of active stream channels.

Small fans with drainages not extending to the mountains were heavily utilized by the Hohokam for farming. Floods originating in the mountains would not provide water to these smaller fans. However, heavy rains on the upper bajada can apparently flow the few miles needed to reach the fan heads on the lower slope.

Success of floodwater farming for individual locations is uncertain from year to year because of the spottiness and irregularity of intense rainfalls. Unpredictability of flow is greater for small fans with small drainage basins. Farming of individual fans is therefore risky on an annual basis. However, observations suggest that any given year may provide excellent opportunities for agricultural water on any alluvial fan if rainfall patterns are favorable.

Other factors can also hinder farming conditions on an alluvial fan. The development of arroyo networks re-sults in channelization of flow and decreases the chances for favorable sheetflow. Such events are most likely at fan toes on the lower bajada where large arroyos along the river can impinge headward into the fan surface. The sudden migration of active fan reaches during large storm events may also hinder the agricultural potential of not only the old but also the new active surfaces. When shifting creates active surfaces farther from the source area, the distance water must travel is increased, thus lowering the frequency at which floods reach these active fan areas.

Although there are 390 square kilometers (150 square miles) of late Holocene alluvial fans in the surveyed area north of Tucson, only approximately 15 percent is active at one time. Within this fraction of fan territory, favorable conditions for floodwater farming without improvements are found where sheetflows dominate. Fans far from the mountain front or with small drainage basins have the lowest bankful discharges, greatest percentage of sheetflow deposits, and consequently offer agricultural advantages with this technology. These favorable conditions for floodwater farming are balanced against the unpredictability of rainfall patterns.

CHAPTER SIX

The Dairy Site: Occupational Continuity on an Alluvial Fan

Paul R. Fish, Suzanne K. Fish, John H. Madsen,
Charles H. Miksicek, and Christine R. Szuter

During the period of early ceramic occupation, when subsistence patterns in the Marana area can first be described in detail, nearly the full range and typical proportions of later Hohokam cultigens are present. By this time, the transition to agriculture appears to have been completed, consistent with evidence for the prior importance of domesticates in Late Archaic sites of the Tucson Basin and surrounding areas (Chapter 2). Studies at the Dairy Site (AZ AA:12:285) document subsistence activities from an initial interval of plain and red ware pottery into the early Colonial period (Fig. 2.1).

The Dairy Site is situated on an alluvial fan of the lower bajada (in Zone 1 of the later Marana Community; Figs. 2.3, 3.9). Floodwaters reaching the fan after storms nourished the fields of its residents and periodically covered the remains of their houses, all the while supplying sediments that continued to build the fan in height and in downslope extent. Features exposed in a cross section of the Dairy fan provide a powerful illustration of floodwater farming and persistent zonal land use, inferred elsewhere from distributions of sites visible on fan surfaces. Occupations spanning more than 600 years between the third and ninth centuries A.D. exemplify the continuing correspondence between agricultural technology and settlement locations throughout the chronological sequence.

THE OCCUPATIONAL SAMPLE

Settlement history at the Dairy Site is derived not from the present surface of the alluvial fan but from remains in a profile 500 m long and 3 m high created by the Shamrock Dairy along its property line (Fig. 6.1). Cultural deposits were exposed 50 cm or more below the present ground surface along all but the western portion of the profile (Fig. 6.2). Intersected features represent a sample of fan occupations through time and space.

The Dairy profile was selected as a study site for investigating floodwater farming as part of research on prehistoric agricultural strategies in the northern Tucson Basin, supported by the National Science Foundation. The profile was cleaned by students in an undergraduate field methods class at the University of Arizona and a detailed profile map was made by John Field, project geomorphologist. Artifact collections and samples of subsistence remains were obtained by first cutting into the profile to a depth of 25 cm to 40 cm above intact deposits in each cultural feature. Excavations then proceeded down from the initial cut through the fill to the floor or bottom of the exposed feature.

Late Archaic Occupation

Initial use of the Dairy fan for agriculture appears to represent a preceramic occupation, although earliest ceramics elsewhere have been dated within the same general time range. The profile intersected only one well-defined feature of probable Late Archaic affiliation. Features 12 and 14, concentrations of charred wood and ash, and a hearth, Feature 34, occur on separate segments of surfaces in the profile for which similar stratigraphic position implies previous continuity (Fig. 6.2). These surface segments are from 1 m to 50 cm below ceramic features in the respective profile sectors. Feature 34 produced a mesquite charcoal date with a midpoint in the late third century A.D. (Table 6.1) and a pollen sample containing corn and distributions of weedy species that suggest agriculture (Table 6.2). Exposed preceramic remains do not necessarily represent the earliest farming activity at this fan location. Determinations on cultigens from several Late Archaic sites in the northern Tucson Basin predate Feature 34 at the Dairy Site by a number of centuries (Table 2.1).

Figure 6.1. View downslope along a section of the Dairy Site profile.

Early Ceramic Occupation

Fifteen pit houses and a variety of other features of the early ceramic sequence were encountered. Profile cross sections suggest large houses, analogous to the Pioneer period structures at the well-studied site of Snaketown in the Phoenix area (Haury 1976). Some floors are well plastered; others are not. Exposed intramural firepits are clay lined. Bell-shaped storage pits are present in the floors of some structures. Two inhumations in pits within houses and two cremations were exposed by profile cleaning, but numbers of burials have been encountered by Dairy employees during a decade of fill removal in front of the existing profile. Dairy employees also reported that numerous areas of dark soil and a variety of artifacts were observed during fill removal from an area covering 72 ha (180 acres). The site extends for an unknown distance behind the present profile.

Decorated ceramics represent types from the Phoenix core and somewhat later types from the Tucson Basin sequence, including Estrella Red-on-gray, Sweetwater Red-on-gray, Snaketown Red-on-buff, Cañada del Oro Red-on-brown, Gila Butte Red-on-buff, and Santa Cruz Red-on-buff (Table 6.1). A polished Tucson red ware unlike the thin Vahki Red at Snaketown is present in all Pioneer period contexts and is classified as Tortolita Red following Bernard-Shaw (1990a: 210). This red ware accounts for up to seven percent of the pottery in some features but only two percent of the total ceramic assemblage. Pottery in the local red-on-brown tradition first appears in the Cañada del Oro style of the early Colonial period. Only two percent of the 7,000 sherd total are painted or incised.

The lack of superpositioning and wide spacing of most features along the profile (Figs. 6.2, 6.3) suggest relatively rapid burial of each unit and a restricted time span for postoccupational fill above the floors. Because there is some overlap between occupied areas of the site during sequential phases and because of the rarity or absence of diagnostic artifacts in individual features, radiometric dates, stratigraphic relationships, and ceramic associations (Table 6.1) have been combined to identify the chronology of profile segments shown in Figures 6.2 and 6.3. Neither dates nor ceramics indicate occupation of the Dairy fan after the early Colonial period.

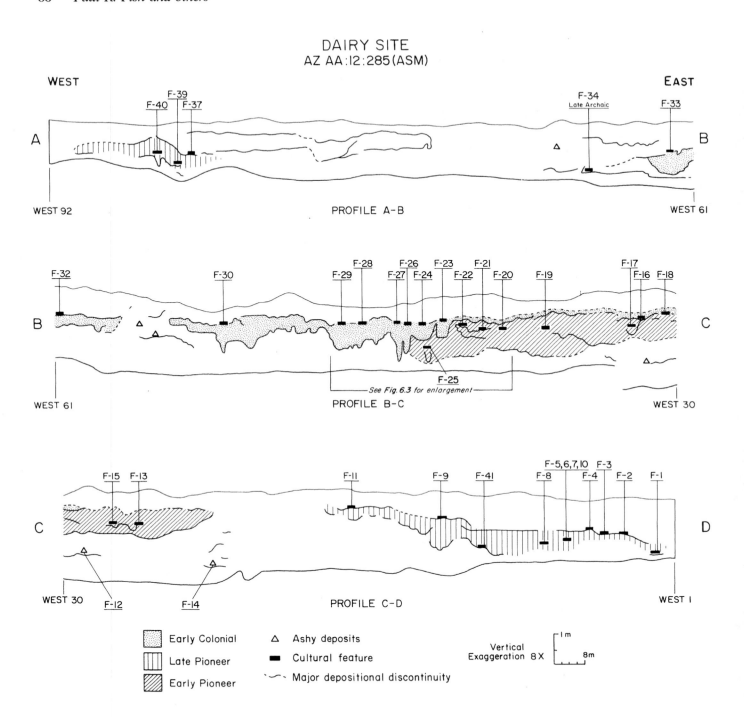

Figure 6.2. Dairy Site profile, showing locations of features.

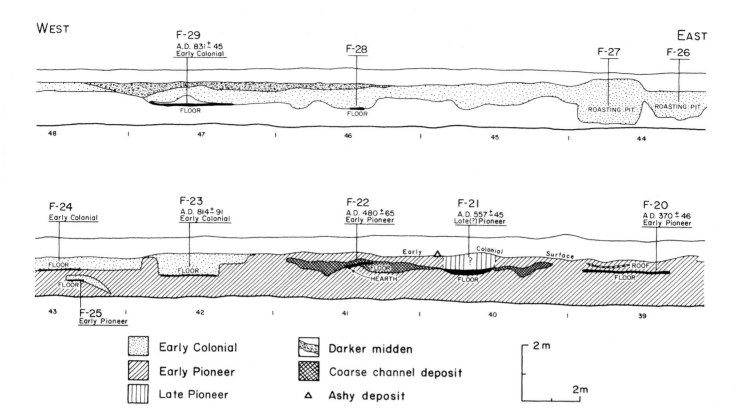

Figure 6.3. Central portion of the Dairy Site profile, showing stratigraphic relationships of chronologically significant features.

FARMING AND RESIDENCE ON THE DAIRY FAN

As the result of opportunities for floodwater farming, late Holocene alluvial fans on the lower bajada are areas of high site density. Interaction of several factors influences the floodwater potential on these alluvial fans, including areal extent of sheetflooding on active fan lobes and minimum discharge needed to induce overbank flooding by drainages. Areas frequently inundated by sheetfloods are highly conducive to floodwater farming techniques because water evenly wets the entire active surface and deposited sediments have relatively high silt content (Chapter 5). At present, the active and most easily farmed portion of the 1.35-square-kilometer (0.75-square-mile) Dairy fan is more than 20 percent of the total surface, compared to the approximate 15 percent average for the study area as a whole.

Occupants of the Dairy Site changed settlement locations on the fan surface as it aggraded and as active portions shifted laterally and along the length of the fan over time. It is likely that contemporary habitation occurred adjacent to active reaches and that remains were subsequently buried by locational shifts in sedimentation. Nearby structures of differing date in the central profile suggest that some fan locales remained relatively stable during occupations of sequential phases. The absence of features postdating the ninth century A.D. and the early Colonial period implies that the profile portion of the fan or the entire fan became inactive and unamenable to farming after this time.

SUBSISTENCE STUDIES

The Dairy fan is advantageously located for efficient exploitation of a variety of plant and animal resources in several topographic zones as well as for receiving floodwaters. The head of the alluvial fan is only 3 km (1.5 miles) from the Santa Cruz River and its riparian habitats. Dense cacti and leguminous trees with edible beans grow in mid and upper basin vegetation immediately above the fan. Resources from both bajada and riparian zones are consistently found among subsistence remains from the Dairy Site.

Table 6.1. Feature and Chronology Information for the Dairy Site (AZ AA:12:285)

Feature		Period	Basis for Temporal Designation				
			Diagnostic ceramics	Number of sherds	Accelerator radiocarbon	Conventional radiocarbon	Archaeomagnetic date
1	Pit house	Late Pioneer	Tortolita Red	1	A.D. 611 ± 63[a]	A.D. 780 ± 60[b]	
2	Channel fill	?					
3	Occupation surface	Late Pioneer*					
4	Hearth	Late Pioneer*					
5	Pit house	Late Pioneer	Tortolita Red	14	A.D. 611 ± 99[a]		
6	Pit house	Late Pioneer	Tortolita Red	1			
7	Pit house	Late Pioneer	Tortolita Red	1			
8	Hearth	Late Pioneer	Tortolita Red	1			
9	Roasting pit	Late Pioneer	Snaketown Red-on-buff	5			
10	Pit house	Late Pioneer	Sweetwater-Snaketown	1			
			Tortolita Red	7			
11	Pit house	Late Pioneer*				A.D. 230 ± 50[b]	
12	Ash lens	Late Archaic?*					
13	Pit house	Early Pioneer	Estrella Red-on-gray	13			
			Sweetwater Red-on-gray	14			
			Snaketown Red-on-buff	5			
			Tortolita Red	3			
14	Burned log	Late Archaic?*					
15	Hearth	Early Pioneer*					
16	Pit house	Early Pioneer*					
17	Pit house	Early Pioneer	Snaketown Red-on-buff	1	A.D. 430 ± 70[c]		
			Estrella Red-on-gray	1			
			Tortolita Red	6			
18	Pit house	Early Pioneer	Sweetwater Red-on-gray	1			
			Santa Cruz Red-on-buff	1			
			Tortolita Red	3			
19	Pit house	Early Pioneer	Tortolita Red	2			
20	Pit house	Early Pioneer	Tortolita Red	7	A.D. 370 ± 46[a]		
21	Pit house	Late Pioneer	Snaketown Red-on-buff	1	A.D. 557 ± 45[a]		
			Tortolita Red	7			
22	Pit house	Early Pioneer	Snaketown Red-on-buff	1	A.D. 480 ± 65[a]		
			Tortolita Red	4			
23	Hearth	Early Colonial	Cañada del Oro Red-on-brown	2	A.D. 814 ± 91[a]		
			Snaketown Red-on-buff	2			
			Tortolita Red	10			
24	Pit house	Early Colonial	Snaketown Red-on-buff	1			A.D. 630–1020
			Sweetwater Red-on-gray	1			
			Gila Butte Red-on-buff	1			
			Tortolita Red	3			
25	Pit house	Early Pioneer*	Snaketown Red-on-buff	1			
			Tortolita Red	2			
26	Roasting pit	Early Colonial*	Snaketown Red-on-buff	1			
			Tortolita Red	4			
27	Roasting pit	Early Colonial*	Snaketown Red-on-buff	2			
			Sweetwater Red-on-gray	1			
			Tortolita Red	3			
28	Pit house	Early Colonial*					
29	Pit house	Early Colonial	Tortolita Red	6	A.D. 831 ± 45[a]		
30	Cremation	Early Colonial	Tortolita Red	7			
31	Ash lens	?					
32	Pit house	Early Colonial*					
33	Pit house	Early Colonial	Snaketown Red-on-buff	8	A.D. 830 ± 49[a]		
			Cañada del Oro Red-on-brown	2			
			Tortolita Red	5			
34	Hearth	Late Archaic				A.D. 290 ± 50[b]	
36	Cremation						
37	Pit house	Early Pioneer*					
39	Ash lens	Early Pioneer	Tortolita Red	1			
40	Pit house	Early Pioneer	Tortolita Red	1	A.D. 661 ± 52[a]		
41	Pit house	Late Pioneer					

Note: Features yielding only plain wares and red wares are included in the Early Pioneer period; feature numbers 35 and 38 were not used.
* Period designation based on stratigraphic relationship only.

Table 6.2. Percentages of Pollen Types in Samples from the Dairy Site
(N = 200)

PERIOD / Provenience	Ambrosia-type, Bursage and related composites	High spine Compositae, Other composites	Cheno-Am, Chenopod and amaranth	Gramineae, Grass	Boerhaavia, Spiderling	Sphaeralcea, Globe mallow	Kallstroemia, Arizona poppy	Onagraceae, Evening primrose	Eriogonum, Wild buckwheat	Cylindropuntia, Cholla	Platyopuntia, Prickly pear	Cereus-type, Saguaro and related cactus	Typha, Cattail	Yucca, Yucca	Other	Zea, Corn (number of occurrences)*	Gossypium, Cotton (number of occurrences)*
LATE ARCHAIC																	
Feature 34 Hearth	16.5	7.5	43.0	3.0	15.0	1.5	0.5		2.0				0.5		10.5	1	
EARLY PIONEER																	
Feature 13 Pit house	18.5	22.0	53.5		1.0										5.0	1	
Feature 16 Pit house	19.0	17.0	43.5	1.5	4.5	2.0			1.5				1.5		9.5	15	
Feature 17 Pit house	10.0	20.5	32.0		17.0	0.5			1.5				2.0		16.5	1	
Feature 18 Pit house	26.5	32.5	14.5	3.0	7.5	1.5	0.5	0.5	1.0	1.0		2.0			9.5		
Feature 19 Pit house	14.0	11.5	58.5	2.5	5.5	2.0	1.0		1.0		1.0				3.0	7	
Feature 20 Pit house	13.0	13.5	66.0	1.0	2.0				0.5	0.5					3.5		
Feature 39 Hearth	13.0	17.5	38.5	2.0	16.0		0.5	2.0	7.5		1.0				2.0		
Feature 40 Pit house	12.5	17.5	54.0	3.5	4.5	1.5					0.5		1.5		4.5	2	
LATE PIONEER																	
Feature 1 Pit house	24.5	22.5	33.5	3.0	5.5	3.0		0.5	0.5		1.0		0.5		5.5	15	
Feature 5 Pit house	10.0	28.5	29.0	2.5	15.0	0.5			4.0	0.5	2.5	1.0			6.5	30	
Feature 6 Pit house	14.5	15.0	52.5	3.0	3.0		0.5		1.0	1.0					9.5	9	
Feature 9 Roasting pit	24.0	13.5	56.5	0.5	0.5						0.5				4.5		
Feature 10 Pit house	14.0	24.0	41.0	4.5	5.5	0.5			0.5						10.0		
Feature 11 Pit house	16.5	27.5	36.5	1.0	5.5	5.0	1.0				1.0		1.0		5.0	6	
Feature 21 Pit house	14.5	8.5	42.5	4.5	8.0			1.0	1.5	10.0			1.5	0.5	7.5	76	1
EARLY COLONIAL																	
Feature 24 Pit house	8.5	18.0	60.0		6.0	1.5				2.0	1.0				3.0	4	
Feature 28 Pit house	41.5	17.0	29.0	2.0	0.5				0.5						9.5	1	
Feature 33 Pit house	9.0	6.5	73.5	2.0	3.5		0.5			1.5	0.5				3.0	2	1
Feature 36 Cremation	16.5	16.0	52.5	1.5	4.0	3.5				1.5	0.5	0.5			3.5	1	

*Cultigen pollen, corn and cotton, was excluded from a standard sum of 200 pollen grains per sample that was used to calculate percentages of all other types. Cultigen pollen was tabulated in addition to this standard sum and is quantified as the number of occurrences encountered during tabulation of the 200 other grains.

Pollen Analysis

Pollen distributions at the Dairy Site (Table 6.2) suggest continuity in land use over the entire course of occupation into the Colonial period. Even in the earliest features, pollen configurations reflect substantial modification of natural vegetation by residential disturbance and surrounding floodwater fields. High chenopod and amaranth (Cheno-Am) percentages are not characteristic of the natural vegetation of the Dairy Site environment (Hevly and others 1965) but are hallmarks of recent Tohono O'odham floodwater fields (S. Fish 1984a, 1985).

Cheno-Am is the dominant pollen type at the Dairy Site. Frequencies are comparable with those at early Classic period sites in the most favorable farming locations farther north along the lower bajada and are greater than at later sites in less agriculturally favored fan situations (S. Fish 1987a). Additional species (spiderling, globe mallow, and Arizona poppy) in an agricultural weed category (S. Fish 1985) are also well represented in Dairy Site samples.

Cultigen values throughout the Dairy profile are also comparable with later Hohokam sites of the study area and Tucson Basin (S. Fish 1988). Again, equivalence is

Table 6.3. Numbers of Flotation Samples Containing
Carbonized Plant Remains at the Dairy Site

PERIOD / Provenience	Number of samples	Zea, Corn	Agave, Agave	Phaseolus vulgaris, Common bean	Lagenaria, Bottle gourd	Gossypium, Cotton	Cucurbita, Squash	Amaranthus, Amaranth	Salvia, Chia	Trianthema portulacastrum, False purslane	Chenopodium, Chenopod	Portulaca, Purslane	Physalis, Ground cherry	Polanisia trachysperma, Clammy weed	Sphaeralcea, Globe mallow	Boerhaavia, Spiderling	Descurainia, Tansy mustard	Atriplex, Weedy saltbush	Euphorbia, Spurge	Astragalus, Locoweed	Sporobolus, Dropseed grass	Opuntia, Prickly pear	Mammillaria, Fishhook cactus	Echinocereus, Hedgehog cactus	Carnegiea gigantea, Saguaro	Prosopis, Mesquite	Celtis, Hackberry
EARLY PIONEER																											
Feature 13 Pit house	1																									1	
Feature 17 Pit house	7	3	1					5	4	1							1					1			2	7	
Feature 19 Pit house	3	3							1		1						1										
Feature 20 Pit house	4	4	1					3	1								1						1			1	
Feature 22 Pit house	6	4	1			1	1	3	2	2					1	1	1								2	3	2
Feature 25 Pit house	2	2						2									1									2	
Feature 37 Pit house	3	2						2									1								1		
Feature 39 Ash lens	1	1						1	1	1			1					1								1	
Feature 40 Pit house	2	2						2									1										1
LATE PIONEER																											
Feature 1 Pit house	3	1						2			1	1			1			1		1	1				2	1	
Feature 5 Pit house	2	2						1				1													2	2	
Feature 6 Pit house	1	1						1				1							1							1	1
Feature 7 Pit house	1	1						1																		1	1
Feature 9 Roasting pit	8	7	2					3	1	1														1	5	3	3
Feature 10 Pit house	1							1																		1	
Feature 21 Pit house	6	6	1	3	1			2		1					1								1	1	2	6	6
Feature 41 Pit house	1							1	1																		
EARLY COLONIAL																											
Feature 23 Hearth	5	5	1					4	1				1	1	1						1				1	2	
Feature 24 Pit house	7	4	2					2			3	1	1	1			1			2						2	
Feature 26 Roasting pit	3	3						2	2	3	1				1		1					1			1	3	1
Feature 27 Roasting pit	4	3	1					4	3	1				1	2		1								1	3	
Feature 29 Pit house	4	4						4		2					1		1						1		1	2	
Feature 30 Cremation	3							1												1					1	1	1
Feature 32 Pit house	2	1	1							1															1	1	
Feature 33 Pit house	6	6				2		4	1	1			2				1						2	2	5	5	1

with sites having the best floodwater potential or even with sites in riverine settings. Corn pollen is widely distributed among the earliest features with plain wares and red wares. Variation in amounts of cultigen pollen does not form consistent temporal trends, but rather appears to have resulted from differential activities involving resources on a feature-by-feature basis during each time segment.

Pollen evidence for use of wild products, best exemplified by cholla and other cacti, is found throughout the occupation but at a moderate level compared to other Tucson sites. Greater emphasis on cacti can be documented at some Zone 1 sites of the early Classic period (S. Fish 1987a, 1987b; S. Fish and Donaldson 1991). At least occasional use of upland resources is apparent in the pollen of yucca in one pit house. The occurrence of cattail pollen from earliest to latest contexts shows access to permanently damp habitats, probably along the Santa Cruz River, over the duration of occupation.

Flotation Analysis

Flotation samples further reveal a diverse subsistence base for the Pioneer and early Colonial periods (Table 6.3). Corn, cotton, squash, and agave remains were identified from features dating to the earliest occupation with

Table 6.4. Faunal Remains from the Dairy Site

PERIOD / Provenience		Lepus sp., Jackrabbit	L. alleni, Antelope jackrabbit	L. californicus, Black-tailed jackrabbit	Sylvilagus sp., Cottontail	Rodentia, Rodent	Sciuridae, Small squirrel	Thomomys bottae, Pocket gopher	Dipodomys sp., Kangaroo rat	Sigmodon hispidus, Cotton rat	Canidae	Canis sp.	C. latrans, Coyote	Artiodactyla	Odocoileus sp.	O. hemionus, Mule deer	Ovis canadensis, Bighorn or Mountain sheep	Unidentified small mammal	Unidentified large mammal	Unidentified bone	Total
EARLY PIONEER																					
Feature 17	Pit house			1																	1
Feature 18	Pit house																		2	1	3
Feature 19	Pit house	4	4	3	3	2	1	1										11	3	2	34
Feature 20	Pit house	7		10		1												31	2	3	54
Feature 22	Pit house	3		3	8					1				3		1		9		2	30
Feature 25	Pit house			1	4									1		1					7
Feature 37	Pit house			1														1		1	3
Feature 39	Ash lens			1														3	2		6
Feature 40	Pit house	1			1													2		4	8
LATE PIONEER																					2
Feature 1	Pit house																	1	3[a]		4
Feature 5	Pit house	6		2	5									1				7	1		22
Feature 7	Pit house													1							1
Feature 8	Hearth											1									1
Feature 9	Roasting pit		2															1			3
Feature 10	Pit house	2	2	1														4	3		12
Feature 11	Pit house																	3	2[b]		5
Feature 21	Pit house	14			5			2	3					1				5			35
Feature 41	Pit house				1				1					1							3
EARLY COLONIAL																					
Feature 23	Hearth	7	6	4	1													12	3		33
Feature 24	Pit house	4		1	4													14	1		25
Feature 26	Roasting pit	2		1			1						16	17			1	1	9	3	51
Feature 27	Roasting pit	5	1	4										1				6	2	1	20
Feature 28	Pit house	1		4														4			9
Feature 29	Pit house	15		4														10			29
Feature 33	Pit house	4	1	8	11		5				1	2	1			2[a]		36	12	5	88
UNDATED		14	5	11	3	1	1					6			8			15	16		80
	Total	89	21	64	45	4	8	3	4	1	1	9	16	27	8	4	1	176	58	26	565

Note: Nonmammalian remains include: Feature 20, *Kinosternon* sp., mud turtle (1 fragment); Feature 21, *Anas* sp. or *Mareca americana*, duck or widgeon (1 fragment); Feature 23, Phasianidae, quail (1 fragment); Feature 29 - Phasianidae, quail (1 fragment); Feature 33, *Crotaphytus* (= *Gambelia*) *wislizeni*, leopard lizard (1 fragment).

a = 1 specimen worked, b = 2 specimens worked.

plain ware ceramics. The only additional cultigens, bottle gourd and common bean, were encountered in the same Late Pioneer feature. Seeds from weedy plants that may represent purposely encouraged species or weeds of agricultural contexts are common throughout the occupational sequence. Recovery rates for mesquite, saguaro, and other cacti suggest an important wild plant component in Dairy Site diet. The frequencies of corn, mes- quite, and saguaro are in the upper range of proportions recorded from most later Sedentary and early Classic period sites in the Tucson Basin (Miksicek 1988).

Identification of a range of plant parts (spines, fibers, leaf and heart fragments) in significant quantities extends the possibility of Hohokam manipulation and cultivation of agave back into the Pioneer period. Except for a few species that may have been introduced into the Hohokam crop repertoire during the Sedentary period (tepary beans, jack beans, and *Amaranthus hypochondriacus*), the data from the Dairy Site suggest Hohokam subsistence patterns were firmly established in the Marana study area by the early part of the ceramic horizon.

Faunal Analysis

As with most Hohokam sites, lagomorphs comprise the majority of identifiable bones (Table 6.4). The faunal assemblage, however, is comparatively diverse. That is, the quantity of distinct taxonomic groups is relatively high for the small sample of identified remains. Fourteen different taxa, including mud turtle, duck or widgeon, leopard lizard, quail, jack rabbit and cottontail, mule deer and bighorn sheep, coyote, ground squirrel, pocket gopher, kangaroo rat, and cotton rat were identified. Compared to other Hohokam faunal assemblages of similar size from settlements occupied during the Sedentary or Classic periods, the Dairy Site assemblage exhibits somewhat greater taxonomic richness.

Additionally, the fauna is characterized by a relatively greater abundance of artiodactyl remains from a variety of features. Artiodactyls comprised 13 percent of the identifiable fauna, were recovered from more than a third of the features, and their skeletal elements represent portions of the entire body. The relative abundance of artiodactyl remains, their widespread spatial distribution, and entire skeletal representation are unique characteristics for Tucson Basin Hohokam sites. Sedentary and Classic period lowland Hohokam sites tend to have few artiodactyl remains and these few represent the cranial and podial portions of the skeleton.

CONTINUITY IN FARMING AND SETTLEMENT

The nature of the Late Archaic presence on the Dairy fan is unclear, although pollen of corn and weedy species suggests floodwater farming had begun. In a similar zonal setting 4 km (2 miles) to the north, trenching at a Late Archaic site revealed pits containing corn with midpoint dates in the fourth century B.C. (Roth 1989). Just south of the study area, structures were preserved at another Late Archaic fan site that yielded corn and a still earlier date in the eleventh century B.C. (Mabry 1990). The earliest feature in the Dairy profile, in the third century A.D., marks an occupation that already postdated more than 1000 years of floodwater farming on alluvial fans of the northern Tucson Basin.

Diagnostic artifacts in houses of the Dairy fan cross section are commensurate with continuous occupations through the early Colonial period. Overall numbers of structures cannot be reconstructed for any specific phase or through time from the profile sample. However, distributions of houses and the presence of ancillary features and burials suggest a settlement structure little different in size and arrangement from the dispersed clusters of dwellings in excavated sites of the Classic period on Zone 1 alluvial fans (Henderson 1987a; G. Rice 1987a).

Domestic water for Dairy Site inhabitants undoubtedly came from the river at a distance of 3 km (1.5 miles). Occupations along the Santa Cruz at the toe of the Dairy fan and at other nearby locations are generally contemporary, according to ceramic attributes and absolute dates. Summer cropping would have predominated on the fans and the river floodplain, prohibiting effective participation in both floodwater farming and riverine irrigation during critical episodes of rainfall, rapid runoff, and peak flows. Nevertheless, fan residents may have increased the labor force that could be tapped for swift repairs of canal intakes following summer floods.

The happenstance of profile creation at the Dairy Site offered a uniquely vertical perspective on settlement continuity that could otherwise be seen only in its horizontal dimensions. Floodwater farming on lower bajada alluvial fans of the northern Tucson Basin was capable of supporting long-term sequential occupations, in this case illustrated by 600 years of sustainable agriculture. The record of such occupation and production in the early years of the Hohokam sequence is surely underrepresented in settlement patterns based on surface visibility. Continuing fan deposition and the scarcity of diagnostic artifacts in early ceramic assemblages makes it difficult to distinguish these phases where settlement is registered by sparse remains. With the apparent demise of favorable hydrological conditions, the Dairy fan was eventually abandoned, but not the zone or this enduring mode of farming.

CHAPTER SEVEN

Evidence for Large-scale Agave Cultivation in the Marana Community

Suzanne K. Fish, Paul R. Fish, and John H. Madsen

Linkage of agave cultivation with a farming technology represented by widespread remains in the Marana Community has been one of the significant consequences of Northern Tucson Basin Survey research (S. Fish, P. Fish, Miksicek, and Madsen 1985; S. Fish, P. Fish, and Madsen 1990a), illuminating a new dimension of prehistoric agriculture in the Sonoran Desert. Fields marked by rockpiles and low stone alignments cover many hundreds of hectares. Interdisciplinary study of these prehistoric agricultural complexes has detailed the nature and extent of agave cultivation during the later portions of the Hohokam sequence.

THE ISSUE OF CULTIVATION

Agave or century plant species have been a source of food and fiber for most aboriginal groups of North America living within the distributional range of these drought-adapted perennial succulents. Stiff, spiny leaves pointing upward in a rosette contain fibers used for cordage, sandals, brushes, textiles, and other items. During its lifetime of from 5 to 20 years, the agave stores carbohydrates in its tissues to fuel a single and final flowering episode in which a tall, blossom-bearing stalk emerges (Fig. 7.1). When agave is harvested prior to energy expenditure in flowering, stored carbohydrates are converted by roasting to a sugary, high calorie, and nutritious food (Fig. 7.2). Large Mesoamerican species were utilized in a somewhat different manner by extraction, just prior to flowering, of copious, sugary sap used primarily in historic times as a fermented base for pulque, mescal, and tequila. Unlike annual crops such as corn, beans, and squash, cultivated agaves exhibit no clear morphological markers that can be used to distinguish archaeological remains of crops from wild, gathered plants.

The importance of agave as a gathered resource among Southwestern Indians is well attested in the ethnographic literature (Castetter and others 1938; Pennington 1963; Felger and Moser 1985). Processed products were circulated widely among groups living at a distance from natural stands. Spanish documentary references to agave "plantations" have been interpreted as evidence of cultivation in Baja California at the time of first Jesuit contact (Castetter and others 1938: 50; Nabhan 1985) and in northern Sinaloa (Perez de Ribas 1968). However, cultivation that has been historically documented in the southwestern United States and adjacent northwestern Mexico is relatively recent, limited to small-scale plantings, and has not established a role for agave as a major aboriginal cultigen.

The apparent absence of cultivated agave among northerly indigenous peoples of the Sonoran Desert and its limited role in the agriculture of southern groups contrasts with the pre-Columbian and historic ubiquity of this crop farther south. Agave is a major cultigen throughout the rest of highland Mexico, including portions of Durango and Zacatecas often considered within the greater Southwestern cultural sphere. The potentially active role of Southwestern Indians in spreading indigenous species beyond their natural ranges was included by Richard Ford (1981: 21) as an issue deserving attention in the definition of an agricultural complex distinctive to the American Southwest.

Agave species of the Sonoran Desert grow mainly on rocky slopes of hills and mountains and are lacking in valleys (Gentry 1972: 1). Many records for the Pimans or O'odham describe acquisition through the harvesting of wild stands in such topographic situations and often at considerable distances from home bases (Castetter and others 1938: 50; Curtin 1981: 48). Upland gathering has been commonly assumed to account for charred agave long known to occur in Hohokam roasting pits at lower elevation habitation sites away from natural populations (Haury 1945: 39; Fewkes 1912; Hayden 1957: 103).

Botanical attributes and distributional associations of *Agave parryi* Englem, *Agave murpheyi* E. Gibson, and other species recovered from archaeological sites have

Figure 7.1. *Agave murpheyi* with flowering stalk. (Photograph by Wendy Hodgson.)

Figure 7.2. Roasted hearts or heads of agave, prepared by removal of leaves and extended baking in a pit. (Photograph by Charles H. Miksicek.)

been cited as suggesting potential aboriginal transport or manipulation of indigenous species (Minnis and Plog 1976; Crosswhite 1981: 58–59; Ford 1981; Gentry 1972, 1982). More recently, extensive flotation analyses for charred plant materials at Hohokam residential sites in the Tucson Basin (Miksicek 1988) and the Phoenix Basin (Miksicek 1984; Bohrer 1987; Gasser 1988a, 1988b; Mitchell 1989) have yielded impressive amounts of agave. Locations of these sites coincide poorly with natural distributions in southern Arizona (Fig. 7.3), yet in each case, charred agave occurs in substantial amounts and is often among the more common kinds of botanical material. Prehistoric cultivation rather than acquisition of gathered plant products from uplands has been proposed on the basis of overall quantity and variety of plant parts (Miksicek 1984; Gasser and Miksicek 1985). Ongoing studies in the Marana Community have demonstrated the cultivation of agave by identifying replicated associations of agricultural features, specialized artifacts, field-side

processing facilities, and charred agave (P. Fish and others 1984; S. Fish, P. Fish, Miksicek, and Madsen 1985; S. Fish, P. Fish, and Madsen 1985, 1990a). Complexes of these agricultural remains document the productive capacity for supplying this abundantly utilized resource.

ARCHAEOLOGICAL INDICATORS OF CULTIVATION

In the northern Tucson Basin, as in most other regions, all facets of prehistoric agricultural activity have not left equally tangible or easily retrieved records. Santa Cruz floodplain canals are buried by active alluvial and colluvial deposition. Surface features are also seldom preserved on arable bottomlands of larger tributaries. Some Piman cultivation methods with probable Hohokam antecedents involve brush diversions, low earthen ridges, and short ditches. Such ephemeral structures

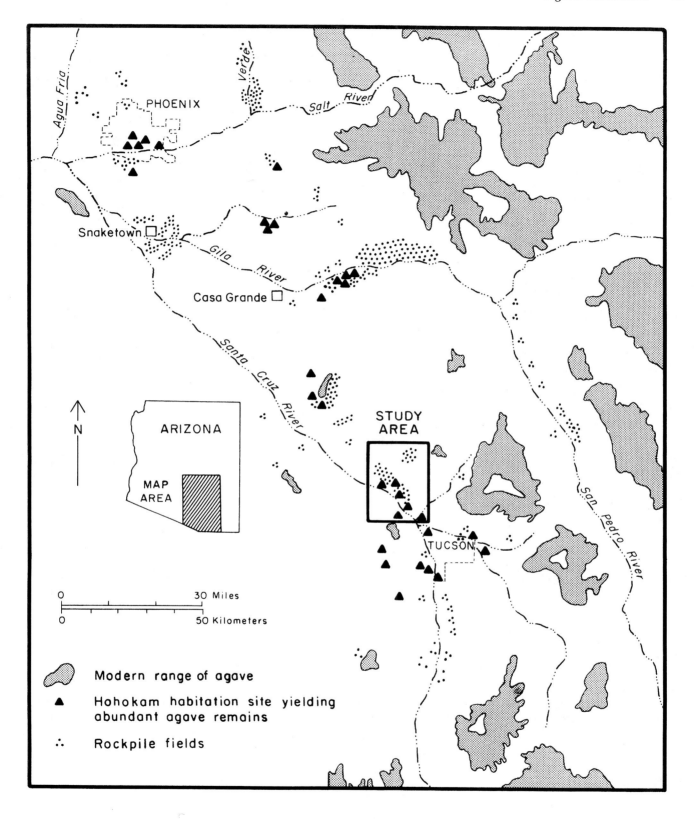

Figure 7.3. A comparison of the modern range of agave species with evidence for prehistoric production and use in southern Arizona.

Figure 7.4. Typical rockpile feature in the Marana survey area.

often are obliterated in single planting seasons and are unlikely to persist archaeologically. Farming that employed ephemeral constructions can only be inferred by reference to ethnographic practices in similar situations of settlement location and topographic opportunity (Chapter 4).

With the exception of floodplains and portions of some alluvial fans, however, stone surface features related to agriculture are relatively well preserved throughout the Marana area. Most are small devices, informally constructed from unshaped local rock. These kinds of remains are readily obliterated by later prehistoric or modern surface disturbance and would be spottily preserved in areas experiencing pervasive historic development. Distributional characteristics hinder systematic recording even where preservation is optimal. The features are areally diffuse, but may be so widespread in the aggregate that boundary definition for large complexes presents problems. Associated artifacts are usually sparse.

The ubiquitous unit of stone features and other associated remains has been termed a "rockpile field," after its most frequent feature. Rockpiles or rounded heaps were constructed from cobbles scattered on the bajadas (Fig. 7.4). Excavated cross sections of undeflated piles reveal that cobbles often cap smaller mounds of soil (Fig. 7.5). Rockpile size is variable but rarely exceeds 1.5 m in diameter and 75 cm in height. Short, linear features of one to several cobble courses that served as contour terraces (Fig. 7.6) and checkdams are often interspersed in small fields and are always present in large complexes.

Most of these rockpile fields are located in Zones 2 and 4 of the Marana Community (Fig. 3.9). Zone 2, the focus of this chapter, occupies middle elevations of the eastern bajada and was rarely chosen for residence. More than 485 hectares (more than 2 square miles) of large, 10-ha to 50-ha fields without habitation have been located here. Segments of three typical fields are mapped in Figures 7.7, 7.8, and 7.9. Rockpiles, terraces, and checkdams occur in substantial numbers in Zone 4 in

Figure 7.5. Cross section of an excavated rockpile.

Figure 7.6. Typical contour terrace in the Marana survey area.

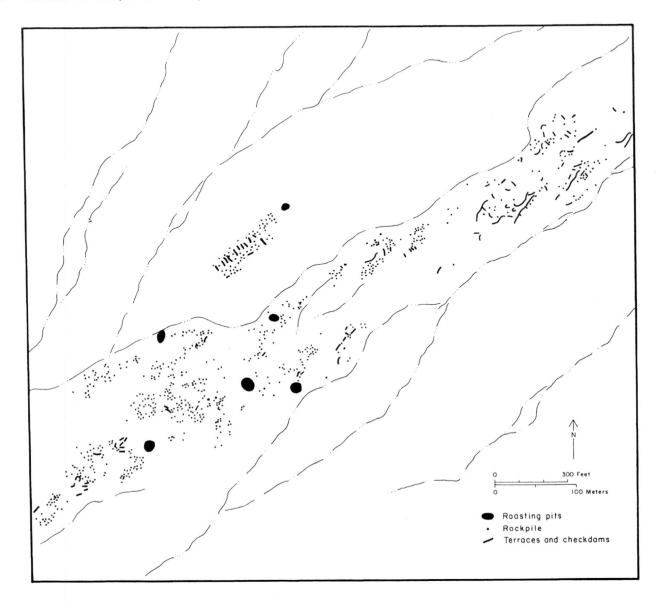

Figure 7.7. Distribution of features in a portion of site AZ AA:12:108,
a large rockpile field in Zone 2 of the Marana Community.

conjunction with large sites, small sites, and isolated structures, but never independent of habitation as in Zone 2 and never of an areal extent comparable to the larger fields below (Fig. 3.9).

Rockpiles and Planting

The presence of rockpile complexes has not been recorded routinely by a majority of archaeologists; the fact that instances have been reported throughout Hohokam territory (Fig. 7.3; S. Fish, P. Fish, Miksicek, and Madsen 1985) is a reflection of their ubiquity. However, these features received little directed study until recently. Multiple lines of evidence now indicate that the rockpiles as well as the terraces and checkdams are facilities of agricultural production. Doyel (1984: 43) has suggested that heaped cobbles in the New River area north of Phoenix originated as residuals of surface clearing, but this seems an improbable explanation for a majority of rockpile occurrences. Rockpiles are sometimes located in the midst of dense concentrations of surface rock and occasionally are found in alluvial situations necessitating

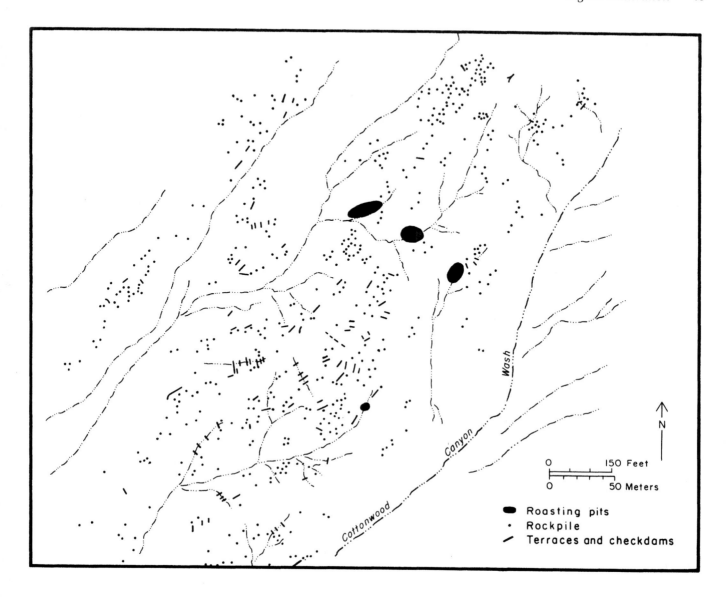

Figure 7.8. Distribution of features in a portion of site AZ AA:12:470,
a large rockpile field in Zone 2 of the Marana Community.

importation of rock for construction. A function of clearing the surface to increase runoff onto more arable land (Evenari and others 1971; Irwin-Williams 1986) also seems unlikely for the Tucson Basin and most other Hohokam locations. Tucson rockpiles on bajadas are topographically situated so as to receive optimal runoff from ridge catchments; diversion devices for directing water to more suitable plots are not present in any field.

Rockpiles enhance the planting environment, as do the more obviously agricultural terraces and checkdams with which they occur. The uneven, porous surface of the piles allows penetration of rainfall and runoff in contrast to surrounding hard-packed and impermeable ground surfaces. The rocks then act as a mulch, slowing evaporation of soil moisture by blocking capillary action and preserving higher moisture levels beneath. This mulching effect of rocks in desert soils has been measured experimentally in Israel (Evenari and others 1971) and by the authors in gauged soil-moisture experiments now underway.

The response of plants today to the microhabitat of rockpiles is demonstrated by the relatively dense seasonal concentrations of annuals, the distribution of perennials, and the presence of lichens and mosses that require

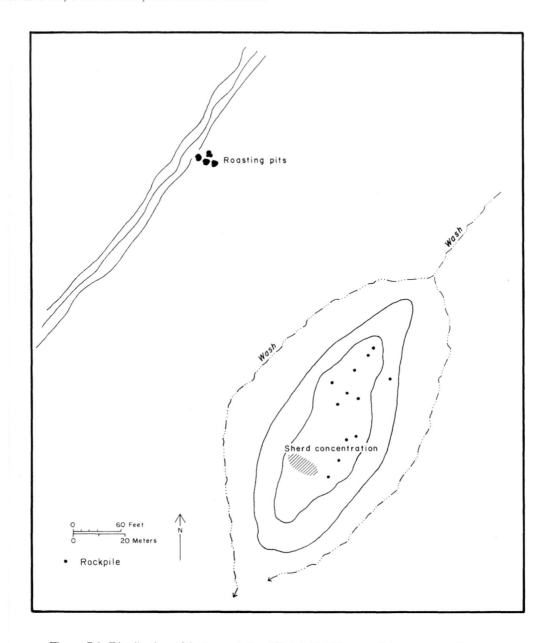

Figure 7.9. Distribution of features at site AZ AA:12:469, one of the many small groups of rockpiles interspersed among the large fields in Zone 2 of the Marana Community.

substantial moisture. Modern plant response has been quantified by comparing root biomass in soil directly beneath rockpiles and in adjacent control areas. Root weight in rockpile soil is an average 80 percent higher than in the controls (S. Fish, P. Fish, Miksicek, and Madsen 1985: 109, Fig. 4). These observations further strengthen an interpretation of rockpiles as moisture-enhancing facilities for crop plants.

An additional benefit of rockpiles became apparent from experimental plantings. Rockpiles provide signifi-

cant protection from rodent predation that damages leaves but is concentrated on stem bases and roots. Animals cannot as easily gain access to these parts by digging beneath the plants in rockpiles as is possible with agaves growing directly in soil. The practices of Mayan traditional farmers in Yucatan (Caballero 1986) provide parallels in the use of piled rocks for protecting young sabal palms. Gary Nabhan, of the Phoenix Botanical Garden and Native Seed Search, has observed similar practices by the Lower Pima of Sonora to protect cucurbits.

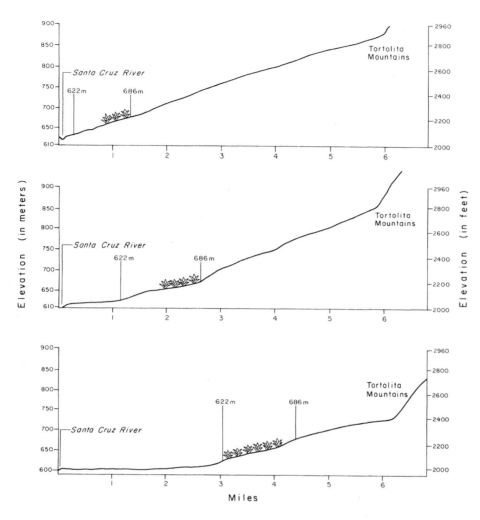

Figure 7.10. Three basin cross sections from north (*top*) to south (*bottom*) in the Marana Commuinity, showing elevational limits of rockpile fields in Zone 2.

Zone 2 Distributions

Although earlier dates for small rockpile loci have been indicated by ceramic associations and radiocarbon determinations (Chapter 8), fields in the large category (10 ha to 50 ha) belong exclusively to the early Classic period. These mid-bajada rockpile fields are homogenous in physical and locational attributes. All are situated on ridges of dissected Pleistocene alluvial fans. Caliche or calcium carbonate layers occur consistently between 20 cm and 40 cm below the surface and form an impermeable barrier that traps moisture in the upper soil within reach of shallow-growing agave roots. Covering a total of about 5 square kilometers (2 square miles), community fields occur within a band less than 2.5 km (1.5 miles) wide and 20 km (12 miles) long. All are positioned between elevations of 625 m and 670 m (2030 and 2200 feet) above sea level (Figs. 3.9, 7.10).

Most of these agricultural complexes derive a linear outline from their locations along ridge tops paralleling trans-bajada drainages. Cobble features are infrequent on bottomlands of secondary drainages between ridges. At least some of these intervening drainage bottoms were farmed with the aid of earthen checkdams, as attested by occasionally preserved berms. Corn pollen was recovered from the upstream planting surface behind one such checkdam during berm excavation at site AZ AA:12:470, a large rockpile field to the east and upslope of the Marana Mound Site.

No indications of field house structures or concentrated domestic refuse occur within Zone 2 fields. Roasting pits filled with ash and fire-cracked rock are found in many fields, and multiple pits usually occur in the largest complexes. Stone artifact assemblages are marked by steep-edged core tools and thin, knifelike implements made from tabular stone with flaked and ground edges. Field size, proportions of agave-related implements in stone tool assemblages, and sizes of roasting pits indicate a production emphasis in mid-bajada fields that is not duplicated in other zones of the Marana Community.

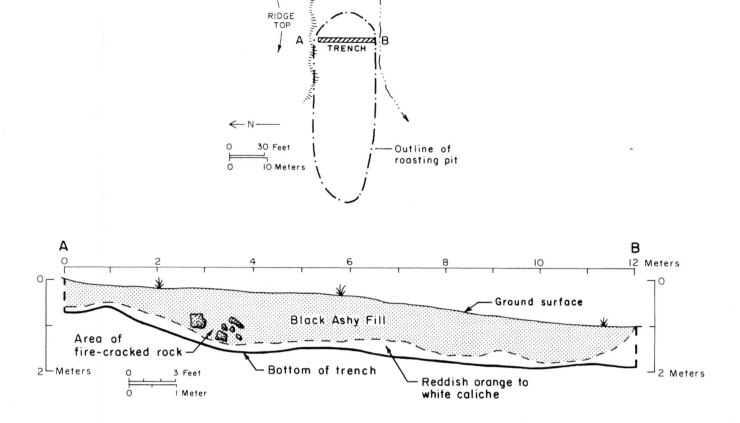

Figure 7.11. Typical large roasting pit located in a large rockpile field in Zone 2 of the Marana Community.

Roasting Pits

Rockpile agricultural complexes are most directly linked to agave by roasting facilities. Pit-roasting is the common method of preparing agave among historic Southwestern Indians (Castetter and others 1938). In some cases, pits were dug relatively deeply into the ground and in other cases, agave was roasted in shallow troughs with earth heaped above. Extended cooking up to 48 hours in sealed pits prepares the nutritious heart, inflorescence, and leaf bases for eating. Briefer, controlled roasting of leaves is also a process that may be used to aid in the removal of leaf fibers for use in cordage and crafts. Rocks lining pits or mixed in the fill retain heat and facilitate the roasting process. Indians of historic times often reused both pits and rocks.

Roasting pits are consistently found in Marana Zone 2 fields, often in loose, easily excavated sediments of shallow and ephemeral drainages. They range from sev-

eral meters up to 50 m in the longest dimension and average 1.5 m in depth (Fig. 7.11). Pit size tends to correlate with field size. Discrete pit shapes from individual roasting episodes cannot be easily distinguished in the large features among the intrusions and accretions of seasonal reuse over many years (Fig. 7.11). Pits are filled with ash, charcoal, fire-cracked rock, and occasional artifacts. Large sherds (discussed further in Chapter 8) appear to have been used to protect food items from scorching during roasting and as scoops in the excavation of pit fill. Whole and partial examples of such formal and informally shaped sherd artifacts with worn edges have been recovered from large mid-bajada pits.

Botanical Evidence

Flotation of more than 600 liters of fill from one or more excavated roasting pits in 16 fields (S. Fish, P. Fish, and Madsen 1990a; Miksicek 1988) has produced charred

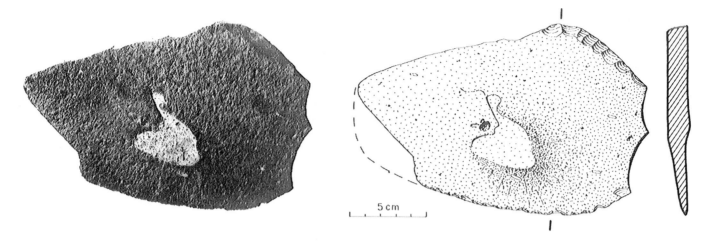

Figure 7.12. Agave knife from the Marana Community.

specimens of agave from each. Fragmentary fibers are most abundant, but recovered plant parts include marginal teeth, terminal spines, leaf bases, and heart (compound stem) fragments. Plentiful wood charcoal, dominated by mesquite and ironwood, has been identified; fuel sources reflect an environment similar to the present and trees readily available in adjoining drainages.

The identity and number of cultivated agave species is currently unresolved. Variation in remains from Marana roasting pits suggests more than one cultivar (S. Fish, P. Fish, Miksicek, and Madsen 1985). Floral and fruit parts for taxonomic determination are unavailable in roasting pits and other site contexts. Arizona species may have been transplanted, particularly *Agave murpheyi* (following Gentry 1972; Crosswhite 1981; S. Fish and Nabhan 1991; Hodgson and others 1989). However, as with most other Southwestern aboriginal crops, cultivars may have included varieties of ultimate Mesoamerican origin.

Inflorescences or flower stalks were gathered from natural agave stands by Southwestern groups. However, by the time the inflorescence had emerged, a majority of stored energy and moisture had been consumed by its growth, leaving a much reduced potential for edible use of the heart. Groups who acquired agave solely by gathering often prevented stalk development in maturing plants intended for future harvest by inhibiting or destroying the precursor tissues (Castetter and others 1938). Cultivators are typically even more rigorous than gatherers in this kind of plant management (Parsons and Parsons 1990). Occasionally the Hohokam may have inadvertently or intentionally allowed flower stalk growth to proceed. Charred stalk remains are rare, but have been recovered in an excavated Marana site in Zone 1

on the lower bajada where they appear to have been used as roofing materials (Miksicek 1987).

Agave pollen is seldom recovered from Hohokam sites, in keeping with the presumed rarity of flowering. It has not been identified in sediments from Marana roasting pits or in agricultural features. As with charred stalk fragments, the infrequent occurrences of pollen in residential sites (Spaulding 1974; S. Fish 1987b, 1989) may represent accidental or intentional instances of inflorescence development for special purposes, or cases in which wild agave products were obtained.

Field Artifact Assemblages

Artifacts recovered in systematic surface collections from the rockpile fields strengthen the inference of agave cultivation. Broad, flat stone tools made on raw materials with naturally tabular fracture (Fig. 7.12) are prominent in field assemblages. The common term in the ethnographic and archaeological literature for this tool type is agave or mescal knife. Varying in outline from rectangular to rounded, such specialized implements were used historically by Southwestern groups to sever agave leaves from the hearts (Castetter and others 1938). Supporting this analogy, calcium oxalate crystals like those present in agave tissues have been observed in microscopic examinations of Hohokam knife surfaces (Bernard-Shaw 1990b). In collections from Marana fields, 9 percent of more than 400 stone artifacts, including flaking debris, and 19.2 percent of retouched tools are agave knives and fragments. Knives are not concentrated near the roasting pits or in any other sector, but are widely scattered throughout the fields.

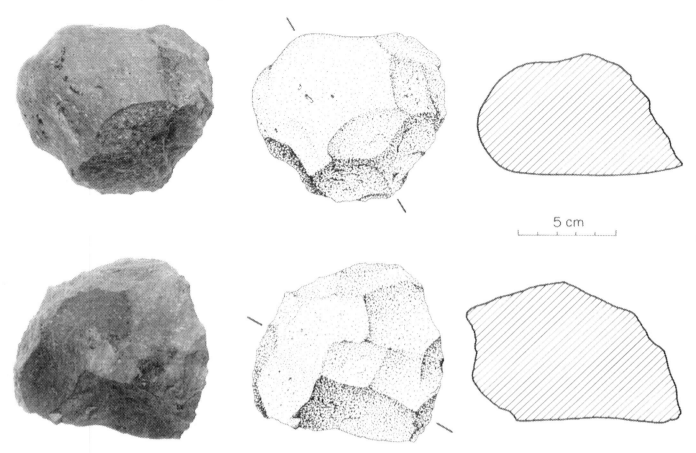

Figure 7.13. Pulping planes from the Marana Community.

A second distinctive and numerous artifact type is a steep-edged core tool often designated a scraping or pulping plane (Fig. 7.13). Such tools have been associated experimentally, and in ethnographic reports, with fiber removal from agave leaves (Salls 1985; Rogers 1939: 51–53; Osborne 1965: 47–49; Kowta 1969: 52–69; Hester and Heizer 1972: 109–110; Bernard-Shaw 1990b). Experiments conducted in the course of this study have shown pulping planes to be efficient in stripping marginal spines from leaves. Precautionary removal of spines from agave leaves and hearts before transport to processing facilities has been observed among modern Otomí cultivators (Parsons and Parsons 1990). As with agave knives, pulping planes are scattered throughout the fields. Together these two artifact types represent 53.9 percent of retouched tools, an assemblage emphasis unique among sites in the Marana survey area.

One complete and two fragmentary ground stone objects of uncertain function were collected from Marana rockpile complexes. These are formally shaped artifacts resembling a "T" in outline. The complete specimen (Fig. 7.14) is approximately 64 cm by 42 cm in maximum dimensions, 11 cm thick, and weighs 12.8 kg (28 pounds). Additional examples have been found in rockpile fields elsewhere (for example, Debowski and others 1976). In a discussion of the distribution and significance of such objects, Alan Ferg (1986) proposed a possible symbolic or ceremonial function. An alternative possibility based on field contexts might be a functional association with agave processing, although detectable use-wear is lacking on the Marana specimens.

Figure 7.14. Ground stone object of uncertain function from a rockpile field in Zone 2 of the Marana Community. (Height is 23 cm.)

Cultivation in Rockpile Fields

Stands of wild agave are absent on northern Tucson Basin bajadas. Within a 100–km (62–mile) radius of the Marana Community, all species but one occur well above community boundaries at elevations greater than 925 m (3035 feet; Gentry 1982). The exception, *Agave murpheyi*, has been collected at lower elevations only under Tohono O'odham cultivation. It is unlikely that naturally occurring prehistoric stands at lower elevations have been extirpated historically. Agave persists widely in other habitats under postcontact conditions such as cattle grazing; natural populations depleted by Hohokam overuse should have had ample opportunity to recover in the intervening 500 to 600 years. Furthermore, according to Robert McDaniel, of the Department of Plant Sciences at the University of Arizona, experiments in commercial agave production at the nearby University of Arizona Marana Farms have shown that reproduction by seed for the most likely species is inhibited by damage to seedlings from the intense summer heat and sun at lower bajada elevations. Successful reproduction appears possible only through cloning by previously established plants or by human transplantation of clones or offsets beyond the seedling state of development. This latter method is the universal means of planting by agave cultivators in historic and modern times, even in environments where heat presents no danger to seedlings.

Mexican agave cultivation of the magnitude suggested by Tucson Zone 2 fields typically involves similar basin slopes (K. Johnson 1977; Parsons and Parsons 1990; West 1948, 1968). Agave is considered a crop primarily for planting on land of secondary agricultural value that cannot be irrigated. On sloping terrain agaves are used to stabilize rock features such as terraces and to trap soil and surface runoff. Adapted to arid conditions, agaves survive droughts and spotty rainfall more successfully than annual crops, producing reliable long-term yields. Annual crops requiring more predictable moisture may be interspersed in the better watered portions of fields or in years when rainfall is judged to be particularly promising.

Intercropping in Marana fields on a minor scale seems indicated by a few instances of corn pollen from soil samples in and around several rockpiles. This pollen also might have been generated by nearby plantings in earthen checkdams across adjoining small drainages. Corn and cotton pollen have been identified at Hohokam rockpile loci elsewhere, such as along the Gila River in situations where floodwater diversion onto the fields may have been possible (S. Fish 1984b).

The combined evidence from Marana fields presents a strong case for large-scale agave cultivation. Roasting pits that are separated from habitations are localized in or near field areas. All excavated pits have contained agave. Both the pits and the associated distinctive stone tools fit Southwestern ethnographic correlates for harvesting and processing agave. Knives and pulping planes are distributed throughout fields rather than clustered about roasting pits or in other circumscribed locations. Finally, the predominant topographic situation of rockpile fields closely resembles dry basin slopes extensively planted with agave in highland Mexico.

ESTIMATES FROM ARCHAEOLOGICAL DISTRIBUTIONS

Construction Labor

The fact that agricultural features in Marana fields persist intact and apparently serviceable until today suggests simultaneous cultivation of the great majority of complexes during at least the latter part of community occupation in the early Classic period. Only a few small fields appear to date to Preclassic times, as indicated by surface ceramics and sherds in excavated roasting pits. Numbers of rockpiles and meters of cobble alignments were tabulated in multiple 50-m squares within three large fields in order to characterize feature densities. Averaged figures were then used to calculate feature totals for the area covered by all large mid-bajada fields. Estimates of 42,000 rockpiles and 120,000 m of alignments were projected. Experimental rockpile construction gave an approximate range of 20 minutes to one hour, depending on size and availability of cobbles. A 40-minute mean per rockpile results in an initial construction effort of 28,000 person-hours or 14 person-years with 5-day work weeks. Experimental building of comparable cobble terrace alignments produced a figure of 1.65 m per hour (P. Fish and S. Fish 1984: 156–157). An initial investment of 72,500 person-hours or slightly more than 36 person-years would have been required to construct the terraces and checkdams in the Zone 2 fields.

A total of more than 100,000 person-hours or 50 person-years are estimated to have been expended by farmers in constructing cobble features prior to the demands of planting, tending, harvesting, and processing crops. Any perishable components of the system and maintenance of field facilities would have been additional. Intriguing but unanswered questions concerning labor investment include whether the large fields were completed as unitary construction events or by accretion over a period of continued use and to what degree field layout may have been a centrally coordinated effort.

Agave Yields

In Mexico, agaves often line terrace walls for soil stabilization and runoff control, and a similar planting pattern seems likely for rockpiles. Quantities of these features are therefore used to estimate potential agave yield. As a minimum estimate, a single plant is posited per rockpile, and one for every 2 m of alignment. According to this formula, 102,000 plants could have been growing at one time in large mid-bajada fields of the Marana Community. Harvest comes at plant maturity, for which an average 10-year figure is used. Thus only one-tenth of the plantings, or 10,200 agaves, would have been available in a given year.

Yield in food and fiber is based on relatively small Southwestern species best suited to lower elevations. Because species identification from charred macrofossils is not yet possible, per plant estimates would be distinctly low should it be determined in the future that large agaves of Mesoamerican origin were also utilized by the Hohokam. Yields for two end products are calculated independently; use of the edible heart should not have precluded fiber extraction from the leaves of the same plant.

Agaves harvested in a single year could have supplied approximately 365 grams of fiber per plant (S. Fish, P. Fish, Miksicek, and Madsen 1985) or a total for the Marana fields of 3.72 metric tons. At an average of 4 kg, agave hearts could have produced 40.8 metric tons of edible product. Hearts furnish 347 calories and 4.5 g of protein per 100 g (Ross 1944). According to FAO recommendations (FAO/WHO 1973), agaves in Zone 2 fields would have supplied the equivalent of annual caloric requirements for 155 individuals and protein requirements for 110. In an alternative projection of nutritional role more in keeping with probable prehistoric diet, 20 percent of caloric needs for 775 persons and protein for 550 could have been met by agave. Although specific variables in estimates are subject to refinement or change, it is clear that these fields could have supplied a significant increment in Classic period Hohokam diet and economy.

The ratios of plants to features used in these calculations are likely to produce a low estimate. Particularly for moderate-sized species, individual rockpiles and 2-m intervals of linear features might have supported several plants at once; agaves produce offsets in natural habitats and tend to form clusters. Superfluous offsets tapping mother plants may have been removed to concentrate nutrients and water for rapid maturity and harvest. However, if two or three plants could mature in tandem or rapid succession, the above yield estimates would be superseded by several magnitudes. Results of experimental plantings suggest that multiple plants per feature would have appeared naturally by cloning and that retaining more than one would have offered a strategy for achieving higher long-term production rather than the most rapid returns.

IMPLICATIONS OF PRODUCTIVE PATTERNS IN THE CLASSIC PERIOD

The regional distribution of rockpile fields has implications for the organization of labor and land tenure. Large complexes may have necessitated communal labor and consensual recognition of intrafield boundaries by many cultivators. In one large field, a small boulder with petroglyphs resembles field boundary markers of the Hopi and Zuni (Forde 1931: 233, 235; Cushing 1920: 153). As among many Southwestern native peoples, kin-based or other corporate groups may have controlled arable land, with use-rights for individuals or households assigned to particular plots. The patterning of fields with respect to habitation also can be compared by time and setting. Small fields on the upper bajada occur in conjunction with habitation. Only fields on the middle bajada are situated at a distance from residential sites, indicating a system of agricultural tenure not based on immediate proximity.

Large fields undoubtedly drew upon the labor of many cultivators, whether solely through individual incentive or more integrated planning. Indicative of communally scheduled efforts in the complexes are the huge roasting facilities. Although features of large size show repetitive use from year to year, excavation produced little evidence of discrete small firings. It appears that numbers of cultivators roasted their harvests together. Communal events would have been an efficient use of woody fuel in a desert environment, but would have entailed coordination of fuel acquisition, harvest, and preroasting preparation of the plants. By contrast, farmers using the modest pits of smaller fields could process their harvest according to individual convenience.

In an environment where aridity circumscribes agricultural activity, opportunities to expand production are limited. Agave cultivation on marginal bajada slopes would have offered an optimal solution to restricted sources of supplemental water. These plants are adapted to low and unreliable moisture to a greater degree than annual crops. More poorly watered and previously uncultivated land could therefore be used to satisfy expanding needs for foodstuffs. In addition, fibers could support craft manufacture and furnish highly portable raw materials and finished products for external trade.

Cultivation of mid-bajada areas with sparse prior use represents an arid land version of intensification

(Boserup 1965), through expansion of extensive land use practices rather than more frequent cropping of land already under cultivation. Intensification is also indicated by an increased labor cost in travel time per unit of production (G. Johnson 1977: 490). Farmers of the mid-bajada complexes had to invest more time going to and from their fields than did farmers whose fields and habitations were adjacent. It is not surprising, then, that large-scale cultivation was concentrated in those community sectors where denser populations coincided with poorer access to irrigable land or floodwater opportunities.

Potential investment in rockpile fields on mid-bajadas was virtually unlimited. Combinations of topographic and hydrologic variables similar to those of the largest fields are duplicated widely in the Classic period Marana Community. The location and extent of rockpile fields can best be understood as the outcome of investment decisions that took into account other productive needs and alternatives.

The largest fields and the greatest total acreage occur above the Zone 1 lower bajada sites with the highest population densities and poorest potential for floodwater farming (Figs. 3.2, 3.9). These fields are located at a distance from habitations and in a slightly drier portion of the bajada than areas to the south. Even though higher labor input per unit return was likely entailed than in fields near residences, expansion of bajada cultivation must have been economically advantageous under local circumstances. To the south in Zone 1, less dense populations with more favorable floodwater situations constructed fewer and mostly small rockpile fields. Farther south still, fields are absent on bajadas opposite the numerous settlements along the river at the Tucson Mountains. The agricultural labor of these river dwellers evidently could be expended more effectively in irrigated farming.

Recognition of the mid-bajada field configuration as a temporal innovation rests on access to comprehensive regional data sets. Such information confirms that the technology and the crop were not new. Only the locational concentration, the remarkable size of individual complexes, the expansion of total acreage in rockpile fields, and a concomitant emphasis on their yield are unique to the early part of the Classic period. Productive strategies at that time seem best understood in light of the demographic conditions described in Chapter 3. Agave production in mid-bajada fields represents an economic reformulation of agricultural effort by particular segments of the community and a form of intensification in response to increasing population and demand.

CHAPTER EIGHT

The Archaeology of an Agave Roasting Location

Mary Van Buren, James M. Skibo, and Alan P. Sullivan III

Rockpiles and roasting pits, distinctive features of fields on mid-bajada slopes in Zone 2 of the Marana Community, form extensive agricultural complexes for cultivating and processing agave (Chapter 7). Site AZ AA:12:205 is one of the smaller examples, containing only a few rockpiles and one roasting pit. The site was investigated in order to clarify the nature of the artifact assemblage and activities associated with such small sets of features.

SITE DESCRIPTION

Site 205 is situated on a gently sloping ridge between two northeast to southwest trending washes (Fig. 8.1). On-site vegetation is dominated by bursage and creosote bush, but saguaro and cholla also occur, and leguminous trees line the adjacent drainages. Site features consist of a roasting pit and three rockpiles (Fig. 8.2). Associated with these is an artifact assemblage comprised primarily of plain ware pottery (870 sherds), although a handful of decorated ceramics (21 sherds) and lithics (55 specimens) were also recovered. Temporally diagnostic designs could not be discerned on the decorated sherds. The artifacts were scattered over 1230 square meters, mostly in and around the roasting pit. No remains of dwellings or temporary shelters were apparent on the surface, nor were any revealed during excavation.

FIELD INVESTIGATIONS

Although mapping and collecting by Northern Tucson Basin Survey crews had provided detailed information about surface characteristics of rockpile fields, understanding the activities that occurred at these locales required more intensive study. To further investigate the agricultural nature of these sites and the presumed culti-

vation of agave, and to provide data regarding their precise functions and periods of use, a sample of rockpiles and 16 roasting pits at a number of locations were excavated during the spring of 1984 and 1985 with the aid of the University of Arizona undergraduate field class.

As a part of this research program, the excavation of Site 205 was motivated by three concerns. The first was to identify the botanical resources produced and processed at the site. A second goal was to provide additional information about the function of rockpiles. The foremost aim was to clarify the nature of the occupation and artifact assemblage so as to better understand how such small sites articulated with the larger subsistence and settlement system.

Surface Collection and Stratigraphic Tests

A grid system of 2-m squares was imposed over the site and an intensive surface collection was conducted. Excavation of the roasting pit and rockpiles was preceded by systematic random testing on nonfeature areas in order to evaluate the relationship between surface and subsurface remains (Fig. 8.2). One to three sherds were found in six 1-m by 1-m units, and others had no cultural material. The stratigraphy of these test pits was fairly uniform. Reddish brown sediment containing pebbles and small cobbles was underlain by a solid layer of caliche from 5 cm to 27 cm below the surface. In one unit, however, ashy fill occurred both above and below a broken layer of caliche. Seven sherds were recovered from the upper 30 cm. These results provided convincing evidence that surface remains were reliable indicators of subsurface deposits, and that few artifacts would be overlooked if only features visible on the surface were excavated.

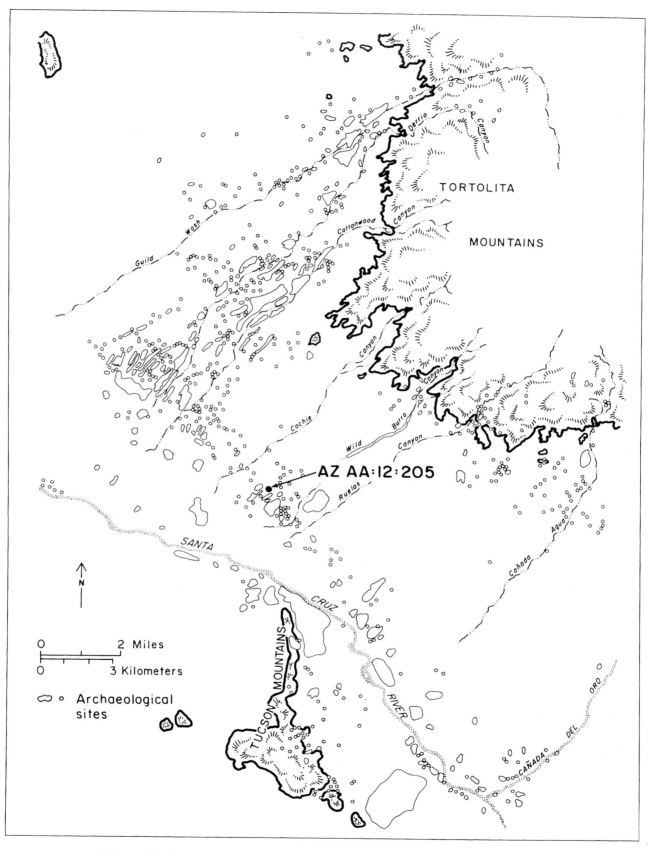

Figure 8.1. Location of site AZ AA:12:205 in the Marana survey area. Other archaeological sites are depicted as irregularly shaped outlines.

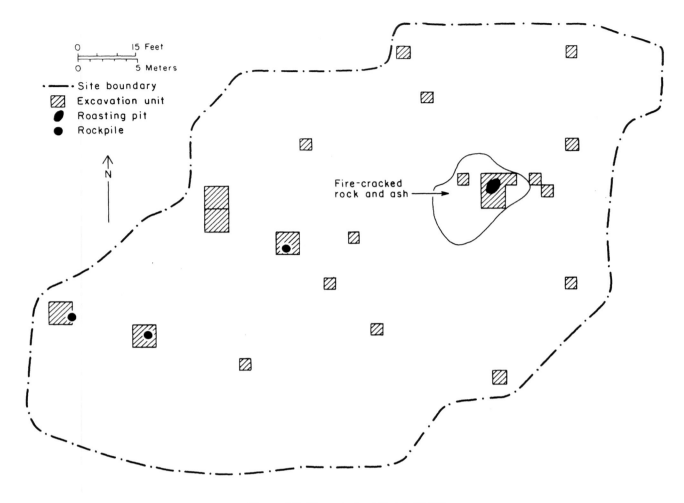

Figure 8.2. Map of site AZ AA:12:205.

Features

Rockpiles

The three rockpiles at Site 205 were located 18 m, 33 m, and 38 m southwest of the roasting pit. Each was approximately 1 m in diameter and 10 cm to 15 cm high. The rocks comprising the piles were identical to those littering the surface of the rest of the site and do not seem to have been selected on the basis of any distinctive characteristics.

The rockpiles were bisected (Fig. 8.3) and completely dismantled after profiles were drawn, and the surrounding soil was then stripped to reveal any signs of related features such as postholes or brush structures for directing runoff. In all cases the rockpiles consisted of a layer of rocks underlain by 2 cm to 10 cm of fine, grayish brown soil intermixed with pebbles and small cobbles. A caliche layer immediately beneath this soil was not broken or otherwise modified by human activity. No arti-

facts were recovered from the rockpiles. The units excavated adjacent to the rockpiles revealed a similar soil and caliche sequence.

Roasting Pit

On the ground surface the roasting pit appeared as a shallow depression surrounded by a band of pebbles and small cobbles. This rock ring was not intentionally constructed, but resulted from the prehistoric excavation of the pit and the subsequent removal of its contents. The depression measured approximately 8 m in diameter and contained soft, ashy fill. The highest concentration of surface artifacts occurred in this area.

Excavation revealed that actual pit dimensions beneath the surface depression were approximately 2.25 m in diameter and 1 m in depth (Fig. 8.4). The pit was slightly conical and was not lined with rocks. Fill consisted of dark, ashy sediment mixed with fire-cracked

Figure 8.3. Cross section of a bisected rockpile, showing the stratigraphy and the relationship to the underlying caliche layer at site AZ AA:12:205.

Figure 8.4. Excavated roasting pit at site AZ AA:12:205, showing the size and depth, fire-cracked rock, and ashy fill containing charred vegetal material.

Table 8.1. Wood Charcoal Recovered by Flotation from the Roasting Pit at Site AZ AA:12:205

Species	Percentage
Prosopis, Mesquite	26
Olneya tesota, Ironwood	61
Cercidium floridum, Blue palo verde	5
Cercidium microphyllum, Foothills palo verde	3
Acacia greggii, Catclaw acacia	1
Carnegiea gigantea, Saguaro	4
Chilopsis linearis, Desert willow	1
(Sum does not equal 100 because percentages were rounded up.)	

rocks and charcoal. Toward the bottom, the fill became black and greasy in texture. A solid mass of fused organic matter measuring about 30 cm in diameter was at the base of the feature. Within the pit were 145 sherds, 16 percent of the total pottery recovered at Site 205.

The roasting area at Site 205 is small compared to excavated pits at several large rockpile fields in the Marana Community. S. Fish, P. Fish, and Madsen (1985; Chapter 7 in this volume) note that pit size tends to follow field size. Excavation did not reveal any stratigraphic traces of repeated use, nor were multiple pits present. However, the large amount of ash and fire-cracked rock at the site, as well as the quantity of artifacts, implies repeated use.

Flotation samples from the roasting pit indicated that only agave was processed, a pattern typifying excavated pits in the northern Tucson Basin. Charred agave was recovered from 23 percent of the samples. Exploitation appears to have focused on the roasting of agave hearts (83% of identified plant parts) and, perhaps, leaves (17%). The predominant fuel species, amounting to 95 percent of the wood charcoal, were ironwood, mesquite, and palo verde (Table 8.1).

A radiocarbon assay on agave yielded a calibrated age of 1040 ± 90 years B.P. (Beta 10801), indicating that the site was used sometime between A.D. 894 and 1148 (one sigma). The midpoint of this determination, A.D. 1011, would place the site somewhat earlier than the large agave fields associated with the Marana Community, which date primarily to the early Classic period (S. Fish, P. Fish, Miksicek, and Madsen 1985).

LITHIC TECHNOLOGY AND AGAVE PROCESSING

Tool and Debitage Analysis

A total of 55 flaked stone artifacts was recovered from surface collections and excavation at Site 205. According to the classification methods employed here

(Sullivan 1983; Rozen 1984; Sullivan and Rozen 1985), this small collection comprised 49 pieces of debitage divided among five categories, two unifacially retouched pieces, and four core tools. The two tools with positive and negative percussion features were found in widely separated units.

Most of the debitage is quartzite (83.7% of the collection), with rhyolite (10.2%) and limestone (6.1%) composing the remainder. Rhyolite and limestone were brought to the site from sources elsewhere. Complete flakes (51.0%) and split flakes (18.4%) dominate the debitage; flake fragments (12.2%), debris (12.2%), and broken flakes (6.1%) equal less than one-third of the assemblage (30.5%). A comparatively high combined frequency for complete flakes, split flakes, and debris (81.6%) strongly suggests an emphasis on hard hammer core reduction (following Rozen 1984: 588).

Patterns of Artifact Selection

In general, it appears that relatively thick debitage, which may have been more resistant to stress failures, was selected for use in activities related to agave harvesting and processing. Half of the debitage with edge damage is rhyolite (although it equals only 10.2% of all debitage), and four out of five pieces of rhyolite debitage show edge damage. Rhyolite seems to have been selected because either its edges are sharper or it holds a sharper edge longer. It is likely that the rhyolite debitage was produced elsewhere and transported to Site 205, because no rhyolite cores were recovered and four of the five rhyolite artifacts were complete flakes.

The two unifacially retouched tools and the four core tools from Site 205 share some functional characteristics in spite of their typological differences. In contrast to the eight pieces of edge-damaged debitage, these relatively "massive" artifacts appear to have been designed not for resistance to lateral stresses, but rather for their resistance to perpendicularly transmitted stress. Similar core tools or "pulping planes" are consistently found in large rockpile fields of the Marana Community (Chapter 7).

CERAMICS AND AGAVE PROCESSING

A review by Doelle of the material correlates of ethnographically documented Southwestern agave exploitation makes no mention of ceramics used in harvesting or roasting activities. However, jars were used in secondary processes such as boiling, storing processed products, and rehydrating dried agave prior to consumption (Doelle 1980: 95–97).

When a liquid product was made from agave (see Castetter and others 1938), impermeable containers were used. For instance, Felger and Moser (1970) state that the Seri sometimes fermented agave leaves in sea turtle shells to make wine, and Doelle (1980: 96) mentions that watertight baskets were used to catch the juice extracted from pounded leaves. Roasted agave was occasionally boiled by the Pima to produce syrup, and many Apache groups as well as the Tarahumara made fermented drinks from the roasted crowns (Castetter and others 1938: 49, 60–63).

Presumably the technology involved in processing liquid from agaves would parallel that used to process saguaro fruit into syrup (Crosswhite 1980) and might leave comparable traces in the archaeological record (following Raab 1973). The relatively abundant pottery at Site 205 could indicate a processing of agave that involved the extraction of liquids. Alternatively, the sherds could have been the remains of vessels broken during the course of water transport and domestic tasks associated with resource production and processing activities. In both cases, breakage of whole vessels would account for the presence of sherds. By determining the number, type, and spatial distribution of vessels, more precise information might be gained about how ceramics had been used at the site, the configuration of activity loci, and the manner in which sherds had entered the archaeological record.

Ceramic Analysis

The separation of sherds into groups representing parent vessels was based on paste characteristics (type, size, and density of temper and the presence, color, and configuration of the carbon streak), surface finish, color, and thickness (Sullivan 1983). Small, severely eroded sherds, and completely charred ones (20% of the total) were not assigned to vessels. Initial homogenous batches were then sorted into vessel fragments, or aggregates of batches that exhibited a degree of internal variability but which were very different from one another. These larger groupings indicated the minimum number of vessels.

The results of the analysis contradicted original assumptions about the assemblage. The ceramics recovered from Site 205 were not the remains of whole vessels used and broken at the site, but instead represented a tool kit composed of sherds that were transported to the site for use in agave processing. Several lines of evidence support this conclusion.

The number of vessels represented at Site 205 is large compared to expectations for such a small, special purpose site. Based on a conservative count, portions of 82 different vessels were identified. None of these vessels

Table 8.2. Weights and Numbers of Sherds for 82 Vessel Fragments from the Ceramic Assemblage at Site AZ AA:12:205

Vessel number	Weight (g)	Number of sherds	Vessel number	Weight (g)	Number of sherds
1	249.9	25	42	155.4	18
2	522.4	88	43	59.4	20
3	28.4	3	44	36.6	9
4	32.5	7	45	66.5	8
5	59.0	9	46	25.4	4
6	85.6	6	47	38.4	4
7	206.0	16	48	85.1	21
8	18.0	4	49	80.1	14
9	479.2	47	50	32.9	15
10	110.6	19	51	49.5	7
11	56.2	2	52	9.2	1
12	468.9	32	53	27.0	8
13	140.7	10	54	48.5	5
14	30.1	6	55	54.5	12
15	121.0	6	56	41.0	11
16	78.6	12	57	69.3	9
17	39.7	8	58	11.1	4
18	13.9	4	59	12.5	4
19	40.8	9	60	9.8	2
20	13.9	4	61	9.5	2
21	70.2	6	62	6.0	2
22	16.6	5	63	15.8	3
23	20.4	9	64	66.4	1
24	8.6	5	65	6.4	1
25	3.6	2	66	15.6	1
26	16.4	2	67	4.9	1
27	17.2	8	68	2.1	1
28	18.3	9	69	3.6	1
29	16.2	7	70	2.5	1
30	5.6	2	71	18.9	1
31	12.4	5	72	13.6	1
32	11.3	2	73	3.4	1
33	75.3	26	74	4.5	1
34	49.8	20	75	2.7	1
35	84.3	21	76	3.0	1
36	52.0	16	77	4.8	1
37	85.6	18	78	3.1	1
38	95.6	19	79	3.4	1
39	30.4	5	80	22.0	1
40	21.8	6	81	10.7	1
41	7.2	3	82	37.9	1

are even partially reconstructible, and conjoinable sherds are rare (7% of the total). Of the 82 vessel fragments identified, 61 (74.4%) are represented by 9 or fewer sherds, and the mean number of sherds per vessel is only 8.7 (Table 8.2; Fig. 8.5).

More informative than sherd counts, however, are the weights of vessels, because they more accurately reflect the degree to which these vessel fragments approximate whole pots. At Site 205, 72 of the vessel fragments weigh 57 g or less. The range is wide, however, with the smallest fragment weighing only 2.1 g and the largest 522.4 g. In comparison, the average weight of 20 whole

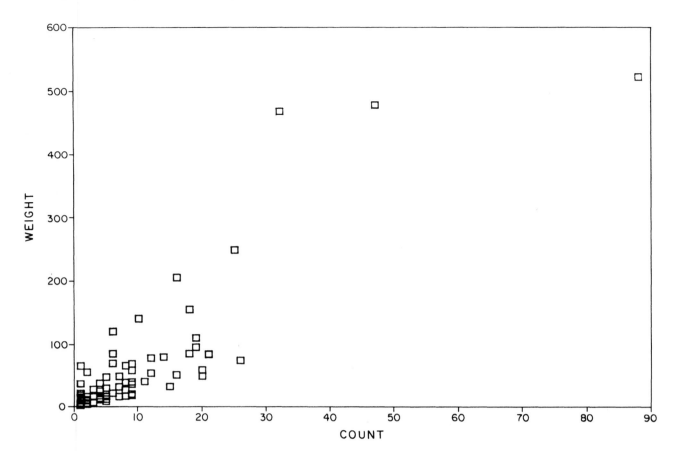

Figure 8.5. Scattergram of the weight and number of sherds
of the 82 refitted vessel fragments from site AZ AA:12:205.

**Table 8.3. Weights of 20 Whole Vessels
from Southern Arizona**

Site	Form	Type	Weight (g)
Hodges Ruin	Jar	Plain	1,616.6
Hodges Ruin	Jar	Plain	1,205.9
Hodges Ruin	Bowl	Plain	1,191.3
Hodges Ruin	Bowl	Plain	518.8
Hodges Ruin	Bowl	Decorated	347.4
AZ AA:16:11	Jar	Plain	2,707.5
AZ AA:16:26	Jar	Plain	3,726.8
AZ AA:16:29	Bowl	Plain (polished)	1,206.6
AZ AA:16:33	Jar	Plain	1,105.8
AZ BB:9:33	Bowl	Sells Red	1,236.4
AZ BB:11:20	Bowl	Gila Polychrome	570.0
AZ BB:13 (quad)	Jar	Plain	1,513.7
AZ BB:13:3	Bowl	Sells Red	779.1
AZ BB:13:16	Jar	Decorated	863.9
AZ BB:13:16	Seed jar	Decorated	1,571.5
AZ BB:13:50	Jar	Plain	805.6
AZ CC:10:5	Bowl	Encinas Red-on-brown	1,001.1
AZ CC:10:5	Bowl	Encinas Red-on-brown	836.0
AZ U:15:18	Jar	Plain	4,180.4
AZ Z:11:1	Bowl	Plain	1,012.8

and nearly intact vessels from southern Arizona in the Arizona State Museum collection is 1401.9 g (Table 8.3). Ten bowls, with a mean weight of 874 g, weigh substantially less than jars, which average 1919.9 g. The smallest bowl weighs 347 g and the largest jar weighs 4180.4 g, 89.4 percent of the total weight of vessel fragments recovered from Site 205. Only three vessel fragments weigh as much as or more than the smallest bowls in the whole vessel sample (Fig. 8.5). Rim sherds included with these vessel portions, however, indicate that these are not small, nearly intact bowls, but heavy, relatively large jars.

The low weights of vessel segments from Site 205, the large number of vessels represented, and their fragmentary condition support the contention that the ceramics from this site are the remains of broken or discarded sherds rather than broken vessels. Data collection techniques were thorough, and this finding was not the result of an incomplete recovery of artifacts. All surface sherds were collected, the features were excavated and screened, and testing revealed that few artifacts occurred outside

Figure 8.6. Sherd tools from roasting pits. The proximal ends of *a* and *b* from site AZ AA:12:205 (fragments of larger sherd tools) and the right side of *b* display rounded edges due to wear. *c* is a complete tool from site AZ AA:12:470 and shows wear along its proximal edge and both lateral edges. Length of *c* is 20.8 cm.

these contexts. In addition, the geological surface on which the site is located is stable. Although some downhill movement of artifacts appears to have occurred, the sherds show no traces of having been subjected to fluvial action strong enough to move them far from the area in which they were deposited (Skibo 1987).

Sherds as Tools

At Site 205 the unusual nature of the ceramic assemblage indicates that sherds, rather than pots, were transported to the site for use in resource processing activities. No intact sherd tools were found, perhaps because they were discarded only after their use-lives had expired. Sherds were probably gathered from trash middens associated with nearby residential sites.

Physical traces on the sherds themselves, and to some extent their spatial contexts, provide information about how these artifacts were used. The concentration of sherds around and within the roasting pit and the presence of burned sherds suggest that most were used directly in the roasting process, perhaps in some cases to keep the agave from contacting the coals or soil. Although ethnographic accounts reveal that sherds were used to parch seeds (Castetter and Underhill 1935: 25; Goodyear 1975: 171), there is no evidence that sherds were used for this purpose at Site 205. Parching food over an open fire might soot the exterior of a sherd, but would not turn it completely gray, a common attribute of pottery at the site and one that is only produced in a nonoxidizing atmosphere (P. Rice 1987: 335, 343).

Sixteen vessel fragments also exhibit distinctive forms of edge wear unlike that produced by fluvial abrasion (Skibo 1987). Most of these have rounded edges that are sometimes associated with parallel striations on the sherd surface (Fig. 8.6). These artifacts appear to have been used as scrapers or scoops, perhaps in the processing of agave flesh or fiber, but more likely in the construction of the pit or in the removal of the hot, ashy contents.

In addition to sherds modified by use, seven sherds from five vessels have been purposefully shaped by chipping or grinding. Four are small disks, one is perforated, and two are square. The function of these artifacts in relation to agave cultivation and processing remains enigmatic.

Only five vessel fragments weighed 200 g or more (Table 8.2). All these heavier fragments have some form of edge wear even though only one-third of all vessel fragments from the site were worn. A complete scoop shaped from a large plain ware sherd was recovered from a roasting pit at a large rockpile field, AZ AA:12:470 (Fig. 8.6c). It weighed 277 g and had obvious traces of abrasion. Large, heavy sherds appear to have been purposefully selected for such tools.

If large sherds were brought to the site as protective coverings or as tools, several possibilities may explain the presence of the numerous small sherds. Small sherds could have been detached from larger ones when the pit was sealed with rocks and soil or when the agave was removed; in either case the potential for sherd breakage is high. If large sherds were used to excavate a pit or to clean it out, small pieces could easily have been snapped off the larger ones. In each case, the small sherds would have been incorporated readily into the matrix of the pit, whereas the larger sherds may have been saved and used on another occasion.

ACTIVITIES AND ARTIFACTS AT SITE 205

Excavation results indicate that the activities that occurred at Site 205 were limited in scope and of short duration. Apparently the site was used only for the cultivation and processing of agave. Agave remains were found in the roasting pit, and if the roasted agave was subsequently converted into syrup or wine, such secondary processing probably did not take place at the site.

No evidence of domestic or maintenance activities was observed, suggesting that the site was used for only short periods of time. Structural remains could not be discerned, and the site also lacked middens composed of domestic debris. The narrow range of artifact types in the assemblage supports the conclusion that agave processing was not associated with the seasonal occupation of a field house or with routine domestic tasks that would be performed during the course of a protracted stay.

The location of the site away from habitations could be due to a number of factors. It might have been more convenient, for instance, to process the agave where it was harvested and then to transport the processed product, rather than the raw material, back to the habitation locus. The depletion of firewood in the immediate vicinity of the residential area (Shackley 1983) as well as the desire to locate grimy roasting pits away from residences (Ambler 1987) may have influenced the spatial separation of agave processing from domestic environs.

The investigation of Site 205 provides some insight into the exploitation of agave by the Tucson Basin Hohokam. However, implications of the ceramic analysis go beyond the identification of the subsistence practices that occurred at this small site. Potsherds are invariably regarded by archaeologists as simply the remains of broken containers, despite ample ethnographic evidence of extensive recycling (P. Rice 1987: 294). By assuming that variability in the attributes and distribution of sherds is directly linked to the prehistoric use of containers, archaeologists may be ignoring a wide range of functionally diagnostic activities associated with the secondary use of sherds as tools.

CHAPTER NINE

The Marana Community in Comparative Context

Suzanne K. Fish and Paul R. Fish

The foregoing chapters have summarized the present state of knowledge concerning one Hohokam community among the many distributed across the central portion of southern Arizona during the Classic period (Fig. 9.1). Description and interpretation of the Marana Community has been shaped by survey results and settlement pattern analysis, based on the most exhaustive data set of this kind yet obtained. The very uniqueness of these findings makes it difficult to place the Marana Community in a comparative context. Such a perspective is necessary, however, for assessing the significance of Marana among like phenomena in time and space for formulating the most meaningful questions for future research.

Much previous study in Hohokam archaeology has been focused at investigative scales bracketing the community: excavation of individual sites on the one hand and supracommunity distributions of elements such as public architecture on the other. Thus, in order to view developments in the northern Tucson Basin against a backdrop of community variability within the Hohokam tradition, measures for relevant attributes must be assembled and synthesized. The majority of available information pertains to the irrigated valleys of the Salt and Gila rivers, where observations regarding the locations of settlements first gave rise to the concept of the Hohokam community.

Hohokam communities embody institutions that integrate both dispersed and concentrated settlement into bounded territorial units. A seminal paper by David Doyel (1974; see also 1980: 31) defined irrigation communities as interrelated sites along a shared canal line, including smaller sites and at least one large site with ceremonial architecture. Wilcox (Wilcox and Sternberg 1983: 195) emphasized the focal and integrative function of central sites with public architecture within their respective communities. Due to zones of dispersed but continuous settlement, relatively noncompact centers, and the critical role of intersite relationships, physical

aspects of Hohokam territorial organization cannot be understood by studying individual sites. Structural changes in Hohokam society are also incompletely expressed at this scale of analysis. Both issues can be fully comprehended only at the level of the multisite community.

Scattered instances of large sites with ballcourts and a few examples of mound construction are known from the early Preclassic period by at least A.D. 750. Relatively standardized organizational modes focused on such centers with public architecture can be recognized by A.D. 1000, when sufficient data reveal regularized spacing of ballcourts in the Phoenix area and numerous occurrences elsewhere (Wilcox and Sternberg 1983). By that time, it appears that the multisite community had become the principal territorial and organizational unit of Hohokam occupations. In the early Classic period after about A.D. 1150, use of ballcourts ceased. Platform mounds, usually constructed in stages, were located in community centers during this time and continued into the late Classic period as the principal form of public architecture (P. Fish 1989; Wasley 1980; Wallace and Holmlund 1984; Wilcox and Sternberg 1983).

HOHOKAM COMMUNITIES IN THE PHOENIX BASIN

Community Spacing

Because sites with public architecture mark replicates of integrative nodes, community extents can be approximated by boundaries between consecutive centers of similar date. In the area of large-scale irrigation in the Hohokam core, a majority of canal networks and sites with mounds and ballcourts were mapped in the earlier years of this century, prior to obliteration by urban sprawl. Distributions of centers, and thus communities, can be largely reconstructed where data are insufficient for precisely enumerating all constituent sites. Spacing of

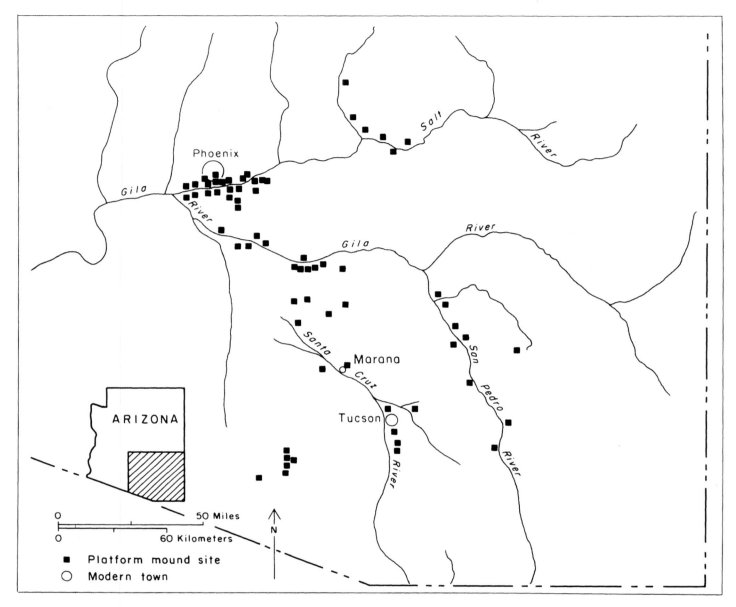

Figure 9.1. Distribution of Classic period mound sites in southern Arizona.

centers has suggested regularities in the size of integrated area. An average of 5.5 km between adjacent ballcourt sites along Phoenix canals was observed by Wilcox (Wilcox and Sternberg 1983: 195) for predominantly late Preclassic ballcourts before A.D. 1150. Sites with more than one ballcourt may indicate a higher level of integration, reflecting coordination in rituals and related social interaction among several ballcourt communities.

The spacing of post-A.D. 1150 Classic period sites with platform mounds along the Salt and Gila river canal systems has been examined with the same methodology (Gregory and Nials 1985; Crown 1987). An average of about 5 km between mound sites is closely similar to the 5.5 km distance for ballcourts (Table 9.1). These averages are derived from an only partially overlapping set of sites with both forms of public architecture. The convergence suggests continuity in basic size of integrated units between Late Preclassic and Classic periods. Classic mound spacing has been associated with distances suitable for regulation of canals and distribution of water along shared networks (Crown 1987: 155–158; Gregory and Nials 1985: 383). Regularities in linear distance between centers, along canals, may reflect optimal distances for agricultural travel and day-to-day communication within a single community or between adjacent community centers.

Table 9.1. Estimated Statistics for Some Key Hohokam Communities

	Phoenix Area (Lower Salt River)	Casa Grande Area (Middle Gila River)
Approximate average total area per community	40 square kilometers	40 square kilometers
Average irrigated acreage per community	21,000 ha (a) 23 communities (c) = 935 ha	6250 ha (b) 6 communities = 1041 ha

Range of irrigated acreage in single Gila community
Estimates by two different methods (b): 389 to 1889 ha, 520 to 1856 ha

According to Piman analogy (d): 1000 irrigated hectares per community could support 2300 to 5800 persons
Phoenix Basin population for 21,000 irrigated hectares = 53,000 to 133,000 persons

Spacing of Phoenix Late Preclassic period ballcourt sites along canals = 5.5 km (e)
Spacing of Phoenix Classic period mound sites along canals = 5 km (f)

Northern Tucson Basin (g): Area of 2 Preclassic period ballcourt communities = 57 square kilometers, 70 square kilometers
Area of Classic period mound community = 146 square kilometers

Sources: (a) Nials, Gregory, and Graybill 1989; (b) Crown 1987; (c) Gregory 1987; (d) Castetter and Bell 1942: 54; (e) Wilcox and Sternberg 1983; (f) Gregory and Nials 1985; (g) S. Fish and others 1989.

Community Area and Layout

Classic period mounds appear evenly spaced within the Phoenix area as a whole (Fig. 9.1), as well as linearly along individual canals. Average community territory can be calculated by generously outlining the extent of canal systems and dividing by the respective number of mound centers, if communities integrate all adjacent space whether irrigated or not. The average territory for each of the 23 Salt River mound communities would be roughly 40 square kilometers. Based on mound sites mapped by Patricia Crown (1987) along the Classic period canal systems on the Gila River, average territories here also approximate 40 square kilometers.

With 5-km spacing along canals and community territory averaging 40 square kilometers, the long axes of communities would tend to be across the canals. Gregory and Nials (1985: 381) noted a linear, cross-canal arrangement of habitation features for major mound sites on the Las Colinas system that would have maximized land available along the canals for agricultural use. A cross-canal shape for communities as a whole, however, may also be a consequence of laterally integrated territory beyond the limits of irrigation. Nonirrigated land likely provided wild food resources, raw materials, fuel, and semicultivated desert species.

Irrigated Acreage

Another general trend for the Salt and Gila basin communities involves magnitudes of prehistorically irrigated acreage. Recent estimates place land irrigated from the Salt River at approximately 21,000 hectares

(Nials and others 1989: 73–76), for an average of 935 hectares per platform mound community. Within the systems on the Gila River, recent estimates of 6250 irrigated hectares (Crown 1987) result in a comparable average of 1040 hectares for each Classic period community. Extents of irrigated acreage, like community size, may involve practical distances for regular communication and travel to fields (Crown 1987: 154; Gregory and Nials 1985: 383–384) or routine transport of agricultural products.

Although reasonably derived modalities can be cited for integrated area and irrigable acreage, these must be regarded as general averages incorporating a degree of community variation. For example, Crown (1987: 154–155) finds a correlation between size of the mound site in Gila communities and amount of irrigable acreage. However, calculations for maximum acreage among Gila communities is no more than twice the average figure.

Population Size

Convergences in irrigated acreage may point to some optimal range for a more elusive and vital parameter of Classic communities: population. As a comparative exercise, estimates of supportable population in the Hohokam core can be made using amounts of cultivated land among late historic Pimans according to Castetter and Bell (1942: 54). A Piman family of five subsisted on 0.86 to 2.15 hectares. If plows, domestic animals, and commercial sale of harvests increased the acreage farmed by historic households, these figures might indicate the lower range for prehistoric populations that cultivated smaller plots. In an average prehistoric community containing about 1000 hectares of irrigated land, 2300 to 5800 persons could have been supported according to Piman analogy (Phoenix area totals would range from 53,000 to 133,000 persons). These figures overlap with previous estimates (Haury 1976: 356; Schroeder 1940: 20; Doyel 1991; P. Fish and S. Fish 1991). However, continuities in inferred Salt River community size between the late Preclassic and Classic periods, based on similar spacing of earlier ballcourt and later mound centers, may or may not equate with a stability in population size determined by irrigated production. A greater interconnectedness of Classic networks through canals linking major trunk lines, as posited by Nicholas and Feinman (1989), may indicate some degree of agricultural intensification. There is also general consensus that networks reached their maximum areal extent during this period (Masse 1981; Nicholas and Neitzel 1984; Nicholas and Feinman 1989; Plog 1980; Upham and Rice 1980).

Processes of ongoing aggregation and agricultural intensification in the Phoenix Basin during the Classic period thus may have created higher population densities within community territories that were of similar size to those of the late Preclassic period. In spite of obliterated segments of settlement pattern and variable archaeological visibility by time period, numbers of sites over time provide one avenue for evaluating this issue. A compilation by Upham and Rice (1980) showed a clear increase in site numbers from the late Preclassic to Classic periods along the lower Salt River. Additional factors of site size and occupational density at large sites that are relevant to relative population magnitudes cannot be chronologically compared with any precision in the Hohokam core. Estimated boundaries for large Classic period sites commonly incorporate the overlapping areal extents of all earlier components.

Settlement Hierarchies

The existence of site hierarchies is basic to the recognition of Hohokam communities. As observed by Doyel (1974, 1980), common canal usage creates a basis for sociopolitical integration embodied at larger sites or centers with administrative functions. Many Phoenix area irrigation networks serve multiple ballcourt or platform mound communities. There is general agreement (Upham and Rice 1980; Gregory and Nials 1985; Crown 1987) that by the Classic period, the largest mound site along a shared network was differentiated from the others by at least some aspects of decision making and consumption, and minimally played a preeminent role in coordination and conflict resolution involving canal use. By the late Classic period after approximately A.D. 1350, a few very large sites such as Pueblo Grande, Mesa

Grande, and Casa Grande contain more massive public architecture than previous or contemporary centers. These sites have been interpreted as representing a further level of hierarchy integrating a number of community units (Howard 1987: 218–220; Crown 1987: 157; Nicholas and Feinman 1989: 225).

A recent analysis of settlement along a major canal system with multiple communities considers attributes of hierarchy in addition to size, public architecture, and spacing of central sites. Howard (1987) documents differential access to high value items between the foremost site of Mesa Grande and lesser sites with and without public architecture along the Lehi canal system. Mesa Grande, the largest site, has the most massive mound, the only known burial offerings of unusual richness, and the greatest access to ceramic trade wares, axes, and turquoise. No artifactual data are available for a second size category of sites with less massive public architecture. A third category of smaller sites with walled adobe compounds but without mounds or ballcourts has lower frequencies of high value goods.

Differentiated Land Use

On the broad, flat, basin floor of the lower Salt River encompassing modern Phoenix, relatively homogenous topography would have fostered similarities in land use among irrigated communities. However, modern urban and agricultural disturbance allows only partial reconstruction of intracommunity patterns for isolated residential, agricultural, and extractive sites. A gradation in land use diversity can be observed between these environmentally most homogenous Phoenix communities, communities within the adjoining but somewhat narrower basin of the middle Gila River, and those in other Hohokam regions without perennial rivers and large-scale irrigation.

Even in the Phoenix vicinity, some degree of differentiation in settlement and land use is correlated with features of the valley floor (Wilcox 1991; Wilcox and Sternberg 1983; Masse 1991; Mitchell 1988). For example, three environmental zones with differential settlement and production characteristics can be defined for segments of the Mesa Grande system at increasing distances from the river (Howard 1987). A low density of small dispersed sites on the first terrace of the Salt River is consistent with a predominantly agricultural land use. A diversity of site types occurs on the densely occupied bluff area of the second terrace. Here, Mesa Grande contains multiple compounds, the largest mound, and a second mound of lesser size. Inland on the second terrace, several sites with public architecture are near the ends of main canal branches.

Greater diversity of land use is exhibited within individual Classic period communities along the Gila River (Crown 1987: 149–153), although all communities are located adjacent to the river due to the lesser width of this basin. Irrigated portions of sequential communities along the Gila occupy the floodplain. Substantial habitation sites occur on adjacent higher terraces, as do complexes of agricultural features dependent on water from storm runoff. Locations of field houses also suggest floodwater farming from tributary drainages in upper terrace and lower bajada situations. This combination of agricultural technologies is generally replicated from community to community.

HOHOHAM COMMUNITIES IN THE TUCSON BASIN AND OTHER NONCORE AREAS

Unlike the perennially flowing Salt and Gila rivers of the Hohokam core, desert rivers in the other basins of this cultural tradition are intermittent, lacking year-round flow over much of their courses. Without equivalent scales of riverine irrigation, spatial and organizational characteristics of communities in these regions cannot be related to shared systems, nor are settlement expressions necessarily identical. Systematic records of central sites were not made by early observers, as along the Salt and Gila, and such distributional data for community identification are absent or incomplete. The delimitation of sites within community boundaries is also more difficult without clear spatial linkages among sites afforded by common canals, as in the Phoenix core. Although currently there are few descriptions of noncore communities, greater potential exists for understanding the role of dispersed populations in these areas where modern development has been less pervasive.

Community Spacing and Size

Ballcourts and even mounds are not yet fully tabulated outside the Salt and Gila core. Recent investigations have added significantly to the known Tucson instances of public architecture. Central sites of the Preclassic and Classic periods occur both along the Santa Cruz River and on the bajadas, reflecting varied and land-extensive agricultural bases. In keeping with this contrast between Phoenix and Tucson subsistence and settlement patterns, spacing between central sites in most sectors of the Tucson Basin is greater and more variable than in the core area. Settlement data revealing details of community size and layout are available only in a few cases.

In an exception to more distant Tucson spacing, William Doelle and others (1987) describe the distribution of primary or larger-sized Preclassic period villages in the southern basin along a stretch of the Santa Cruz with persistent surface flow. Most of these villages contain ballcourts. Spacing is approximately every 3 km along the river, a shorter distance than the 5.5 km between Preclassic ballcourts along canals in the Phoenix area. Although riverine irrigation is probable on this part of the Santa Cruz, Tucson topography and hydrology would have restricted the size of systems. Closer spacing of central sites than in the core area is not associated with denser populations, since territory surrounding these Tucson primary villages includes only an average of two small habitation sites.

Continuities in average spacing between centers of earlier ballcourt and later mound communities in the Phoenix Basin are not duplicated near Tucson. Sociopolitical reorganization throughout the Hohokam tradition occurred at the end of the Preclassic period, at which time some Phoenix ballcourt sites were abandoned. In other Phoenix ballcourt sites, patterned arrangements have been identified between ballcourts and the mounds built in the earliest part of the Classic period (Gregory 1987), but use of Hohokam ballcourts appears to have ceased before the late Classic period. A disjuncture between Preclassic and Classic period centers is more strongly expressed in noncore regions. Classic mounds are not constructed at Tucson ballcourt sites, for example, and may be located at considerable distances. Hohokam reorganization culminating in the early Classic period may be more freely expressed by changing site primacy and other community dynamics outside the core area, where locational strictures of preexisting canal networks did not apply.

In the northern Tucson Basin, settlement clusters are concentrated along the Santa Cruz River and along mountain flanks at the basin edge (S. Fish and others 1989, Chapter 3 in this volume). Spatially separated Preclassic communities with ballcourt centers in each of these locations, at 70 and 57 square kilometers, are larger than the 40-square-kilometer average for core communities of the Classic period. These two earlier communities merged into the subsequent Marana Community. Sites appeared in the formerly intervening area, including the newly settled central mound site. The resulting early Classic period community spanned the basin from river to mountains, encompassing 146 square kilometers.

Settlement Hierarchies

Hierarchy in Tucson Preclassic period communities has been approached largely through site size and presence of ballcourts. A three-tiered settlement hierarchy in the Marana Community of the Classic period is based on site size, architecture, and ceramics. The four largest sites are distinguished by low frequencies of imported ceramics, higher consumption of decorated pottery, walled adobe compounds, and, in one case, the mound (see Chapter 3). The mound site is geographically central within the community, but in a location of secondary subsistence potential, suggesting an important role for intracommunity exchange. Intermediate-sized sites contain cobble outlines of adobe surface structures. More than three-fourths of the smallest residential sites, presumably with pit houses or less substantial surface dwellings, have no visible architectural remains. Contemporary sites fitting these Marana categories have been recorded widely in the Tucson Basin (Doelle 1985b; Wallace and Holmlund 1984), likely reflecting similar hierarchies in other Classic period communities.

Large portions of most Phoenix core communities have been destroyed and smaller elements of settlement pattern cannot be systematically recovered. However, sets of interrelated communities along the same network are demarcated by well-mapped canals. Relationships among the better preserved but more diffuse and widely spaced Tucson communities, on the other hand, could be similarly well established only through prohibitively broad retrieval of settlement patterns. These spatial parameters of communities and available settlement data are sufficiently divergent between the Phoenix and Tucson basins to confuse comparison of hierarchical arrangements within and among communities. For example, it is unclear whether the previously described site hierarchy within the 146-square-kilometer Marana Community is organizationally more equivalent to a single mound community covering about 40 square kilometers along a major Phoenix canal or to the set of communities sharing that network.

Within proposed hierarchies involving Classic period communities along shared canal lines in the Salt and Gila core, developmental histories of the communities and their centers are incompletely known. It is generally unclear whether rankings based on size and magnitude of public architecture in central sites pertain equally to the early division of the Classic period or only to late Classic times. The Marana Community and contemporary entities are separated by vacant areas or attenuated settlement. Hierarchical relationships involving the Marana Community and early Classic counterparts in the northern Tucson Basin are not apparent, although merger of the two prior Preclassic communities within its boundaries seems to reflect a consolidation of territorial sway at the beginning of the Classic period. The developmental trajectories of the other early Classic communities are more poorly understood, including

chronological details concerning centers and their mounds.

In the Late Classic period, hierarchical relationships are possible among the set of communities located in the southern Tucson Basin and among those near the Picacho Mountains to the north. If so, a common irrigation network cannot have provided a relational basis, nor have preeminent centers and communities been identified. North of the Picacho Mountains along the Gila River, Classic mound centers sharing the Casa Grande canal system have been considered hierarchically related to the large and elaborate site of Casa Grande (Crown 1987). Interestingly, the mound site of the Tom Mix Community near the Picacho Mountains is no farther from Casa Grande than the more distant centers on that common canal system.

Differentiated Land Use

Internal differentiation in settlement and subsistence activities by topographic zones seems to characterize communities outside the core area (Wood and McAllister 1980, 1984; Doelle 1985b; G. Rice 1987b) to a greater degree than ones within it (Crown 1987; Cable and Mitchell 1987; Howard 1987). Noncore communities frequently include segments along major drainages that could support irrigation of modest scale compared to core systems. Irrigated acreage may have contributed disproportionately to total production of annual crops, but substantial remainders of community land were farmed with alternative technologies.

In the northern Tucson Basin Marana Community, six zones of functionally and topographically differentiated settlement cover almost the full range of basin environments (Chapters 3 and 4). Inhabitants of individual sites in the community may have pursued subsistence activities in one or more adjacent zones, but distances and environmental diversity necessarily entailed variable participation in agricultural technologies among the population as a whole. The geographic concentration of rockpile fields also demonstrates an appreciable degree of agricultural specialization (S. Fish and others 1989).

Irrigation networks, series of adjacent floodwater fields, and the large rockpile complexes all involved common interests and efforts for subsets of community members. Households and villages likely participated in more than one agricultural association or water users group that coordinated joint tasks, scheduling, or water allocation. Relations based on consensus and cooperation in these contexts would have crosscut and sequentially interlinked members across the community. Such networks of interrelationship may have served as a social and economic cement across productively diversified communities in a manner resembling the interdependence created by shared use of massive canal systems in the Hohokam core.

Population

Even with the best distributional data, population in noncore regions can be approached only through the broadest comparative estimates. Agricultural acreage cannot be approximated in a manner similar to the extent of irrigable land in the core as a basis for calculating supportable totals. However, without the same degree of settlement continuity imposed by canals in the Phoenix Basin, superpositioning of successive occupations over hundreds of years occurs in fewer sites. It is therefore less difficult to assess individual components in settlement and regional trends over time. Indeed, population shifts and rearrangements can be recognized in the developmental histories of these areas.

In the northern Tucson Basin, population is a variable in community dynamics. Densities in the early Classic period Marana Community seem only partially accounted for by inhabitants of the two preceding communities within its territory. Habitation site area in the Preclassic period communities totals about 2,000,000 square meters compared to just under 6,000,000 square meters in the early Classic period community, which represents a shorter time span. Although local population growth must have contributed to this increase, it is probable that some members of the Marana Community were newly arrived. Habitation site area averages 16,000 square meters for each kilometer of the 127 square kilometers covered by the two Preclassic entities compared to 40,000 square meters for each kilometer in the 146-square-kilometer Classic period community.

Population dynamics further accelerate during the following Hohokam sequence in the Tucson Basin. The Marana Community and an adjacent early Classic community in the northern basin are abandoned by the beginning of the late Classic interval marked by Salado polychromes after A.D. 1350. Nearly 1300 square kilometers (500 square miles) surrounding these communities lack habitation sites of that time. Rather than wholesale population loss, these dramatic shifts in settlement are probably related to processes of aggregation.

On either side of this abandoned area, late Classic communities cluster in the southern Tucson Basin and near the Picacho Mountains to the north. In some cases it appears that mounds were first constructed at the central sites during the late Classic period. As with the largest sites of that date in the Hohokam core, late Classic mound sites in both the northern and southern

clusters of communities exhibit the densest architectural and artifactual remains for any period, suggesting that population densities within central sites reached a peak. These late Classic communities near Tucson also coincide with hydrological situations most suited to agricultural intensification through irrigation and other means.

Population magnitudes of the late Classic period McClellan Community, surveyed by the same full-coverage method as the Marana study area (Fig. 1.8), are greater than those of the earlier Marana Community. The McClellan Community shares the developmental pattern of an incorporation of two earlier Preclassic period settlement concentrations into a single Classic period unit. Population then peaks in Late Classic settlement covering 136 square kilometers or 10 square kilometers less than the Marana Community. Total habitation site area for the McClellan Community of this date is about 16,000,000 square meters. Increased population density in the later community is registered by an average of 118,000 square meters of habitation site per square kilometer compared to the 40,000 square meters per square kilometer at Marana.

COMMUNITIES AS INTEGRATIVE INSTITUTIONS

Although locational and organizational imperatives of massive irrigation may have been critical along the Salt and Gila rivers, shared canals were not the impetus for Hohokam communities of the Tucson Basin and other regions. Cooperation, coordination, and any central decision making could not have been shaped by such interaction. Yet similar community patterns began in the Preclassic, and by the Classic period included settlement hierarchies and mound precincts. Risk sharing and subsistence exchange for larger populations in regions lacking dependable irrigation are among probable community functions in these cases. A concept of integrated communities transcending irrigation or other locationally specific needs must have existed and been transmutable to a variety of environmental situations. This basic organizational structure provided the integrative framework for settlement and society throughout the Hohokam tradition.

In worldwide developmental sequences, there is a repetitive correlation between integrative structure and public architecture. The relationship between these phenomena may be particularly significant for the Hohokam. Mounds are diagnostic elements by which archaeologists define Classic period communities, and they may have been similarly perceived by their builders. Frequently identified with public ceremony and leadership roles for the individuals using or inhabiting their precincts, mounds are also the most imposing and visible structures of the Hohokam community. Construction episodes, which in at least some cases were periodic and enlarged mound size by stages, must have involved participation and logistical support from many social groups. Mounds likely embodied symbols of community identity, cohesiveness, and differentiation from other such entities in surrounding areas.

The most massive instances of Hohokam public architecture appear in the late Classic period, in sites often regarded as representing an additional level of hierarchy linking several lesser mound communities. The erection of mounds may have served in the expression of intercommunity relations involving both hierarchy and competition. One aspect of such "peer polity interaction" (Price 1977; Renfrew 1986: 1–8) in the Tucson Basin may have been competition for population. Both early and late Classic communities of this region apparently grew to their ultimate extents through increments of population, drawn from preceding or contemporary communities. Agricultural intensification and a general increase in productive specialization may have provided incentives for more concentrated settlement in late prehistoric time.

THE MARANA COMMUNITY IN THE HOHOKAM WORLD

The Marana Community represents no superlatives in the Hohokam world. Its developmental history begins with preceramic agriculturalists, but ends while other communities continue to grow. The mound at its center is small compared to most Classic period edifices. The areal extent of the Marana Community is greater than the average for territories surrounding mound centers in the Hohokam core, but size information is inadequate for noncore comparisons. Although population estimates derived from irrigated acreage in the core cannot be directly compared to measures of habitation area in Marana sites, it is doubtful that Marana and other outlying communities attained Phoenix Basin densities. According to site area measures, a population of greater magnitude lived within the late Classic period McClellan Community of the same noncore region.

Delineation of the Marana Community has unfolded in a context of settlement pattern unparalleled in Hohokam archaeology. Survey in the northern Tucson Basin is the first instance of full-coverage examination of similarly large contiguous blocks and systematic coverage at a truly regional scale. Although survey results have provided the primary source of interpretations concern-

ing the Marana Community to date, the major advantage of a regional backdrop is an increased depth for interconnected inquiries at multiple scales. The most powerful insights have arisen through an interplay among outcomes from several investigative levels, studies of broad and narrow focus, and findings from survey and excavation. This interplay is perhaps best illustrated by the topic of agave cultivation. Fine-scale studies of features, artifacts, and biotic remains at individual sites interdigitate with regional distributions of cultural and environmental variables to provide a basis for economic interpretation. The role of the mound center in community organization and dynamics is another example of such evidence merger. As future excavations are undertaken, the ability to place site-specific studies in a community framework will simultaneously sharpen understanding at smaller and larger scales.

Quantification presents an ongoing challenge in Hohokam studies. The benefits of a large data set for deriving relative magnitudes where more precise estimates cannot be achieved is illustrated by comparative measures for the Marana Community. Habitation area in community sites as a proxy for population is a prime example. Trends derived from community-wide distributions are clear and convincing, as in the tripling of Preclassic habitation area in the Marana Community during the Early Classic period. Increasing community densities over time are strongly indicated by averages for site habitation area per square kilometer. The Preclassic Marana level of 16,000 square meters per square kilometer increases to 40,000 square meters in the early Classic period, and rises again to 118,000 square meters per square kilometer in the McClellan Community of the late Classic period. These quantitative data may be subject to substantial future refinement, but reversal of magnitudes is highly improbable.

If not distinctive among its prehistoric counterparts, the Marana Community is nevertheless archaeologically unique in several respects. Precisely because there has been relatively minor use of community territory from the beginning of the Late Classic period until the present, the record of growth and change from earliest ceramic occupations through the Early Classic period is particularly clear. Marana studies provide the first comprehensive view of community parameters in a Hohokam region outside the valley of the Salt and Gila rivers. Nowhere else has such a detailed and complete record yet been obtained of the settlement components of a Hohokam community, their spatial relationships to one another, and to features of the desert environment. Investigations in the Marana Community have revealed a social and territorial configuration that incorporated broad environmental diversity, but constituted a well-integrated subsistence system. Agricultural technologies were distinctive from zone to zone, varying with topography and sources of water. Because of localized risks among zones, it is unlikely that individual community segments could have sustained Classic period population densities in isolation; reciprocity and circulation of subsistence items within the community undoubtedly contributed to the long-term welfare of all members. For inhabitants in the desert basins of intermittent rivers, such communities encompassed the basic requirements for population sustenance and reproduction and provided the means for equal participation in the Hohokam tradition.

At the end of the Hohokam sequence sometime after A.D. 1400, a long-term developmental trajectory ceased and community organization disappeared. Less aggregated and smaller successor populations in southern Arizona echoed many aspects of Hohokam lifeways, including the eventual Pima resurrection of large-scale canals on the Gila River in the mid-nineteenth century, but the previous integrative principles and their expression in public architecture never reappeared. The level of integration embodied in communities is a hallmark of Hohokam society and distinguishes their tradition from all others in the southern deserts of the southwestern United States.

References

ABRUZZI, WILLIAM S.
1989   Ecology, Resource Redistribution, and Mormon Settlement in Northeastern Arizona. *American Anthropologist* 91(3): 642–655.

ACKERLY, NEAL, JERRY HOWARD, AND RANDALL H. McGUIRE
1987   La Ciudad Canals: A Study of Hohokam Irrigation Systems at the Community Level. *Arizona State University Anthropological Field Studies* 17. Tempe: Department of Anthropology, Arizona State University.

ADAMS, ROBERT McC.
1965   *Land behind Baghdad: A History of Settlement on the Diyala Plains*. Chicago: University of Chicago Press.
1981   *Heartland of Cities: Surveys of Ancient Settlement and Land Use on the Central Floodplain of the Euphrates*. Chicago: University of Chicago Press.

AGENBROAD, LARRY D.
1967   The Distribution of Fluted Points in Arizona. *The Kiva* 32(4): 113–120.
1970   Cultural Implications from the Statistical Analysis of a Prehistoric Lithic Site in Arizona. MS, Master's thesis, Department of Anthropology, University of Arizona, Tucson.

AMBLER, J. RICHARD
1987   AZD–11–9, A Locus for Pueblo II Grimy Activities on Central Black Mesa, Northeastern Arizona. *Archaeological Series* 2. Flagstaff: Department of Anthropology, Northern Arizona University.

ANDERSON, R. SCOTT, AND THOMAS VAN DEVENDER
1991   Comparison of Pollen and Macrofossils in Packrat (*Neotoma*) Middens: A Chronological Sequence from the Waterman Mountains of Southern Arizona, U.S.A. *Review of Paleobotany and Palynology* 68: 1–28.

ASCHMANN, HOMER
1959   The Central Desert of Baja California Demography and Ecology. *Ibero-Americana* 42: 1–282. Berkeley: University of California Press.

BARTLETT, JOHN
1854   *Personal Narrative of Explorations and Incidents in Texas, New Mexico, California, Sonora, and Chihuahua, Connected with the United States and Mexican Boundary Commission, during the Years 1850, '51, and '53*. New York: Appleton.

BAYHAM, FRANK E., DONALD H. MORRIS, AND M. STEVEN SHACKLEY
1986   Prehistoric Hunter-Gatherers of South Central Arizona: The Picacho Reservoir Archaic Project. *Arizona State University Anthropological Field Studies* 13. Tempe: Department of Anthropology, Arizona State University.

BEAN, LOWELL J., AND HARRY W. LAWTON
1973   Some Explanations for the Rise of Cultural Complexity in Native California with Comments on Proto-agriculture and Agriculture. In "Patterns of Indian Burning in California: Ecology and Ethnohistory," by Henry T. Lewis, pp. v-xlvii. *Anthropological Papers* 1. Ballena, California: Ballena Press.

BEAN, LOWELL J., AND K. S. SAUBEL
1972   *Temelpakh*. Banning, California: Malki Museum.

BELL, WILLIS H., AND EDWARD F. CASTETTER
1937   The Utilization of Mesquite and Screwbean by the Aborigines in the American Southwest. *University of New Mexico Biological Series* 4: 3–63. Albuquerque: University of New Mexico.

BERNARD-SHAW, MARY
1984   The Stone Tool Assemblage of the Salt-Gila Aqueduct Project Sites. In "Hohokam Archaeology Along the Salt-Gila Aqueduct Central Arizona Project: Material Culture," edited by Lynn S. Teague and Patricia L. Crown. *Arizona State Museum Archaeological Series* 150 (8, Part I): 373–443. Tucson: Arizona State Museum, University of Arizona.
1988   Hohokam Canal Systems and Late Archaic Wells: The Evidence from the Los Morteros Site. In "Recent Research on Tucson Basin Prehistory," edited by William H. Doelle and Paul R. Fish. *Institute for American Research Anthropological Papers* 10: 153–174. Tucson: Institute for American Research.
1989   Archaeological Investigations at the Redtail Site, AA:12:149 (ASM), in the Northern Tucson Basin. *Center for Desert Archaeology Technical Report* 89-8. Tucson: Desert Archaeology.
1990a   Archaeological Excavations at the Lonetree Site, AZ AA:12:120 (ASM), in the Northern Tucson Basin. *Center for Desert Archaeology Technical Report* 90-1. Tucson: Desert Archaeology.
1990b   Experimental Agave Fiber Extraction. In "Rincon Phase Seasonal Occupation in the Northern Tucson Basin," edited by Mary Bernard-Shaw and Frederick Huntington. *Center for Desert Archaeology Technical Report* 90-2: 181–196. Tucson: Desert Archaeology.

BETANCOURT, JULIO L., AND RAYMOND TURNER
1988   Historic Arroyo-cutting and Subsequent Channel Changes at the Congress Street Crossing, Santa Cruz River, Tucson, Arizona. In *Arid Lands: Today and Tomorrow*, edited by E. Whitehead, C. Hutchinson, B. Timmerman, and R. Varady, pp. 1353–1373. Boulder: Westview Press.

BINFORD, LEWIS
1980   Willow Smoke and Dogs' Tails: Hunter-Gatherer Settlement Systems and Archaeological Site Formation. *American Antiquity* 45(1): 4–20.
1982   The Archaeology of Place. *Journal of Anthropological Archaeology* 1: 5–31.

BLANTON, RICHARD E., STEPHEN A. KOWALEWSKI, GARY M. FEINMAN, AND JILL APPEL
1981   *Ancient Mesoamerica: A Comparison of Change in Three Regions.* Cambridge: Cambridge University Press.

BOHRER, VORSILA L.
1987   The Plant Remains from La Ciudad, a Hohokam Site in Phoenix. In "Specialized Studies in the Economy, Environment, and Culture of La Ciudad, Part III: Environmental Data," edited by Jo Ann E. Kisselburg, Glen E. Rice, and Brenda L. Shears. *Arizona State University Anthropological Field Papers* 20: 67–238. Tempe: Department of Anthropology, Arizona State University.

BOSERUP, ESTER
1965   *The Conditions of Agricultural Growth: The Economics of Agrarian Change under Population Pressure.* Chicago: Aldine.

BRYAN, KIRK
1922   Routes to Desert Watering Places in the Papago Country, Arizona. *U.S. Geological Survey Water Supply Paper* 491. Washington.
1925   The Papago Country, Arizona: A Geologic Reconnaissance with a Guide to Desert Watering Places. *U.S. Geological Survey Water Supply Paper* 499. Washington.
1929   Floodwater Farming. *Geographical Review* 19: 444–456.

BULL, WILLIAM B.
1977   The Alluvial-fan Environment. *Progress in Physical Geography* 1: 222–270.

CABALLERO NIETO, JAVIER
1986   Uses and Incipient Cultivation of Palmetto (*Sabal* spp.) in the Mayan Area of Yucatan, Mexico IV. Paper presented at the 9th Annual Ethnobiology Conference, Albuquerque, New Mexico.

CABLE, JOHN S., AND DOUGLAS R. MITCHELL
1987   La Lomita Pequeña in Regional Perspective. In "Excavations at La Lomita Pequeña: A Santa Cruz/ Sacaton Phase Hamlet in the Salt River Valley," edited by Douglas R. Mitchell. *Soil Systems Publications in Archaeology* 10: 395–446. Phoenix: Soil Systems.

CALLEN, ERIC
1967   Analysis of Tehuacan Coprolites. In *Prehistory of the Tehuacan Valley: Environment and Subsistence,* edited by Douglas S. Byers, pp. 261–289. Austin: University of Texas Press.

CASTETTER, EDWARD F., AND WILLIS H. BELL
1942   *Pima and Papago Indian Agriculture.* Albuquerque: University of New Mexico Press.

1951   *Yuman Indian Agriculture: Primative Subsistence on the Lower Colorado and Gila Rivers.* Albuquerque: University of New Mexico Press.

CASTETTER, EDWARD F., AND RUTH M. UNDERHILL
1935   The Ethnobiology of the Papago Indians. *University of New Mexico Bulletin, Biological Series* 4(3): 3–84. Albuquerque: University of New Mexico.

CASTETTER, EDWARD F., WILLIS H. BELL, AND ALVIN R. GROVE
1938   Ethnobotanical Studies of the American Southwest VI: The Early Utilization and Distribution of Agave in the American Southwest. *University of New Mexico Bulletin* 6(4). Albuquerque: University of New Mexico.

CHRISTALLER, WALTER
1966   *Central Places in Southern Germany.* Englewood Cliffs: Prentice-Hall.

CLOTTS, H. V.
1915   Report on Nomadic Papago Surveys. Report prepared by the U.S. Indian Services. MS, Arizona State Museum Library, University of Arizona, Tucson.
1917   History of the Papago Indians and History of Irrigation, Papago Indian Reservations, Arizona. Report prepared by the U.S. Indian Services. MS, Arizona State Museum Library, University of Arizona, Tucson.

COOKE, RONALD U., AND RICHARD W. REEVES
1976   *Arroyos and Environmental Change in the American Southwest.* Oxford: Clarendon Press.

CRAIG, DOUGLAS B., AND HENRY D. WALLACE
1987   Prehistoric Settlement in the Cañada del Oro Valley, Arizona: The Rancho Vistoso Survey Project. *Institute for American Research Anthropological Papers* 8. Tucson: Institute for American Research.

CROSSWHITE, FRANK S.
1980   The Annual Saguaro Harvest and Crop Cycle of the Papago, with Reference to Ecology and Symbolism. *Desert Plants* 2: 4–61.
1981   Desert Plants, Habitat, and Agriculture in Relation to the Major Patterns of Cultural Differentiation in O'odham People of the Sonoran Desert. *Desert Plants* 3: 47–76.

CROWN, PATRICIA L.
1987   Classic Period Hohokam Settlement and Land Use in the Casa Grande Ruin Area, Arizona. *Journal of Field Archaeology* 14(2): 147–162.

CURTIN, LEONORA
1981   *By the Prophet of the Earth: Ethnobotany of the Pima.* Tucson: University of Arizona Press.

CUSHING, FRANK H.
1920   Zuni Breadstuff. *Indian Notes and Monographs* 8. New York: Museum of the American Indian, Heye Foundation.

CZAPLICKI, JON S. (Compiler)
1984   A Class III Survey of the Tucson Aqueduct Phase A Corridor, Central Arizona Project: An Intensive Archaeological Survey in the Lower Santa Cruz River

Basin, Picacho Reservoir to Rillito, Arizona. *Arizona State Museum Archaeological Series* 165. Tucson: Arizona State Museum, University of Arizona.

CZAPLICKI, JON S., AND JOHN C. RAVESLOOT
1988   Hohokam Archaeology Along Phase B of the Tucson Aqueduct Central Arizona Project. *Arizona State Museum Archaeological Series* 178(2). Tucson: Arizona State Museum, University of Arizona.
1989   Excavations at Hawkes Nest (AZ AA:12:484). In "Hohokam Archaeology Along Phase B of the Tucson Aqueduct Central Arizona Project, Small and Specialized Reports," edited by Jon S. Czaplicki and John C. Ravesloot. *Arizona State Museum Archaeological Series* 178(4): 1–136. Tucson: Arizona State Museum, University of Arizona.

DART, ALLEN
1986   Archaeological Investigations at La Paloma: Archaic and Hohokam Occupations at Three Sites in the Northeastern Tucson Basin. *Institute for American Research Anthropological Papers* 4. Tucson: Institute for American Research.

DEAN, JEFFREY S.
1991   Thoughts on Hohokam Chronology. In *Exploring the Hohokam: Prehistoric Desert Peoples of the American Southwest*, edited by George J. Gumerman, pp. 61–150. Albuquerque: University of New Mexico Press.

DEBOWSKI, SHARON S., ANIQUE GEORGE, RICHARD GODDARD, AND DEBORAH MULLON
1976   An Archaeological Survey of the Buttes Reservoir. *Arizona State Museum Archaeological Series* 93. Tucson: Arizona State Museum, University of Arizona.

DOELLE, WILLIAM H.
1980   *Past Adaptive Patterns in Western Papagueria: An Archaeological Study of Nonriverine Resource Use.* Doctoral dissertation, University of Arizona, Tucson. Ann Arbor: University Microfilms.
1985a   Excavations at the Valencia Site: A Preclassic Hohokam Village in the Southern Tucson Basin. *Institute for American Research Anthropological Papers* 3. Tucson: Institute for American Research.
1985b   The Southern Tucson Basin Rillito-Rincon Subsistence, Settlement, and Community Structure. In "Proceedings of the 1983 Hohokam Symposium, Part I," edited by Alfred E. Dittert, Jr., and Donald E. Dove. *Arizona Archaeological Society Occasional Papers* 2: 183–198. Phoenix: Arizona Archaeological Society.

DOELLE, WILLIAM H., FREDERICK W. HUNTINGTON, AND HENRY D. WALLACE
1987   Rincon Phase Reorganization in the Tucson Basin. In *The Hohokam Village: Site Structure and Organization*, edited by David E. Doyel, pp. 71–96. Glenwood Springs, Colorado: Southwestern and Rocky Mountain Division of the American Association for the Advancement of Science.

DOOLITTLE, WILLIAM E.
1984   Agricultural Change as an Incremental Process. *An-*

nals of the Association of American Geographers 74: 124-137.
1988   Prehispanic Occupance in the Valley of Sonora, Mexico. *Anthropological Papers of The University of Arizona* 48. Tucson: University of Arizona Press.

DOWNUM, CHRISTIAN E.
1986   The Occupational Use of Hill Space in the Tucson Basin: Evidence from Linda Vista Hill. *The Kiva* 51(4): 219-232.
1991   The Los Robles Survey: Archaeological Investigations of the Lower Santa Cruz Basin, from Marana to Red Rock, Arizona. MS on file, Arizona State Museum Library, University of Arizona, Tucson.

DOWNUM, CHRISTIAN E., JOHN E. DOUGLAS, AND DOUGLAS B. CRAIG
1985   Community Structure and Agricultural Strategies at Cerro Prieto (AZ AA:7:11). In "Proceedings of the 1983 Hohokam Symposium, Part II," edited by Alfred E. Dittert, Jr., and Donald E. Dove. *Arizona Archaeological Society Occasional Papers* 2: 545–556. Phoenix: Arizona Archaeological Society.

DOYEL, DAVID E.
1974   Excavations in the Escalante Ruin Group, Southern Arizona. *Arizona State Museum Archaeological Series* 37. Tucson: Arizona State Museum, University of Arizona.
1977   Rillito and Rincon Period Settlement Systems in the Middle Santa Cruz River Valley: Alternative Models. *The Kiva* 43(2): 93–110.
1980   Hohokam Social Organization and the Sedentary to Classic Transition. In "Current Issues in Hohokam Prehistory, Proceedings of a Symposium," edited by David E. Doyel and Fred T. Plog. *Arizona State University Anthropological Research Papers* 23: 23–40. Tempe: Department of Anthropology, Arizona State University.
1984   Sedentary Period Hohokam Paleo-economy in the New River Drainage, Central Arizona. In "Prehistoric Agricultural Strategies in the Southwest," edited by Suzanne K. Fish and Paul R. Fish. *Arizona State University Anthropological Research Papers* 33: 35–52. Tempe: Department of Anthropology, Arizona State University.
1991   Hohokam Cultural Evolution in the Phoenix Basin. In *Exploring the Hohokam: Prehistoric Desert Peoples of the Southwest*, edited by George J. Gumerman, pp. 133–161. Albuquerque: University of New Mexico Press.

ELSON, MARK D., AND WILLIAM H. DOELLE
1987   Archaeological Assessment of the Mission Road Extension: Testing at AZ BB:13:6 (ASM). *Institute for American Research Technical Report* 87–6. Tucson: Institute for American Research.

EVENARI, MICHAEL, LESLIE SHANAN, AND NAPHTALI TADMOR
1971   *The Negev: The Challenge of a Desert.* Cambridge: Harvard University Press.

FAO/WHO
1973   Energy and Protein Requirement: Report of a FAO/ WHO Ad Hoc Expert Committee. *World Health Organization Technical Report Series* 522. New York: World Health Organization, United Nations.

FELGER, RICHARD S., AND MARY B. MOSER
1970   Seri Use of Agave (Century Plant). *The Kiva* 35(4): 159–167.
1971   Seri Use of Mesquite. *The Kiva* 37(1): 53–60.
1976   Seri Indian Food Plants: Desert Subsistence without Agriculture. *Ecology, Food, and Nutrition* 5: 13–27.
1985   *People of the Desert and Sea: Ethnobotany of the Seri Indians.* Tucson: University of Arizona Press.

FERG, ALAN
1986   Hohokam T-shaped Stones. Paper presented at the Second Tucson Basin Conference, Tucson.

FEWKES, J. WALTER
1912   Casa Grande, Arizona. *Twenty-Eighth Report of the Bureau of American Ethnology, Bulletin* 51. Washington.

FIELD, JOHN J.
1985   Depositional Facies and Hohokam Settlement Patterns on Holocene Alluvial Fans, Northern Tucson Basin, Arizona. MS, Master's thesis, Department of Geosciences, University of Arizona, Tucson.

FISH, PAUL R.
1967   Gila Dunes: A Chiricahua Stage Cochise Site near Florence, Arizona. MS, Department of Anthropology, Arizona State University, Tempe.
1989   The Hohokam: 1000 Years of Prehistory in the Sonoran Desert. In *Dynamics of Southwestern Prehistory*, edited by Linda S. Cordell and George J. Gumerman, pp. 19–63. Washington: Smithsonian Institution Press.

FISH, PAUL R., AND SUZANNE K. FISH
1984   Agricultural Maximization in the Sacred Mountain Basin. In "Prehistoric Agricultural Strategies in the Southwest," edited by Suzanne K. Fish and Paul R. Fish. *Arizona State University Anthropological Research Papers* 33: 147–160. Tempe: Department of Anthropology, Arizona State University.
1991   Hohokam Social Organization. In *Changing Views of the Hohokam*, edited by George J. Gumerman, pp. 84–101. Albuquerque: University of New Mexico Press.

FISH, PAUL R., SUZANNE K. FISH, AND JOHN H. MADSEN
1984   Northern Tucson Basin Survey: Research Summary and Recommendations for the Marana Complex. In "A Supplemental Class III Archaeological Survey of the Phase A, Reach 3 Corridor, Tucson Aqueduct, Central Arizona Project," by Jon S. Czaplicki and Adrianne G. Rankin. *Arizona State Museum Archaeological Series* 165 (Supplement): 83–89. Tucson: Arizona State Museum, University of Arizona.
1991   (Editors) The Northern Tucson Basin Survey: Research Directions and Background Studies. MS on file, Arizona State Museum Library, University of Arizona, Tucson.

FISH, PAUL R., SUZANNE K. FISH, AUSTIN LONG, AND CHARLES H. MIKSICEK
1986   Early Corn Remains from Tumamoc Hill, Southern Arizona. *American Antiquity* 51(3): 563–572.

FISH, SUZANNE K.
1984a   Agriculture and Subsistence Implications of the Salt-Gila Aqueduct Project Pollen Analysis. In "Hohokam Archaeology Along the Salt-Gila Aqueduct, Central Arizona Project, Environment and Subsistence," edited by Lynn S. Teague and Patricia L. Crown. *Arizona State Museum Archaeological Series* 150(7): 111–138. Tucson: Arizona State Museum, University of Arizona.
1984b   The Modified Environment of the Salt-Gila Aqueduct Sites: A Palynological Perspective. In "Hohokam Archaeology along the Salt-Gila Aqueduct, Central Arizona Project, Environmental and Subsistence," edited by Lynn S. Teague and Patricia L. Crown. *Arizona State Museum Archaeological Series* 150(7): 39–51. Tucson: Arizona State Museum, University of Arizona.
1985   Prehistoric Disturbance Floras of the Lower Sonoran Desert and their Implications. In "Late Quaternary Vegetation and Climates of the American Southwest," edited by B. Jacobs, P. Fall, and O. Davis, pp. 77–78. *American Association of Stratigraphic Palynologists Contribution Series* 16.
1987a   An Evaluation of Subsistence and Specialization at the Marana Sites. In "Studies in the Hohokam Community of Marana," edited by Glen E. Rice. *Arizona State University Anthropological Field Studies* 15: 235–248. Tempe: Department of Anthropology, Arizona State University.
1987b   Marana Sites Pollen Analysis. In "Studies in the Hohokam Community of Marana," edited by Glen E. Rice. *Arizona State University Anthropological Field Studies* 15: 161–170. Tempe: Department of Anthropology, Arizona State University.
1988   Environment and Subsistence: The Pollen Evidence. In "Recent Research on Tucson Basin Prehistory," edited by William H. Doelle and Paul R. Fish. *Institute for American Research Anthropological Papers* 10: 31–38. Tucson: Institute for American Research.
1989   Grand Canal Ruins Pollen Results. In "Archaeological Investigations at the Grand Canal Ruins: A Classic Period Site in Phoenix, Arizona," edited by Douglas Mitchell. *Soil Systems Publications in Archaeology* 12: 559–579. Phoenix: Soil Systems.

FISH, SUZANNE K., AND MARCIA DONALDSON
1991   Production and Consumption in the Archaeological Record: A Hohokam Example. *Kiva* 56(3): 255–275.

FISH, SUZANNE K., AND PAUL R. FISH
1990   An Archaeological Assessment of Ecosystem in the Tucson Basin of Southern Arizona. In *The Ecosystem Concept in Anthropology*, edited by Emilio Moran, pp. 159–190. Ann Arbor: University of Michigan Press.

1991 Comparative Aspects of Paradigms for the Neolithic Transition in the Levant and the American Southwest. In *Perspectives on the Past: Paradigmatic Biases in Hunter-Gatherer Research*, edited by Geoffrey A. Clark, pp. 396–410. Philadelphia: University of Pennsylvania Press.

FISH, SUZANNE K., AND STEPHEN A. KOWALEWSKI (Editors)
1990 *The Archaeology of Regions: The Case for Full-Coverage Survey.* Washington: Smithsonian Institution Press.

FISH, SUZANNE K., AND GARY P. NABHAN
1991 Deserts as Context: The Hohokam Environment. In *Changing Views of the Hohokam*, edited by George J. Gumerman, pp. 35–54. Albuquerque: University of New Mexico Press.

FISH, SUZANNE K., PAUL R. FISH, AND CHRISTIAN E. DOWNUM
1984 Terraces and Hohokam Agricultural Production in the Tucson Basin, Arizona. In "Prehistoric Agricultural Strategies in the Southwest," edited by Suzanne K. Fish and Paul R. Fish. *Arizona State University Anthropological Research Papers* 33: 55–72. Tempe: Department of Anthropology, Arizona State University.

FISH, SUZANNE K., PAUL R. FISH, AND JOHN H. MADSEN
1985 A Preliminary Analysis of Hohokam Settlement Pattern and Agriculture in the Northern Tucson Basin. In "Proceedings of the 1983 Hohokam Symposium, Part I," edited by Alfred E. Dittert, Jr., and Donald E. Dove. *Arizona Archaeological Society Occasional Papers* 2: 75–106. Phoenix: Arizona Archaeological Society.
1989 Classic Period Hohokam Community Integration in the Tucson Basin. In *The Sociopolitical Structure of Prehistoric Southwestern Societies*, edited by Steadman Upham and Kent G. Lightfoot, pp. 237–267. Boulder: Westview Press.
1990a Analyzing Regional Agriculture: A Hohokam Example. In *The Archaeology of Regions: The Case for Full-Coverage Survey*, edited by Suzanne K. Fish and Stephen A. Kowalewski, pp. 189–218. Washington: Smithsonian Institution Press.
1990b Sedentism and Settlement Mobility in the Tucson Basin prior to A.D. 1000. In *Perspectives on Southwestern Prehistory*, edited by Paul E. Minnis and Charles L. Redman, pp. 76–91. Boulder: Westview Press.

FISH, SUZANNE K., PAUL R. FISH, CHARLES H. MIKSICEK, AND JOHN H. MADSEN
1985 Prehistoric Agave Cultivation in Southern Arizona. *Desert Plants* 7(2): 107–112.

FLANNERY, KENT
1968 Archaeological Systems Theory and Early Mesoamerica. In *Anthropological Archaeology in the Americas*, edited by Betty Meggers, pp. 67–87. Washington: Anthropological Society of Washington.

FONTANA, BERNARD L.
1983a Pima and Papago Introduction. In *Handbook of North American Indians, Southwest*, Vol. 10, edited by Alfonso A. Ortiz, pp. 125–136. Washington: Smithsonian Institution.
1983b History of the Papago. In *Handbook of North American Indians, Southwest*, Vol. 10, edited by Alfonso A. Ortiz, pp. 137–148. Washington: Smithsonian Institution.

FORD, RICHARD I.
1972 An Ecological Perspective on the Eastern Pueblos. In *New Perspectives on the Pueblos*, edited by Alfonso A. Ortiz, pp. 1–21. Albuquerque: University of New Mexico Press.
1981 Gardening and Farming Before A.D. 1000: Patterns of Prehistoric Cultivation North of Mexico. *Journal of Ethnobiology* 1(1): 6–27.

FORDE, C. DARYLL
1949 *Habitat, Economy and Society: A Geographical Introduction to Ethnology.* New York: E. P. Dutton.

FREEMAN, LESLIE G.
1968 A Theoretical Framework for Interpreting Archaeological Materials. In *Man the Hunter*, edited by Richard B. Lee and Irven DeVore, pp. 262–267. Chicago: Aldine.

GASSER, ROBERT E.
1988a Casa Buena Flotation Analysis. In "Excavations at Casa Buena: Changing Hohokam Land Use along the Squaw Peak Parkway," edited by J. Howard. *Soil Systems Publications in Archaeology* 11: 561–586. Phoenix: Soil Systems.
1988b Flotation Studies. In "Hohokam Settlement along the Slopes of the Picacho Mountains: Environment and Subsistence," edited by Donald Weaver. *Museum of Northern Arizona Research Papers* 35: 30–142. Flagstaff: Museum of Northern Arizona.

GASSER, ROBERT E., AND CHARLES H. MIKSICEK
1985 The Specialists: A Reappraisal of Hohokam Exchange and the Archaeobotanical Record. In "Proceedings of the 1983 Hohokam Symposium, Part II," edited by Alfred E. Dittert, Jr., and Donald E. Dove. *Arizona Archaeological Society Occasional Papers* 2: 483–498. Phoenix: Arizona Archaeological Society.

GENTRY, HOWARD S.
1972 The Agave Family in Sonora. *U.S. Department of Agriculture Handbook* 399. Washington.
1982 *Agaves of Continental North America.* Tucson: University of Arizona Press.

GILMAN, PATRICIA A.
1987 Architecture as Artifact: Pit Structures and Pueblos in the American Southwest. *American Antiquity* 52(3): 538–564.

GOODYEAR, ALBERT C., III
1975 Hecla II and III: An Interpretive Study of Archaeological Remains from the Lakeshore Project, Papago Indian Reservation, South-Central, Arizona. *Arizona State University Anthropological Research Papers* 9. Tempe: Department of Anthropology, Arizona State University.

GRAYBILL, DONALD A.
1989 The Reconstruction of Prehistoric Salt River Streamflow. In "The 1982–1984 Excavations at Las Colinas: Environment and Subsistence," by Donald A. Graybill, David A. Gregory, Fred L. Nials, Suzanne K. Fish, Robert E. Gasser, Charles H. Miksicek, and Christine R. Szuter. *Arizona State Museum Archaeological Series* 162: 25–38. Tucson: Arizona State Museum, University of Arizona.

GREBINGER, PAUL F.
1971 *Hohokam Cultural Development in the Middle Santa Cruz River Valley, Arizona*. Doctoral dissertation, University of Arizona, Tucson. Ann Arbor: University Microfilms.

GREEN, CHRISTINE R., AND WILLIAM D. SELLERS
1964 *Arizona Climate*. Tucson: University of Arizona Press.

GREGORY, DAVID A.
1987 The Morphology of Platform Mounds and the Structure of Classic Hohokam Sites. In *The Hohokam Village: Site Structure and Organization*, edited by David E. Doyel, pp. 183–210. Glenwood Springs, Colorado: Southwestern and Rocky Mountain Division of the American Association for the Advancement of Science.
1991 Form and Variation in Hohokam Regional Settlement Patterns. In *Chaco and Hohokam: Prehistoric Regional Systems in the American Southwest*, edited by Patricia L. Crown and W. James Judge, pp. 159–194. Santa Fe: School of American Research Press.

GREGORY, DAVID A., AND FRED L. NIALS
1985 Observations Concerning the Distribution of Classic Period Hohokam Platform Mounds. In "Proceedings of the 1983 Hohokam Symposium, Part I," edited by Alfred E. Dittert, Jr., and Donald E. Dove. *Arizona Archaeological Society Occasional Papers* 2: 373–388. Phoenix: Arizona Archaeological Society.

GUMERMAN, GEORGE J.
1969 *Archaeology of the Hopi Buttes District, Arizona*. Doctoral dissertation, University of Arizona, Tucson. Ann Arbor: University Microfilms.

GUMERMAN, GEORGE J., AND R. ROY JOHNSON
1971 Prehistoric Human Population Distribution in a Biological Transition Zone. In "The Distribution of Prehistoric Population Aggregates," edited by George J. Gumerman, pp. 83–101. *Prescott College Anthropological Reports* 1. Prescott: Prescott College.

HARD, ROBERT
1990 Agricultural Dependence in the Mountain Mogollon. In *Perspectives on Southwestern Prehistory*, edited by Paul E. Minnis and Charles L. Redman, pp. 135–149. Boulder: Westview Press.

HASTINGS, JAMES R., AND RAYMOND M. TURNER
1965 *The Changing Mile: An Ecological Study of Vegetation Change with Time in the Lower Mile of an Arid and Semi-arid Region*. Tucson: University of Arizona Press, Tucson.

HAURY, EMIL W.
1945 The Excavation of Los Muertos and Neighboring Ruins in the Salt River Valley, Southern Arizona. *Papers of the Peabody Museum of American Archaeology and Ethnology* 24(1). Cambridge: Harvard University.
1950 *The Stratigraphy and Archaeology of Ventana Cave, Arizona*. Tucson: University of Arizona Press and Albuquerque: University of New Mexico Press.
1976 *The Hohokam: Desert Farmers and Craftsmen*. Tucson: University of Arizona Press.

HAYDEN, JULIAN D.
1957 Excavations, 1940, at University Indian Ruin. *Southwestern Monuments Association Technical Series* 5. Globe, Arizona: Southwestern Monuments Association.

HEMMINGS, THOMAS, M. D. ROBINSON, AND R. N. ROGERS
1968 Field Report on the Pantano Site (AZ EE:2:50). MS on file, Arizona State Museum Library, University of Arizona, Tucson.

HENDERSON, T. KATHLEEN
1987a Field Investigations at the Marana Community Complex. *Arizona State University Anthropological Field Studies* 14. Tempe: Department of Anthropology, Arizona State University.
1987b Ceramics, Dates, and the Growth of the Marana Community. In "Studies in the Hohokam Community of Marana," edited by Glen E. Rice. *Arizona State University Anthropological Field Studies* 15: 49–78. Tempe: Department of Anthropology, Arizona State University.

HESTER, THOMAS RAY, AND ROBERT F. HEIZER
1972 Problems in the Functional Interpretation of Artifacts: Scraper Planes from Mitla and Yagul, Oaxaca. *University of California Archaeological Facility Papers* 14: 109–110. Los Angeles: Department of Anthropology, University of California.

HEVLY, RICHARD H., PETER J. MEHRINGER, JR., AND HARRISON G. YOCUM
1965 Studies of the Modern Pollen Rain in the Sonoran Desert. *Journal of the Arizona Academy of Science* 3(3): 123–135.

HEWITT, JAMES M., AND DAVID STEPHEN
1981 Archaeological Investigations in the Tortolita Mountains Region, Southern Arizona. *Archaeological Field Report* 10. Tucson: Pima Community College.

HODGSON, WENDY, GARY P. NABHAN, AND LIZ ECKER
1989 Conserving Rediscovered Agave Cultivars. *Agave: Quarterly Magazine of the Desert Botanical Garden* 3: 9–11.

HOOKE, R. L. B.
1967 Processes on Arid-region Alluvial Fans. *Journal of Geology* 75(4): 438–460.

HOWARD, JERRY
1987 The Lehi Canal System: Organization of a Classic Period Community. In *The Hohokam Village: Site Structure and Organization*, edited by David E. Doyel, pp. 211–222. Glenwood Springs, Colorado:

Southwestern and Rocky Mountain Division of the American Association for the Advancement of Science.

HUCKELL, BRUCE B.

1987   Agriculture and Late Archaic Settlements in the River Valleys of Southeastern Arizona. Paper presented at the Third Hohokam Symposium: The Archaic-Pioneer Transition. Arizona State University, Tempe.

1988   Late Archaic Archaeology of the Tucson Basin: A Status Report. In "Recent Research on Tucson Basin Prehistory," edited by William H. Doelle and Paul R. Fish. *Institute for American Research Anthropological Papers* 10: 57–80. Tucson: Institute for American Research.

1990   Late Preceramic Farmer-Foragers in Southeastern Arizona: A Cultural and Ecological Consideration of the Spread of Agriculture into the Arid Southwestern United States. MS, Doctoral dissertation, Arid Lands Resource Sciences, University of Arizona, Tucson.

HUCKELL, BRUCE B., MARTYN D. TAGG, AND LISA W. HUCKELL

1987   The Corona de Tucson Project: Prehistoric Use of a Bajada Environment. *Arizona State Museum Archaeological Series* 174. Tucson: Arizona State Museum, University of Arizona.

IRWIN-WILLIAMS, CYNTHIA

1986   Prehistoric Water-harvesting Techniques in the Northern Great Basin. Paper presented at the annual meeting of the Society for American Archaeology, New Orleans.

JAMES, STEVEN

1987   Hohokam Patterns of Faunal Exploitation at Muchas Casas. In "Studies in the Hohokam Community of Marana," edited by Glen E. Rice. *Arizona State University Anthropological Field Studies* 15: 171–196. Tempe: Department of Anthropology, Arizona State University.

JOHNSON, GREGORY A.

1977   Aspects of Regional Analysis in Archaeology. *Annual Review of Anthropology* 6: 479–508.

JOHNSON, KIRSTEN

1977   Disintegration of a Traditional Resource Use Complex: The Otomi of the Mezquital Valley, Hidalgo, Mexico. *Economic Geography* 53(2): 364–367.

KELLY, ISABEL T.

1978   The Hodges Ruin: A Hohokam Community in the Tucson Basin. *Anthropological Papers of The University of Arizona* 30. Tucson: University of Arizona Press.

KINKADE, GAY M., AND GORDON L. FRITZ

1975   The Tucson Sewage Project: Studies of Two Archaeological Sites in the Tucson Basin. *Arizona State Museum Archaeological Series* 64. Tucson: Arizona State Museum, University of Arizona.

KISSELBERG, JO ANN E.

1987   Economic Specialization in the Community System at Marana. In "Studies in the Hohokam Community of Marana," edited by Glen E. Rice. *Arizona State University Anthropological Field Studies* 15: 143–160. Tempe: Department of Anthropology, Arizona State University.

KOWALEWSKI, STEPHEN A., RICHARD E. BLANTON, GARY M. FEINMAN, AND LAURA FINSTEN

1983   Boundaries, Scale, and Internal Organization. *Journal of Anthropological Archaeology* 2: 32–56.

KOWTA, MAKOTO

1969   The Sayles Complex: A Late Millingstone Assemblage from Cajon Pass and the Ecological Implications of Its Scraper Planes. *University of California Publications in Anthropology* 6. Berkeley: University of California.

LANGE, RICHARD C., AND WILLIAM L. DEAVER

1989   The 1979–1983 Testing at Los Morteros (AZ AA: 12:57 ASM): A Large Hohokam Village Site in the Tucson Basin. *Arizona State Museum Archaeological Series* 177. Tucson: Arizona State Museum, University of Arizona.

LIGHTFOOT, KENT G., AND FRED T. PLOG

1984   Intensification Along the North Side of the Mogollon Rim. In "Prehistoric Agricultural Strategies in the Southwest," edited by Suzanne K. Fish and Paul R. Fish. *Arizona State University Anthropological Research Papers* 33: 179–195. Tempe: Department of Anthropology, Arizona State University.

LOMBARD, JAMES, AND PAUL R. FISH

1991   Sand Temper Composition of Pioneer Period Hohokam Ceramics. In "The Northern Tucson Basin Survey: Research Directions and Background Studies," edited by Paul R. Fish, Suzanne K. Fish, and John H. Madsen. MS on file, Arizona State Museum Library, University of Arizona, Tucson.

MABRY, JONATHAN B.

1990   A Late Archaic Occupation at AZ AA:12:105 (ASM). *Center for Desert Archaeology Technical Report* 90-6. Tucson: Desert Archaeology.

MARTIN, PAUL S., AND JOHN B. RINALDO

1950   Sites of the Reserve Phase, Pine Lawn Valley, Western New Mexico. *Fieldiana: Anthropology* 38(3). Chicago: Field Museum of Natural History.

MASSE, W. BRUCE

1979   An Intensive Survey of Prehistoric Dry Farming Systems near Tumamoc Hill in Tucson, Arizona. *The Kiva* 45(1–2): 141–186.

1981   Prehistoric Irrigation Systems in the Salt River Valley, Arizona. *Science* 214: 408–415.

1987   (Editor) Archaeological Investigations of Portions of the Las Acequias-Los Muertos Irrigation System. *Arizona State Museum Archaeological Series* 176. Tucson: Arizona State Museum, University of Arizona.

1991   The Hohokam Quest for Sufficiency and Civilization in the Sonoran Desert. In *Chaco and Hohokam: Prehistoric Regional Systems in the American Southwest*, edited by Patricia L. Crown and W. James Judge, pp. 195–224. Santa Fe: School of American Research Press.

MATSON, R. G., AND BRIAN CHISHOLM
1991   Basketmaker II Subsistence: Carbon Isotopes and Other Dietary Indicators from Cedar Mesa, Utah. *American Antiquity* 56(3): 444–459.

MIKSICEK, CHARLES H.
1984   Historic Desertification, Prehistoric Vegetation Change, and Hohokam Subsistence in the Salt-Gila Basin. In "Hohokam Archaeology along the Salt-Gila Aqueduct, Central Arizona Project, Environment and Subsistence," edited by Lynn S. Teague and Patricia L. Crown. *Arizona State Museum Archaeological Series* 150(7): 53–80. Tucson: Arizona State Museum, University of Arizona.
1987   Late Sedentary and Early Classic Period Hohokam Agriculture: Plant Remains from the Marana Community Complex. In "Studies in the Hohokam Community of Marana," edited by Glen E. Rice. *Arizona State University Anthropological Field Studies* 15: 197–216. Tempe: Department of Anthropology, Arizona State University.
1988   Rethinking Hohokam Paleoethnobotanical Assemblages: A Progress Report for the Tucson Basin. In "Recent Research on Tucson Basin Prehistory," edited by William H. Doelle and Paul R. Fish. *Institute for American Research Anthropological Papers* 10: 47–56. Tucson: Institute for American Research.

MINNIS, PAUL E.
1985   Domesticating People and Plants in the Greater Southwest. In "Prehistoric Food Production in North America," edited by Richard I. Ford. *Museum of Anthropology, Anthropological Papers* 75: 309–339. Ann Arbor: University of Michigan.
1989   Prehistoric Diet in the Northern Southwest: Macroplant Remains from Four Corners Feces. *American Antiquity* 54(3): 543–563.

MINNIS, PAUL E., AND STEPHEN E. PLOG
1976   A Study of the Site Specific Distribution of *Agave parryi* in East Central Arizona. *The Kiva* 41(3–4): 299–308.

MITCHELL, DOUGLAS R.
1988   La Lomita Pequeña: Relationships between Plant Resource Variability and Settlement Patterns in the Phoenix Basin. *Kiva* 54(2): 127–146.

MUELLER-WILLE, CATHERINE, AND D. BRUCE DICKSON
1991   An Examination of Some Models of Late Pleistocene Society in Southwestern Europe. In *Perspectives on the Past: Theoretical Biases in Mediterranean Hunter-Gatherer Research*, edited by Geoffrey A. Clark, pp. 23–55. Philadelphia: University of Pennsylvania.

NABHAN, GARY P.
1983   Papago Fields: Arid Lands Ethnobotany and Agricultural Ecology. MS, Doctoral dissertation, Arid Lands Resource Sciences, University of Arizona, Tucson.
1985   *Gathering the Desert.* Tucson: University of Arizona Press.
1986   Ak-chin "Arroyo Mouth" and the Environmental Setting of the Papago Indian Fields in the Sonoran Desert. *Applied Geography* 6(2): 61–75.

NABHAN, GARY P., AND THOMAS E. SHERIDAN
1977   Living Fence-rows of the Rio San Miguel, Sonora, Mexico: Traditional Technology for Floodplain Management. *Human Ecology* 5(2): 97–110.

NELSON, BEN A.
1990   Comments: Southwestern Sedentism Reconsidered. In *Perspectives on Southwestern Prehistory*, edited by Paul E. Minnis and Charles L. Redman, pp. 157–166. Boulder: Westview Press.

NELSON, RICHARD S.
1981   *The Role of the Pochteca System in Hohokam Exchange.* Doctoral dissertation, New York University, New York. Ann Arbor: University Microfilms.

NIALS, FRED L., DAVID A. GREGORY, AND DONALD A. GRAYBILL
1989   Salt River Streamflow and Hohokam Irrigation Systems. In "The 1982–1984 Excavations at Las Colinas: Environment and Subsistence," by Donald A. Graybill, David A. Gregory, Fred L. Nials, Suzanne K. Fish, Robert E. Gasser, Charles H. Miksicek, and Christine R. Szuter. *Arizona State Museum Archaeological Series* 162: 59–78. Tucson: Arizona State Museum, University of Arizona.

NICHOLAS, LINDA, AND GARY M. FEINMAN
1989   A Regional Perspective on Hohokam Irrigation in the Lower Salt River Valley, Arizona. In *The Sociopolitical Structure of Prehistoric Southwestern Societies*, edited by Steadman Upham, Kent G. Lightfoot, and Roberta Jewett, pp. 199–236. Boulder: Westview Press.

NICHOLAS, LINDA, AND JILL NEITZEL
1984   Canal Irrigation and Sociopolitical Organization in the Lower Salt River Valley: A Diachronic Analysis. In "Prehistoric Agricultural Strategies in the Southwest," edited by Suzanne K. Fish and Paul R. Fish. *Arizona State University Anthropological Research Papers* 33: 161–178. Tempe: Department of Anthropology, Arizona State University.

O'LAUGHLIN, THOMAS C.
1980   The Keystone Dam Site and Other Archaic and Formative Sites in Northwest El Paso, Texas. *Publications in Anthropology* 8. El Paso: El Paso Centennial Museum, University of Texas.

OSBORNE, CAROLYN M.
1965   The Preparation of Yucca Fibers: An Experimental Study. In "Contributions of the Wetherill Mesa Archeological Project," assembled by Douglas Osborne. *Society for American Archaeology Memoir* 19: 45–50.

PACKARD, F. A.
1974   *The Hydraulic Geometry of a Discontinuous Ephemeral Stream on a Bajada near Tucson, Arizona.* Doctoral dissertation, University of Arizona, Tucson. Ann Arbor: University Microfilms.

PARSONS, JEFFREY R., AND MARY PARSONS
1990   Maguey Utilization in Highland Central Mexico: An

Archaeological Ethnography. *Museum of Anthropology, Anthropological Papers* 82. Ann Arbor: Museum of Anthropology, University of Michigan.

PENNINGTON, CAMPBELL W.
1963 *The Tarahumar of Mexico: Their Environment and Material Culture.* Salt Lake City: University of Utah Press.

PEREZ DE RIBAS, ANDRES
1968 *My Life among the Savage Nations of New Spain.* Translated by Thomas Robertson. Los Angeles: Ward Ritchie Press.

PLOG, FRED T.
1980 Explaining Culture Change in the Hohokam Preclassic. In "Current Issues in Hohokam Prehistory: Proceedings of a Symposium," edited by David E. Doyel and Fred T. Plog. *Arizona State University Anthropological Research Papers* 23: 4–22. Tempe: Department of Anthropology, Arizona State University.

PRICE, BARBARA J.
1977 Shifts in Production and Organization: A Cluster Interaction Model. *Current Anthropology* 18(2): 209–223.

RAAB, L. MARK
1973 AZ AA:5:2, A Prehistoric Cactus Camp in Papagueria. *Journal of the Arizona Academy of Science* 8: 116–118.

RAHN, P.
1967 Sheetfloods, Stream Floods, and the Formation of Pediments. *Annals of the Association of American Geographers* 57: 593–604.

RAVESLOOT, JOHN C.
1987 Archaeology of the San Xavier Bridge Site (AZ BB:13:14), Tucson Basin, Southern Arizona. *Arizona State Museum Archaeological Series* 171. Tucson: Arizona State Museum, University of Arizona.

READING, H. G.
1978 *Sedimentary Environments and Facies.* Oxford, England: Blackwell Scientific.

REICHHARDT, KAREN
1991 Vegetation of the Northern Tucson and Picacho Basins. In "The Northern Tucson Basin Survey: Research Directions and Background Studies," edited by Paul R. Fish, Suzanne K. Fish, and John H. Madsen. MS on file, Arizona State Museum Library, University of Arizona, Tucson.

REICHHARDT, KAREN, AND GARY P. NABHAN
1982 Application of Remote Sensing in Evaluating Floodwater Farming on the Papago Reservation. MS, Office of Arid Land Studies, University of Arizona, Tucson.

RENFREW, COLIN
1986 *Peer Polity Interaction and Socio-Political Change.* Cambridge: Cambridge University Press.

RICE, GLEN E.
1980 An Analytical Overview of the Mogollon Tradition. In "Studies in the Prehistory of the Forestdale Region, Arizona." *Arizona State University Anthropological Field Studies* 1. Tempe: Department of Anthropology, Arizona State University.
1987a (Editor) Studies in the Hohokam Community of Marana. *Arizona State University Anthropological Field Studies* 15. Tempe: Department of Anthropology, Arizona State University.
1987b Working Hypotheses for the Study of Hohokam Community Complexes. In "Studies in the Hohokam Community of Marana," edited by Glen E. Rice. *Arizona State University Anthropological Field Studies* 15: 249–254. Tempe: Department of Anthropology, Arizona State University.
1987c The Marana Community Complex: A Twelfth Century Hohokam Chiefdom. In "Studies in the Hohokam Community of Marana," edited by Glen E. Rice. *Arizona State University Anthropological Field Studies* 15: 255–272. Tempe: Department of Anthropology, Arizona State University.

RICE, PRUDENCE M.
1987 *Pottery Analysis: A Sourcebook.* Chicago: University of Chicago Press.

ROGERS, MALCOM J.
1939 Early Lithic Industries of the Lower Basin of the Colorado River and Adjacent Desert Areas. *San Diego Museum Papers* 3. San Diego: San Diego Museum.

ROSKRUGE, GEORGE J.
1896a Township 12 South, Range 12 East, Gila and Salt River Meridian Ariz. Survey General's Office, Tucson, Arizona, November 28th, 1896.
1896b Township 11 South, Range 12 East Gila and Salt River Meridian Ariz. Survey General's Office, Tucson, Arizona, November 28th, 1896.

ROSS, WINIFRED
1944 The Present Day Dietary Habits of the Papago Indians. MS, Masters thesis, Department of Home Economics, University of Arizona, Tucson.

ROTH, BARBARA J.
1988 Recent Research on the Late Archaic Occupation of the Northern Tucson Basin. In "Recent Research on Tucson Basin Prehistory," edited by William H. Doelle and Paul R. Fish. *Institute for American Research Anthropological Papers* 10: 81–85. Tucson: Institute for American Research.
1989 *Late Archaic Settlement and Subsistence in the Tucson Basin.* Doctoral dissertation, Department of Anthropology, University of Arizona, Tucson. Ann Arbor: University Microfilms.

ROZEN, KENNETH C.
1984 Flaked Stone. In "Hohokam Habitation Sites in the Northern Santa Rita Mountains," by Alan Ferg, Kenneth C. Rozen, William L. Deaver, Martyn D. Tagg, David A. Phillips, Jr., and David A. Gregory. *Arizona State Museum Archaeological Series* 147(2, Part I): 421–604. Tucson: Arizona State Museum, University of Arizona.

SALLS, ROY
1985   The Scraper Plane: A Functional Interpretation. *Journal of Field Archaeology* 12(2): 99–106.
SANDERS, WILLIAM T., JEFFREY R. PARSONS, AND ROBERT S. SANTLEY
1979   *The Basin of Mexico: Ecological Processes in the Evolution of a Civilization.* New York: Academic Press.
SAYLES, EDWIN B., AND ERNST ANTEVS
1941   The Cochise Culture. *Medallion Papers* 29. Globe, Arizona: Gila Pueblo.
SCHROEDER, ALBERT H.
1940   A Stratigraphic Survey of Pre-Spanish Trash Mounds of the Salt River Valley, Arizona. Master's thesis, Department of Anthropology, University of Arizona, Tucson.
1960   The Hohokam, Sinagua and the Hakataya. *Society for American Archaeology Archives of Archaeology* 5.
1966   Unregulated Diffusion from Mexico into the Southwest prior to A.D. 700. *American Antiquity* 30(3): 297–309.
SCHUSTER, J. E., AND KEITH KATZER
1984   The Quaternary Geology of the Northern Tucson Basin, Arizona, and Its Archaeological Implications. MS, Master's thesis, Department of Geosciences, University of Arizona, Tucson.
SELLERS, WILLIAM D., RICHARD H. HILL, AND M. SANDERSON-RAE
1985   Arizona Climate: The First Hundred Years. MS on file, Institute of Atmospheric Physics, University of Arizona.
SHACKLEY, M. STEVEN
1983   Late Prehistoric Agave Resource Procurement and a Broad-Spectrum Subsistence Economy in the Mountain Springs Area, Western Imperial County, California. Paper presented at the Annual Meeting of the Society for California Archaeology, San Diego.
SIMMONS, ALAN H.
1982   (Assembler) Prehistoric Adaptive Strategies in the Chaco Canyon Region, Northwestern New Mexico. *Navajo Nation Papers in Anthropology* 9. Window Rock: Navajo Nation Cultural Resource Management Program.
1986   New Evidence for the Early Use of Cultigens in the American Southwest. *American Antiquity* 51(1): 73–89.
SKIBO, JAMES M.
1987   Fluvial Sherd Abrasion and the Interpretation of Surface Remains on Southwestern Bajadas. *North American Archaeologist* 8(2): 125–141.
SMITH, BRUCE
1989   Origins of Agriculture in Eastern North America. *Science* 246(4937): 1566–1570.
SMITH, C. E., JR.
1967   Plant remains. In *The Prehistory of the Tehuacan Valley,* Vol. 1, *Environment and Subsistence,* edited by Douglas S. Byers, pp. 220–255. Austin: University of Texas Press.

SPAULDING, W. GEOFFREY
1974   A Preliminary Statement on the Pollen Analysis from the Escalante Ruin Group. In "Excavations in the Escalante Ruin Group, Southern Arizona," by David E. Doyel. *Arizona State Museum Archaeological Series* 37: 262–268. Tucson: Arizona State Museum, University of Arizona.
STEPONAITIS, VINCAS P.
1981   Settlement Hierarchies and Political Complexity in Nonmarket Societies: The Formative Period in the Valley of Mexico. *American Anthropologist* 83(2): 320–363.
STEWARD, JULIAN H.
1938   Basin-Plateau Aboriginal Sociopolitical Groups. *Bureau of American Ethnology Bulletin* 120. Washington.
SULLIVAN, ALAN P., III
1983   Storage, Nonedible Resource Processing, and the Interpretation of Sherd and Lithic Scatters in the Sonoran Desert Lowlands. *Journal of Field Archaeology* 10(4): 309–325.
SULLIVAN, ALAN P., III, AND KENNETH C. ROZEN
1985   Debitage Analysis and Archaeological Interpretation. *American Antiquity* 50(4): 755–779.
SZUTER, CHRISTINE R.
1991   *Hunting by Horticulturalists in the American Southwest.* New York: Garland Publishing.
TANI, MASAKAZU, AND REGINA CHAPIN
1991   Descriptive Summaries of Sites Located During the Northern Tucson Basin Survey. MS, Arizona State Museum Library, University of Arizona, Tucson.
TURNER, RAYMOND M., AND DAVID E. BROWN
1982   Sonoran Desertscrub. *Desert Plants* 4(1–4): 181–221.
UNDERHILL, RUTH M.
1939   *Social Organization of the Papago Indians.* New York: Columbia University Press.
UPHAM, STEADMAN, AND GLEN E. RICE
1980   Up the Canal Without a Pattern: Modeling Hohokam Interaction and Exchange. In "Current Issues in Hohokam Prehistory: Proceedings of a Symposium," edited by David E. Doyel and Fred T. Plog. *Arizona State University Anthropological Research Papers* 23: 78–105. Tempe: Department of Anthropology, Arizona State University.
VAN DEVENDER, THOMAS R., AND W. GEOFFREY SPAULDING
1979   Development of Vegetation and Climate in the Southwestern U.S. *Science* 204(4415): 701–710.
WALLACE, HENRY D.
1983   The Mortars, Petroglyphs, and Trincheras on Rillito Peak. *The Kiva* 48(3): 137–246.
WALLACE, HENRY D., AND JAMES P. HOLMLUND
1984   The Classic Period in the Tucson Basin. *The Kiva* 49(3–4): 167–194.
WASLEY, WILLIAM W.
1980   The Classic Period Hohokam. (Edited and Introduced by David E. Doyel.) *The Kiva* 45(4): 337–352.

WASLEY, WILLIAM W., AND ALFRED E. JOHNSON
1965   Salvage Archaeology in Painted Rocks Reservoir, Western Arizona. *Anthropological Papers of The University of Arizona* 9. Tucson: University of Arizona Press.

WATERS, MICHAEL R.
1987   Holocene Alluvial Geology and Geoarchaeology of AZ BB:13:14 and the San Xavier Reach of the Santa Cruz River, Arizona. In "Archaeology of the San Xavier Bridge Site (AZ BB:13:14), Tucson Basin, Southern Arizona," edited by John C. Ravesloot. *Arizona State Museum Archaeological Series* 171: 39–60. Tucson: Arizona State Museum, University of Arizona.
1988   The Impact of Fluvial Processes and Landscape Evolution on Archaeological Sites and Settlement Patterns along the San Xavier Reach of the Santa Cruz River, Arizona. *Geoarchaeology* 3(3): 205–219.

WATERS, MICHAEL R., AND JOHN J. FIELD
1986   Geomorphic Analysis of Hohokam Settlement Patterns on Alluvial Fans along the Western Flank of the Tortolita Mountains, Arizona. *Geoarchaeology* 1(4): 329–345.

WEAVER, DONALD E., JR.
1972   A Cultural-Ecological Model for the Classic Hohokam Period in the Lower Salt River Valley, Arizona. *The Kiva* 38(1): 43–52.

WEST, ROBERT C.
1948   Cultural Geography of the Modern Tarascan Area. *Smithsonian Institution, Institute of Social Anthropology Publication* 7. Washington.
1968   Population Densities and Agricultural Practices in Precolumbian Mexico, with a Special Emphasis on Semi-terracing. *Proceedings of the 33rd International Congress of Americanists* 2: 361–369. Buenos Aires.

WHALEN, NORMAN M.
1971   *Cochise Culture Sites in the Central San Pedro Drainage, Arizona.* Doctoral dissertation, University of Arizona, Tucson. Ann Arbor: University Microfilms.

WILCOX, DAVID R.
1991   Hohokam Political Organization. In *Chaco and Hohokam: Prehistoric Regional Systems in the American Southwest*, edited by Patricia L. Crown and W. James Judge, pp. 253–275. Santa Fe: School of American Research Press.

WILCOX, DAVID R., AND CHARLES STERNBERG
1983   Hohokam Ballcourts and Their Interpretation. *Arizona State Museum Archaeological Series* 160. Tucson: Arizona State Museum, University of Arizona.

WILLS, WIRT H., III, AND BRUCE B. HUCKELL
In press   Economic Implications of Changing Land-use Patterns in the Late Archaic. In *The Structure and Evolution of Prehistoric Southwest Societies*, edited by George J. Gumerman. Santa Fe: School of American Research Press (1993).

WILSON, JOHN P.
1985   Early Piman Agriculture: A New Look. In "Southwestern Culture History: Collected Papers in Honor of Albert H. Schroeder," edited by Charles H. Lange. *The Archaeological Society of New Mexico* 10: 129–138. Santa Fe: Archaeological Society of New Mexico.

WINDMILLER, RIC C.
1973   The Late Cochise Culture in the Sulphur Spring Valley, Southeastern Arizona: Archaeology of the Fairchild Site. *The Kiva* 39(2): 131–169.

WITHERS, ARNOLD M.
1973   Excavations at Valshni Village. *The Arizona Archaeologist* 7. Phoenix: Arizona Archaeological Society.

WOOD, JON SCOTT, AND MARTIN E. MCALLISTER
1980   Foundation and Empire: The Colonization of the Northeastern Hohokam Periphery. In "Current Issues in Hohokam Prehistory: Proceedings of a Symposium," edited by David E. Doyel and Fred T. Plog. *Arizona State University Anthropological Research Papers* 23: 180–200. Tempe: Department of Anthropology, Arizona State University.
1984   Second Foundation: Settlement Patterns and Agriculture in the Northeastern Hohokam Periphery, Central Arizona. In "Prehistoric Agricultural Strategies in the Southwest," edited by Suzanne K. Fish and Paul R. Fish. *Arizona State University Anthropological Research Papers* 33: 271–289. Tempe: Department of Anthropology, Arizona State University.

WRIGHT, HENRY T.
1979   Archaeological Investigations in Northeastern Kuzestan, 1976. *University of Michigan Technical Reports* 10. Ann Arbor: Museum of Anthropology, University of Michigan.

WRIGHT, HENRY T., AND GREGORY A. JOHNSON
1975   Population, Exchange, and Early State Formation in Southwestern Iran. *American Anthropologist* 77(2): 267–289.

Index

Abandonment
    of the Dairy fan, 72
    of the Marana Community, 39–40
    regional, 40
Adobe architecture, 1, 27–31, 38, 39,
    100, 102
Agate, 37
Agave, xii, 31, 32, 34, 36, 47, 70–71,
    72–96, 104
    roasted, 74, 82, 86, 93
Agave fiber, 37, 73, 82, 83, 84, 86–87,
    96
Agave murpheyi, 73, 74, 83, 85
Agave parryi, 73
Aggregation. *See* Population densities
Agricultural intensification, 87, 100, 103,
    104
Agriculture, 1, 3, 5, 8, 10, 11–19, 20, 21,
    26, 31, 40, 41–52, 53–63. *See also* Ak
    chin farming; Canals; Floodwater
    farming; Irrigation; Rockpiles; Runoff
    cultivation; Terraces; Trincheras
Ak chin farming, 41, 49, 53–63
Alluvial fans, 3, 15, 16, 17, 18, 19, 31, 47,
    49–50, 53–63, 64, 65, 67, 72, 76
Amaranth, 68, 69, 70, 72
Andesite, 37
Apache Indians, 13, 93
Archaeological sites
    AZ AA:12:108, 78
    AZ AA:12:205, 88–96
    AZ AA:12:284, 16
    AZ AA:12:469, 80
    AZ AA:12:470, 79, 81, 95, 96
    AZ AA:18:486, 16, 18, 19
    See also Brady Wash platform mound;
    Casa Grande; Cerro Prieto Site; Con-
    tinental Ranch Site; Dairy Site;
    Hodges Site, Huntington Site; La
    Paloma Site; Las Colinas; Los
    Morteros Site; Los Ojitos Site; Los
    Robles Community and platform
    mound; Marana Community; Matty
    Canyon sites; McClellan Community
    and platform mound; Mesa Grande;
    Milagro Site; Pantano Site; Pueblo
    Grande Site; San Augustin Site; San
    Xavier Bridge Site; Snaketown; Solar
    Well Site; Tcacca platform mound;
    Tom Mix Community and platform
    mound; Tumamoc Hill sites; Valencia
    Road Site
Archaic
    Middle, 11
    Late, 1, 3, 8, 11–19, 20, 64, 68, 69, 72

Architecture, domestic, 34. *See* Adobe
    architecture; Cobbles, architectural
    use of; Compounds, at sites
Architecture, public, 1, 4, 5, 10, 20, 34,
    38, 40, 97, 98, 100, 103–104. *See also*
    Ballcourts; Kivas; Platform mounds.
Arizona poppy, 69
Arizona State Historic Preservation
    Office, xi–xii
Arizona State Land Department, xi–xiii
Arizona State Museum, 20, 94

Ballcourts, ballcourt communities, 1, 5, 7,
    9, 20, 21, 26, 34, 39–40, 97–98,
    100–101
Bajadas
    agriculture on, 31, 37, 44, 45, 47, 50,
        51, 53–63, 67, 69, 72, 73–87, 101
    settlement on, 3, 8, 11, 14, 16, 20, 21,
        24, 26, 27, 31, 38, 39, 44, 46, 50,
        64–72, 86
Beans, 73
    common, 47, 70, 71
    jack, 71, 72
    mesquite, 14
    tepary, 71, 72
Bighorn sheep, 37, 71-72
Bogard Wash, 9, 56
Bottle gourd, 70, 71
Bowls, pottery, 94
Brady Wash, 6, 9, 56
Brady Wash platform mound, 9
Braided channels, 44, 45
Brawley Wash, 6, 9
Bureau of Reclamation, xi–xii
Bursage, 2, 34, 69, 88

Cache, in pit, 37
Calcium oxalate crystals, 84
Cañada Agua, 44–46
Cañada del Oro phase, 3
Cañada del Oro Red-on-brown pottery,
    65, 68
Cañada del Oro Wash, 6, 9, 40
Canals, 1, 3–5, 20, 21, 27, 31, 34, 39,
    40–41, 42, 46, 47, 49, 50, 51, 72,
    97–105. *See also* Irrigation
Casa Grande, site of, 99–100, 102
Casa Grande Red-on-buff pottery, 24
Catalina Mountains, 6, 14
Catclaw, 46
Cattail, 69, 70
Censers, pottery, 1
Central sites, integrative function of, 5,
    20–40, 97–105

Ceramics. *See* Pottery
Cerro Prieto Site, 9, 37
Cerro Prieto washes and alluvial fans, 56,
    60
Checkdams, 31, 43, 47, 76–79, 81,
    85–86
Chenopods, 69–70
Chia, 70
Chiefdom, 39
Cholla, 14, 69–70, 88
Civano phase, 3
Clammy weed, 70
Classic period, xi, xii, 1, 20–40, 72, 86,
    87, 97–105
    Early Classic, 3, 8, 10, 20–40, 71,
        80–87, 97
    Late Classic, 3, 8, 10, 12–19, 24–25,
        34, 39–40, 97, 103–104
Clovis culture, evidence of, 11
Cobbles
    agricultural use of. *See* Rockpiles;
        Terraces
    architectural use of, 28, 31, 34, 38, 102
Cochie Wash, 44, 46
Colonial period, 3, 27
    Early Colonial, 3, 64, 65, 66, 67,
        68–72
Comals (griddles), 1
Common beans, 47, 70, 71
Communities
    definition of, 20–21
    Los Robles, 9, 10, 37, 44
    Marana, xi–xii, 8–10, 20–40, 56–57,
        76, 80–87, 97–105
    McClellan, 10, 103–104
Community exchange, 37. *See also* Long-
    distance exchange; Trade
Compositae, 69
Compounds, at sites, 1, 20, 27–30, 31,
    34, 38, 39, 100, 102
Continental Ranch Site, 18, 19
Coprolites, 17
Core area, of Hohokam, xi, 2–5, 19, 20,
    24, 40, 65, 97–104
Core-periphery dichotomy, of Hohokam
    tradition, 4, 19, 20, 24, 26, 40, 97–105
Corn, 14, 17, 19, 31, 44, 47, 64, 68–72,
    73, 81, 85
Cotton, 69–70, 85
Cottontail rabbit, 71, 72
Cottonwood Wash and alluvial fan, 22,
    31, 44–46, 56, 57, 60–62
Craft specialization, 37, 38, 87
Cremation, 65, 68, 69. *See also*
    Inhumations

Abstract

The prehistoric Hohokam Indians are best known for their massive canals in a core area surrounding Phoenix, Arizona. In other desert basins inhabited by the Hohokam, large-scale irrigation was not possible, nor did shared canal lines create a similar basis for common interests among sites that were integrated within units of settlement called "communities." This account of Classic period settlement in the Tucson Basin between A.D. 1100 and 1300 is the first comprehensive description of the organization of territory, subsistence, and society in a community of an outlying region.

Systematic examination of more than 700 square miles and full-coverage survey of extensive blocks provide a regional framework for the Marana Community in the northern Tucson Basin. Broad recovery of settlement pattern reveals in unique detail the developmental history of the Marana Community and its hierarchical structure about a central site with a platform mound. Two earlier communities centered on sites with ballcourts merge at the beginning of the Classic period to form a single entity covering 56 square miles across the basin width. A settlement hierarchy is defined by co-occurring attributes of site size, architectural styles, and ceramic consumption.

Remains of diverse agricultural technologies demonstrate the means for supporting Classic period populations of previously unrecognized size. The beginnings of zonal patterns of land use can be seen in settlements of Late Archaic cultivators. Riverine irrigation, floodwater farming on alluvial fans, and cobble features for concentrating runoff on gentle slopes were employed for agricultural production in a variety of topographic and hydrological settings.

Data from the Marana Community indicate an economic system that interlinked desert farmers through differentiated production and exchange. Extensive fields of rockpile features for the cultivation of agave on marginal land offer dramatic evidence of agricultural specialization. Full documentation of the importance of agave as a food and fiber crop among the Hohokam is a major contribution of Marana research to the ethnobotany of the Southwest.

Resumen

Los indios Hohokam prehistóricos son conocidos por sus grandes canales en el área nuclear alrededor de Phoenix, Arizona. En otras cuencas desérticas habitadas por los Hohokam no era posible practicar irrigación en gran escala. En ausencia de redes de canales, no existían bases de interés común que agruparan a los sitios. Estos se encontraban integrados en unidades de asentamiento denominadas "comunidades." El presente estudio del asentamiento durante el Período Clásico en la Cuenca de Tucson entre 1100 y 1300 d.C. es la primera descripción exhaustiva de la organización territorial, subsistencia, y sociedad en una comunidad de la región periférica.

El examen sistemático de más de 700 millas cuadradas y la prospección mediante cobertura total de extensos bloques ofrecen un marco regional para la Comunidad de Marana en el norte de la Cuenca de Tucson. El análisis de patrones de asentamiento revela con singular detalle el proceso de desarrollo de la Comunidad de Marana y de su estructura jerárquica organizada alreadedor de un sitio central con montículo-plataforma. Dos comunidades tempranas centradas en sitios con canchas de pelota se fusionaron a comienzos del Período Clásico para formar una sola entidad que se extendía por 56 millas a través del ancho de la cuenca. La jerarquía de asentamientos se define por la co-ocurrencia de atributos tales como tamaño de sitios, estilos arquitectónicos y consumo de cerámica.

Los restos de diversas técnicas agrícolas durante el Período Clásico ponen en evidencia la existencia de medios para sustentar poblaciones de una magnitud sin precedentes. El comienzo de patrones zonales de uso de la tierra se advierte en los asentamientos de cultivadores del Arcaico Tardío. La irrigación fluvial, el cultivo por inundación en abanicos aluviales y el uso de estructuras de rodados para concentrar las aguas superficiales en pendientes poco pronunciadas fueron las técnicas empleadas para la producción agrícola en una variedad de contextos topográficos e hidrológicos.

Los datos procedentes de la Comunidad de Marana indican un sistema económico que vinculaba a agricultores del desierto a través de la producción diferenciada y el intercambio. Los extensos campos con estructuras de rocas apiladas para el cultivo de agave en tierras marginales ofrecen un testimonio elocuente de la especialización agrícola. La documentación exhaustiva de la importancia del agave como fuente de alimento y de fibra entre los Hohokam constituye una importante contribución de la investigación en Marana a la etnobotánica del Suroeste de los Estados Unidos.

ANTHROPOLOGICAL PAPERS OF THE UNIVERSITY OF ARIZONA

44. Settlement, Subsistence, and Society in Late Zuni Prehistory.   Keith W. Kintigh. 1985.

45. The Geoarchaeology of Whitewater Draw, Arizona.   Michael R. Waters. 1986.

46. Ejidos and Regions of Refuge in Northwestern Mexico.   N. Ross Crumrine and Phil C. Weigand, eds. 1987.

47. Preclassic Maya Pottery at Cuello, Belize.   Laura J. Kosakowsky. 1987.

48. Pre-Hispanic Occupance in the Valley of Sonora, Mexico.   William E. Doolittle. 1988.

49. Mortuary Practices and Social Differentiation at Casas Grandes, Chihuahua, Mexico.   John C. Ravesloot. 1988.

50. Point of Pines, Arizona: A History of the University of Arizona Archaeological Field School.   Emil W. Haury. 1989.

51. Patarata Pottery: Classic Period Ceramics of the South-central Gulf Coast, Veracruz, Mexico.   Barbara L. Stark. 1989.

52. The Chinese of Early Tucson: Historic Archaeology from the Tucson Urban Renewal Project.   Florence C. Lister and Robert H. Lister. 1989.

53. Mimbres Archaeology of the Upper Gila, New Mexico.   Stephen H. Lekson. 1990.

54. Prehistoric Households at Turkey Creek Pueblo, Arizona.   Julie C. Lowell. 1991.

55. Homol'ovi II: Archaeology of an Ancestral Hopi Village, Arizona.   E. Charles Adams and Kelley Ann Hays, eds. 1991.

56. The Marana Community in the Hohokam World.   Suzanne K. Fish, Paul R. Fish, and John H. Madsen, eds. 1992.

57. Between Desert and River: Hohokam Settlement and Land Use in the Los Robles Community.   Christian E. Downum. 1993.

58. Sourcing Prehistoric Ceramics at Chodistaas Pueblo, Arizona   María Nieves Zedeño. 1994.